Academics Responding
to Change

SRHE and Open University Press Imprint
General Editor: Heather Eggins

Current titles include:

Mike Abramson *et al.* (eds): *Further and Higher Education Partnerships*
Catherine Bargh, Peter Scott and David Smith: *Governing Universities*
Ronald Barnett: *Improving Higher Education: Total Quality Care*
Ronald Barnett: *The Idea of Higher Education*
Ronald Barnett: *The Limits of Competence*
Ronald Barnett: *Higher Education: A Critical Business*
John Bird: *Black Students and Higher Education*
Jean Bocock and David Watson (eds): *Managing the Curriculum*
David Boud *et al.* (eds): *Using Experience for Learning*
Angela Brew (ed.): *Directions in Staff Development*
Ann Brooks: *Academic Women*
Robert G. Burgess (ed.): *Beyond the First Degree*
Frank Coffield and Bill Williamson (eds): *Repositioning Higher Education*
Rob Cuthbert: *Working in Higher Education*
Heather Eggins (ed.): *Women as Leaders and Managers in Higher Education*
Roger Ellis (ed.): *Quality Assurance for University Teaching*
Maureen Farish *et al.*: *Equal Opportunities in Colleges and Universities*
Shirley Fisher: *Stress in Academic Life*
Sinclair Goodlad: *The Quest for Quality*
Diana Green (ed.): *What is Quality in Higher Education?*
Susanne Haselgrove (ed.): *The Student Experience*
Robin Middlehurst: *Leading Academics*
Sarah Neal: *The Making of Equal Opportunities Policies in Universities*
David Palfreyman and David Warner (eds): *Higher Education and the Law*
Graham Peeke: *Mission and Change*
Moira Peelo: *Helping Students with Study Problems*
John Pratt: *The Polytechnic Experiment*
Tom Schuller (ed.): *The Changing University?*
Peter Scott: *The Meanings of Mass Higher Education*
Harold Silver and Pamela Silver: *Students*
Anthony Smith and Frank Webster: *The Postmodern University?*
Imogen Taylor: *Developing Learning in Professional Education*
Paul R. Trowler: *Academics Responding to Change*
David Warner and Elaine Crosthwaite (eds): *Human Resource Management in Higher and Further Education*
David Warner and Charles Leonard: *The Income Generation Handbook* (Second Edition)
David Warner and David Palfreyman (eds): *Higher Education Management*
Graham Webb: *Understanding Staff Development*
Sue Wheeler and Jan Birtle: *A Handbook for Personal Tutors*

Academics Responding to Change

New Higher Education Frameworks and Academic Cultures

Paul R. Trowler

The Society for Research into Higher Education
& Open University Press

Published by SRHE and
Open University Press
Celtic Court
22 Ballmoor
Buckingham
MK18 1XW

email:enquiries@openup.co.uk
world wide web:http://www.openup.co.uk

and 325 Chestnut Street
Philadelphia, PA 19106, USA

First published 1998

A catalogue record of this book is available from the British Library

ISBN 0 335 19934 8 (pb)   0 335 19935 6 (hb)

Library of Congress Cataloging-in-Publication Data
Trowler, Paul.
  Academics responding to change : new higher education frameworks
and academic cultures / Paul R. Trowler.
    p. cm.
  Includes bibliographical references (p.) and index.
  ISBN 0–335–19935–6 (hardbound). — ISBN 0–335–19934–8 (pbk.)
  1. Education, Higher—Great Britain. 2. College teachers—Great
Britain. 3. Educational change—Great Britain. 4. Universities and
colleges—Great Britain—Administration. I. Title.
LA637.T67 1998
378.41—dc21   97–38819
                                                            CIP

Typeset by Graphicraft Typesetters Limited, Hong Kong
Printed in Great Britain by St Edmundsbury Press Ltd,
Bury St Edmunds, Suffolk

To Terry and Oliver with my love.

Contents

Acknowledgements

I would like to thank Professor Oliver Fulton and Dr Murray Saunders, both of Lancaster University, for the support and encouragement they gave me throughout this project. Both gave their valuable time unstintingly and their wisdom unfailingly. Professor Rosemary Deem and Dr Geoffrey Squires' perceptive comments and questions provided probably the most intensive learning experiences of my life and I would like to thank both of them for that. Thanks also go to the many colleagues who gave me advice and help while I conducted this research, particularly those in my own department. To those who so willingly gave up their valuable time to be interviewed by me I owe a particular debt, as I do to the members of the management team of NewU for giving me permission to conduct the research and for supporting it during all its stages. Finally I owe a great debt to my wife, Terry Wareham, for the intellectual and other forms of support she gave me. She was involved with this project during its development and gave invaluable advice and feedback. She also took on more than her fair share of the duties of daily life to give me the time I needed to complete the task. Now it is time to reciprocate. The views expressed in the book, and any errors in it, are of course my own.

Note

In order to maintain respondent anonymity references in the text to interviewees are by interview number only except where it is essential to give details of their subject area. In these cases the interview number is not given.

Introduction

The motivation behind this book lies in my own puzzlement at the rapid changes in higher education. When I re-entered it as a lecturer in 1991 after a gap of 15 years I found it to be a completely new and strange world, and one still in a state of considerable flux. Despite superficial similarities, the character, assumptions, practices and even language of higher education had become unrecognizable during the time I had been away from it. I found myself asking 'what is going on here?', not yet being sophisticated enough to add Mats Alvesson's (1993) anthropological rider 'apart from the obvious'.

One of the critical aspects of these changes was what I came to call 'the credit framework': those features of the higher education curriculum facilitated by the assignment of credit to assessed learning including modularity, the semester system, franchising, accreditation of work-based learning and of prior learning, all being implemented in a context of expanding student numbers and a declining unit of resource. The introduction of the framework appeared important *per se* and important too because of the other changes that it facilitated, including shifts in the 'idea of higher education' itself (Barnett, 1990).

Slowly my questions became more sophisticated and eventually shaped into the project (the in-depth study of a single higher education institution between 1991 and 1996) from which this book was born. In terms of formal 'research questions' the project sought to do three things: first to explore the regularities in academics' attitudes to change in higher education, particularly to the credit framework; second to understand how these attitudes and values translate into credit framework policy implementation strategies (and how these change policy); third to explain the empirical findings concerning the first two questions.

As these questions reveal, the focus is at the ground level, examining the role and power of actors there in shaping policy. This is deliberate. My review of the literature in the area had revealed a picture which was minutely worked in some areas but only sketched in or entirely missing in others. There was no shortage of material for the reader interested in perspectives 'from the top' (Watson, 1989; Middlehurst, 1993; Bocock and Watson, 1994; Robertson, 1994a; Weil, 1994; Allen and Layer, 1995) even among work apparently aimed at exploring change 'from within' (Slowey, 1995). By contrast, good, theoretically located, ethnographic studies of higher education organizations were decidely thin on the ground, as a number of authors have noted (Cuthbert, 1996; Rothblatt, 1996).

The consistency of the focus on the upper level of higher education had led to what I came to call the 'managerialist model of change' in the study of higher education: one which stressed the guiding role of senior managers in pulling the levers of change and in so doing 'changing the essence' (Beckhard and Pritchard, 1992) of their organization, particularly its culture. The study of the management of change in other contexts had moved away from this perspective towards a focus on the role and power of 'street level bureaucrats' (Lipsky, 1980) in shaping policy at the point of implementation – a move, in other words, from a 'top-down' to a 'bottom-up' approach to understanding change (Sabatier, 1986). This was even true of work conducted in other sectors of the education system (Pollard, 1985; Reynolds and Saunders, 1987; Deem and Davies, 1991; Fullan, 1993).

This emphasis in the higher education literature struck me as strange given the greater autonomy and power that those on the ground in that system still possessed compared with, for example, schoolteachers. It also presented me with the question of how I should go about researching the issues I had set out, given the lack of attention to them in the literature generally. If a fine-grained understanding of academics' values and attitudes, of the cultural context in which they operate, is important for the understanding of policy implementation and policy change, then how should 'culture' in higher education organizations be conceptualized and studied? In a sense the tools to do the job had to be largely invented, though there had been a few 'good starts' as Rothblatt puts it (Rothblatt, 1996) in this endeavour, not least from Tony Becher (1989) and Burton Clark (1987a) as well as some earlier work (Clark and Trow, 1966). The second set of objectives of this book, then, is to propose an approach to the understanding and study of higher education organizations 'close up' (Huberman and Miles, 1984). The project led to a set of conclusions which together act as a 'corrective' to the approaches which currently dominate thinking and writing about higher education. I will summarize here the main issues it addresses in this respect:

- An over-emphasis on the importance of the epistemological characteristics of disciplines in conditioning academic professional cultures as against, for example, social background and factors outside the university.
- An over-emphasis on the ideational aspects of culture and a lack of concern with the implications of cultures for policy implementation.
- An over-simple understanding of the nature of 'culture' in higher education in general, rooted in a view of culture as primarily 'enacted' rather than also 'constructed'.

- Gender blindness, or at least a lack of appreciation of the gendered nature of cultures and the importance of gender in policy implementation.
- A passive model of academic responses to change.

These issues are highlighted by this study partly because it breaks a tradition of studying high status individuals, disciplines and institutions. Unlike many studies in that tradition I do not argue that what is true at 'NewU', the site of this study, is true elsewhere. In particular the findings about the credit framework are specific to a context of greatly increased student numbers and declining resources; the threads of causality linking these factors are inseparably intertwined. However, while the specific details reported here are not generalizable to other sites, the theoretical and conceptual approach developed is commended as having heuristic value elsewhere.

The book is organized as follows. Chapter 1 gives the background to recent changes in the higher education system as a whole, focusing in the latter part on the development of the credit framework in particular. It also describes the institution studied, contextualizing its history, background and current characteristics in a national picture. Chapter 2 critically addresses the claims made about the credit framework by its detractors and supporters while Chapter 3 examines the factors that condition academic responses to the implementation of the framework. Chapter 4 is primarily a literature review chapter, demonstrating the need for a more sophisticated understanding of the implementation of policy generally in higher education; this chapter can be skipped by those most interested in the ethnographic detail in this book. Chapter 5 builds on this to develop a schema of different types of academic response to change. Chapter 6 uses the empirical evidence from the study and the theoretical account which arises from it to reassess a number of earlier approaches to higher education, particularly our understanding of the role of women academics. The final chapter summarizes and discusses the conclusions of the study and considers their implications, primarily for managers in higher education.

1

Contexts

Changes in higher education

This book concerns the responses of academics to a changing environmental and policy context in higher education. The locus of the study is the credit framework, by which is meant those aspects of the higher education curriculum facilitated by giving credit value to assessed learning. These include modularity, the semester system, franchising, accreditation of work-based learning and of prior learning. This is considered in an environment of increasing student numbers and a relative decline in resources. Academics' attitudes towards and implementation of the credit framework is the specific area of change considered here, but the framework is considered in the context that pertained during the first half of the 1990s.

The credit framework: the current situation

Although this book as a whole concentrates on the results of an ethnographic study of a single university, referred to here as NewU, the credit framework has very rapidly become a feature of a large part of what we normally refer to as the higher education 'system' in the United Kingdom. Taking each of the features listed above in turn, by the early 1990s about 80 per cent of universities had developed or were committed to developing modular programmes (Robertson, 1994a). These are learning programmes which are constituted by a designated number (and possibly sequence) of discretely taught and assessed units of study. Modules have uniform size and duration and lead to the attainment of a specified qualification (Church, 1975; Theodossin, 1986). By 1996 the situation was as set out in Table 1.1.

By 1993 around 65 per cent had or planned to adopt a two-semester structure – a division of the academic year into two equal parts usually of 12 to 14 weeks' duration, rather than the traditional three terms (Robertson, 1994a). Around 40,000 full-time equivalent (FTE) students were studying on

Table 1.1 Modular development: England and Wales

	Universities	Colleges
Mainly linear	7	26
Unitized/partly unitized	26	13
Modularized/partly modularized	67	61
Modular/unitized since 1992	60	41

Source: Jackson, 1996, quoted in Tysome, 1996, p. 4 (see glossary for the distinction between a 'modular' and 'unitized' curriculum).

franchised courses, ones in which all or part of higher education occurs in further education colleges under the supervision, in one form or another, of a higher education institution (Bocock and Scott, 1995: 3). Seventy per cent of universities allowed credit for work-based and other forms of experiential learning; that is, learning acquired through experience at work or elsewhere rather than in university classrooms on validated courses (Robertson, 1994a: 10). Nearly 85 per cent of universities had introduced or planned to introduce a credit accumulation and transfer (CAT) scheme (Robertson, 1994a) and 75 per cent of the chartered universities recognized and accepted credit systems, or at least indicated their willingness to consider credit as a suitable form of intellectual exchange.

Meanwhile, the combined degree, one in which two or more disciplines or domains are studied, was becoming the standard, with more (40.3 per cent) higher education students in 1994 taking a combined degree than any other degree type (HESA, 1995: 9). The majority of these were studying with the Open University, an institution created from its inception with a modular curriculum in order to cater for its part-time adult student group (Fulton, 1991a).

The origins of the credit framework

The immediate origins of the components of the credit framework lie in the USA, as does the underlying notion of assigning credit value to assessed learning. While some characteristics of modularity, for example, can be found in the more distant past at Edinburgh University and in Oxford's Greats and PPE (politics, philosophy and economics) schemes (Rothblatt, 1991), the Harvard system of elective courses seems to have been the inspiration for its spread across the USA and latterly to the UK (Squires, 1986; Rothblatt, 1991). In the UK there have been two distinct 'waves' of enthusiasm for modularity. The first, in the 1960s, was motivated by the idea of breaking out of disciplinary restrictions and into inter-disciplinary schemes with names like 'Modern Studies' or 'American Studies' (Church, 1975). This was taken up by the University of London in the mid-1960s, and many new universities and newly-promoted polytechnics used a modular approach.

It was recommended by the Organization for Economic Cooperation and Development (OECD) in the early 1970s, the James Committee on teacher training in 1972, the Russell Report on adult education in 1973 (DES, 1973), the Council for National Academic Awards (CNAA) in 1974 and so on. Even the University Grants Committee 'cautiously recommended' it (Burgess, 1995a). There were, however, misgivings in some quarters, particularly concerning the fragmentation of studies (Mansell *et al.*, 1976) and the loss of control of the curriculum to the centre (Carter, 1980).

The introduction of modularity was, however, slow and limited in the main to the 'public sector' rather than the chartered universities. Church (1975) maps the spread of this phase of modularity from public sector institutions in London, where the practice spread first, to the south-west (Oxford, Bristol, Plymouth) and then to the North (Sunderland, Newcastle, Preston).

The second wave of modularity during the 1980s and 1990s (this time often simultaneously associated with the American semester system) is more concerned with 'multi-disciplinarity' than inter-disciplinarity (Fulton, 1991: 150), flexibility rather than integration and a managerial as well as an educational and access agenda. With the government's 'attack on higher education' (Kogan and Kogan, 1983) of the early 1980s and the steadily declining unit of resource in the context of a push towards a mass higher education system thereafter, it was clear that new, more economical and efficient methods of 'delivery' were required, and modularity, together with other aspects of the credit framework, appeared to offer this. The CNAA discussion papers (1989, 1990) endorsed the view, for example, that 'In the conditions of the 1990s . . . going modular is a serious and useful option' (1990: 11). Indeed, the late 1980s saw a rapid growth in modularization (Fulton and Elwood, 1989) and some of the other features of the framework, first in the polytechnic sector, then in the chartered universities, culminating in the position summarized above.

Franchising, a term used here to refer to any validated delivery of university modules at accredited centres outside the university, is a 'first generation immigrant, the offspring of American parents of doubtful compatibility' (Woodrow, 1993: 208). These 'parents' are, respectively, commercial franchising and the community college movement, both of which mushroomed in the USA in the 1970s. Franchising has been enthusiastically adopted by some institutions in the UK, especially unchartered ones, with general success according to some sources (DES, 1991b; Evans *et al.*, 1991; Abramson, 1993; Abramson *et al.*, 1993), though this is disputed by others (Opacic, 1994). Woodrow (1993) describes the boom in this activity in the early 1990s as the 'quiet revolution', a revolution greatly encouraged by the potential of franchising to facilitate rapid institutional growth when funding mechanisms rewarded this (CNAA, undated). The growth in students on franchised courses has certainly been impressive, steadily rising at a rate of 25 per cent per year to around 5000 students in 1991–2 (Baxter and Bird, 1992; Woodrow, 1993) but then jumping to nearly 40,000 in 1992–3 (Woodrow,

1993: 212–13). In 1993, however, the funding mechanism changed to make franchising a less attractive proposition for Higher Education Institutions (HEIs). Franchising became less profitable than before and some types of collaborative arrangement made planning student numbers more difficult; an important consideration in a funding environment where failing to hit planned targets of student numbers had severe financial consequences.

The assessment and accreditation of prior experiential learning spread quickly across the USA in the 1980s so that by 1991 around 1200 colleges offered it (Simosko, 1991). In the UK it was legitimated at both bachelors and masters levels in the English and Welsh polytechnic sector by the 1987 regulations of the Credit Accumulation and Transfer Registry at the CNAA. By the end of the 1980s there were 'probably more than twenty polytechnics [accurate figures were nowhere recorded], which were developing APEL [accreditation of prior experiential learning] schemes to serve students with a variety of needs' (Evans and Turner, 1993: 2). However, the chartered universities have been more cautious in their adoption of it, as they have to accreditation of prior learning (APL) and accredited work-based learning (AWBL), with one or two exceptions, such as Nottingham. A modest form of APEL has operated in the admissions system of many institutions for mature students, however. While this rarely goes so far as the granting of advanced standing on courses of study, it demonstrates that the components of the credit framework are not mutually dependent and are often found in isolation. The development of a full-blown credit exemption and credit transfer system in the UK, by contrast, has been very slow to develop. Despite the work done by Peter Toyne for the DES-funded Toyne Report in 1979 (Toyne, 1979), the Leverhulme reports in the early 1980s and the Robertson Report in 1994 (Robertson, 1994a, 1994b), all of which recommended setting up such a system, it is still a very long way from being in place.

The rationale for introducing the credit framework

The watchwords of proselytizers of the credit framework are access, flexibility, choice and efficiency. In their ideal form, modular structures should include optionality to promote choice, though 'regressive' (Robertson, 1994a) or 'phantom' (CNAA, 1990) structures do exist which claim to be modular but do not offer choice. The semesterized academic year is also designed to offer more choice to students than year-long courses can, and also to provide consistency for the delivery of equal-sized modules and cost-effectiveness in terms of the amount of material that can be studied in one academic year. The two features combined result in short, self-contained modules which are said to enable part-time students to study at their own pace and when they are free to attend. Franchising too is said to extend choice, this time to the locale of study as well as the content, and additionally facilitates the expansion of student numbers where the university infrastructure is stretched to its limits. The accreditation of prior learning means that credit value

Table 1.2 Principles of a credit culture

From	To
Exclusion	Inclusion
Teacher	Learner
Process	Outcome
Direction	Guidance
Failure	Achievement
Margins	Mainstream
Professional control	Individual choice
Structures	Cultures

Source: Robertson, 1994a: 315.

can be given to learning wherever it takes place, including other universities, the workplace and even the home. As a result it recognizes the knowledge, understanding and abilities gained outside their current university. It means that 'time serving' on courses of a fixed length is no longer necessary and students can choose those elements of programmes that they really need, having been through a careful prior-learning assessment process. The assignment of credit to assessed learning enables part-time students in particular to 'bank' their credits so that they can 'cash them in' when they are ready, not only after three years. Credit transfer enables them to carry those credits with them if they move around the country in pursuit of employment or promotion.

The claim is, then, that the credit framework frees up British higher education to become a 'mass' system. The constellation of features that the framework encompasses makes the boundaries of higher education more permeable, thus broadening and diversifying the student body. Moreover (and importantly) it allows this to be done 'without commensurate increases in . . . resources' (Wagner, 1992). It facilitates curriculum innovation and individual choice so that the higher education 'diet' is digestible by the new types of students found within the academy. Finally it more closely aligns the higher education system to the highly diversified and fluid demands of a 'postmodern' society.

Duke (1992: 21) argues that the introduction of the credit framework is moving higher education towards 'a new paradigm' and it is clear that this 'paradigm' (the scare quotes are there because the word should properly imply universal acceptance) will differ from the established higher education 'paradigm' in the UK insofar as it implies different assumptions about the nature, intentions and outcomes of university education, its potential clientele and the processes experienced within it. Watson (1989) describes the roots of modularity as 'idealistic' and Squires (1986) as 'libertarian' approaches to knowledge and learning. Robertson (1994a: 315) summarizes the shift this paradigm involves in table form, and this is shown in Table 1.2.

Duke (1992) claims that this shift brings with it important changes in the nature of the student experience of higher education and, eventually, changes in its role in the wider community, from what he calls (borrowing from Clark Kerr, 1972) a 'finishing school' to a 'service station' model, as well as new perceptions of the role of higher education in the wider society.

Table 1.2 highlights the important implications of this new 'paradigm' for academic staff. The credit framework 'attempts to undermine the central assumption of much of the UK higher education system, namely that learning best takes place within one institution, over a fixed and limited period of time, according to rules best determined by academic staff' (Allen and Layer, 1995: 25–6). Academic learning is brought to the same level as learning acquired at work or elsewhere rather than being seen as superior. The distinctions between academic, experiential and other forms of learning blur. Control over the curriculum is conditioned by consumer choice rather than 'producer control', a key aspect of neo-liberal thinking.

There are important implications for institutions too. Academic departments become de-coupled from control over individual students' programmes and some centralization of control will occur as institutions reorganize to administer a homogeneous curriculum structure. Assessment of students increasingly becomes an institution-wide issue with academic staff collectively making decisions and departments forced to collaborate, often involving students with whom they have had very limited contact. The administrative centre increasingly mediates the tutor-student relationship as information flow shifts away from academic-student to student-centre-academic. The introduction of the credit framework has also led to a change in the discursive character of those institutions which have adopted it, for example in the adoption of the language of business and currency exchange, as Duke points out (1992: 16).

The changing HE system

Many of the changes to higher education which the credit framework is designed to facilitate have, in fact, been occurring, though this need not mean that there is a causal relationship. Some important developments are summarized below.

The size of the system

In 1982 the age participation index (API) increased from 6.9 to 13.3, and had risen to 27.8 by 1992 (DES, 1991c; DfE, 1994). Between 1982 and 1992 the number of first year full-time students in higher education in the UK increased by 91 per cent, from 228,000 to 436,000 (DfE, 1994: 1). In the latter stages of those ten years the rate of increase quickened, with the API jumping eight points in the first two years of the 1990s (DfE, 1994: 2). In 1992 the total number of students in the UK (both full and part-time) was almost 1.5 million, 11 per cent up on the previous year and two-thirds higher than in 1982 (DfE, 1994: 2). The situation began to change in late 1993, however, with the government's 'autumn statement' of that year. This marked a switch from the *laissez-faire* policy on higher education growth which had essentially allowed growth to occur without commensurate increases in funding (Tarsh, 1992; Williams, 1992: 4). The government now used the funding mechanism to halt growth, reducing the planned number of places to be offered in 1994 by 10,000, penalizing institutions for exceeding target numbers, reducing tuition fees and funding council grants, and cutting student grants (CVCP, 1993a; Richards, 1993). This signalled not only a change in policy on student numbers after the 1993 figures overshot the target but a move from 'steering at a distance' (Kickert, 1991) towards more overt dirigisme. Growth slowed as a result, to give a total of 1,720,000 higher education students in the UK by 1995–6 (HESA, 1997).

Composition of the student body

At many universities and polytechnics during the 1980s and 1990s it became more likely that one would meet students who were female, older, working class, and studying part-time than it had been before. Some institutions, however, retained a traditional student profile, as Ainley's contrast between a chartered and an unchartered institution shows (Ainley, 1994).

The most significant change was in the gender of students. Only 42 per cent of first year higher education students were women in 1982, rising to 47 per cent in 1989 and staying at that figure between 1989 and 1992 (DfE, 1994: 1), though clearly they were unevenly distributed around different curriculum areas. By 1994 the genders became equally represented among first year full-time undergraduates for the first time (HESA, 1995). These changes were however not matched by parallel improvements for women *staff* in universities, either numerically or in terms of seniority (Acker, 1992a; Morley, 1994).

Meanwhile the young mature entry index (YMEI: see glossary for a definition of this) increased from 7.2 per cent in 1982 to 9.5 per cent in 1992, though it dipped to 6.4 per cent in 1990 (DfE, 1994: 2) and the older mature participation index (OMPI) increased from 0.2 per cent in 1982 to 0.6 per cent in 1992, with much of the gain being made in the final two years of that period (an increase of 0.3 per cent) (DfE, 1994: 2). By 1992 the percentage of all students aged 21 and over in the UK was 42 per cent, compared with 33 per cent in 1982, with most of the growth occurring in the undergraduate population (DfE, 1994: 3, Table 3). The widening of access to older students has been of benefit to those from the intermediate and working classes but this has been concentrated in the unchartered universities and colleges (Egerton and Halsey, 1993).

However, despite absolute increases in access the 'service' class (professionals and managers) has maintained its relative advantage so that children from this class are more likely to gain prestigious qualifications from universities than the children of other social groups, and are likely to do so earlier in life (Egerton and Halsey, 1993: 187, 189). By 1997, when the Dearing Report (Dearing, 1997) on higher education was published, the following was the case:

- The professional classes constituted 20 per cent of the population. Eighty per cent of young people from these classes went on to higher education. For the least skilled only around 10 per cent went on to higher education and in no other social group did the figure exceed 50 per cent.
- Even when equipped with the necessary qualifications people from the lower three of five social classes were only 70 per cent as likely to enter universities or colleges as those from the top two social groups (and they were more likely to study locally and part-time).
- Students from less-skilled backgrounds accounted for only 20 per cent of students in chartered universities (and many were mature students). Unchartered universities attracted 60 per cent more applications from these groups (Meikle and Major, 1997: i).

The number of part-time students has risen rapidly in the decade between 1982 and 1992: by 41 per cent in the Open University; by 101 per cent in other chartered universities; and by 60 per cent in polytechnics and colleges, though the percentage varied considerably between the level of course studied (HESA, 1995: 5). The increase in part-time student numbers has been steepest from 1990, around the same time as the credit framework, or aspects of it, was being introduced more widely throughout the system (HESA, 1995: 2).

The changes for other groups previously regarded as disadvantaged in terms of access to higher education have been even less marked. Statistics on the numbers of disabled students were collected for the first time in 1994. They showed that 3.8 per cent of the sampled subset had a disability (HESA, 1995: 27), a figure that remained relatively static subsequently (HESA, 1997). Though it is not possible to compare this with earlier years, it can be compared with the general population, 20 per cent of whom reported long-standing illness, disability or infirmity in 1993 (OPCS, 1995: 21, Table 7.10). In terms of ethnicity, using the OPCS categories and looking only at full and part-time first-year students of known ethnicity in the UK in 1995–6, 4.1 per cent were black, 3.2 per cent Indian, 1.6 per cent Pakistani and 4 per cent were other groups (HESA, 1997: 184). Again it is not possible to compare this reliably with earlier periods because the data are so patchy, especially from the chartered universities. Reasonably reliable figures were collected by Tariq Modood for 1990–1 (Modood, 1993) and comparison with these demonstrates that there was relatively little change in the early years of the 1990s, though Modood's figures do highlight the differences in representation across the binary divide that existed at that time, now masked by a nominally unitary system. Modood's conclusion (Modood,

1993: iv) probably still stands – that some groups are over-represented in higher education in general, notably Africans, Indians, East Africans, Asians and Chinese, while others are severely under-represented, notably Bangladeshis and 'other blacks'.

The resources available

This overall increase in numbers and the additional challenge presented by an increasingly diverse student body were not matched by concomitant increases in public resources. Gareth Williams (1996) notes that public expenditure per student fell by 25 per cent between 1988 and 1993. The 1997 Dearing Report puts the 20 year figure to 1996 at a 40 per cent reduction. This average masks different levels of reduction within the system, however. David Watson (1996) has calculated the public funding of each FTE in higher education in real terms between 1979 and 1998 (projected). With a base index of 100 in 1979–80 he found that the chartered universities had increased to 103 while the polytechnics declined to 75 by 1988–9. Brookman (1992) has also attempted to trace the changing resource allocation in the two sectors, this time in cash terms. His conclusions are similar to, but do not exactly match, Watson's in terms of the general trends. He calculates that in 1979–80 the polytechnics received £5470 per student and the chartered universities £6970, but by 1989–90 the figures were £3121 and £6296 respectively. However he notes that the two sectors are not strictly comparable as the chartered university sector carries some very expensive courses such as medicine, veterinary science and dentistry. The chartered universities had student numbers squeezed in their sector in the early 1980s and so did not suffer the prolonged relative decline felt by the polytechnics who soaked up the demand for higher education despite not receiving commensurate resources for doing so (Kogan and Kogan, 1983: 126; Pratt and Silverman, 1988). The chartered universities did suffer a short period of particular misery, however, during the early 1980s, as Kogan and Kogan (1983) document.

Watson analyses more recent changes in public funding allocation by re-setting the index to 100 for 1989–90. From this date the combined sectors fell 25 points by 1994–5 and are projected to fall to 69 by 1997–8. What this has meant for institutions is an increase in student-staff ratios (SSRs), rising from 9:1 to 12:1 in the chartered universities and from 8:1 to 16:1 in the polytechnics between 1982–92 (Ball, 1992). This represented a reduction in resources available for research, teaching and learning and a decline in the physical structure of the universities themselves. There were other consequences too, for example in management structures and processes, such as a move towards managerialism, as Williams (1992) outlines. The steady decline in the unit of resource has also led to recent calls for remedial action such as top-up fees from students – discussed by the Committee of Vice-Chancellors and Principals (CVCP) in 1996 but then postponed – and the government's private finance initiative. Despite this, the total spending on higher education has grown enormously: only £219 million of public money was spent per year on higher education in England, Scotland, and Wales combined in the early 1960s (Robbins, cited in Scott, 1995: 200, Table 54) compared to £7 billion on English universities alone in 1992–3, two-thirds of which was provided by the state in the form of the Higher Education-Funding Council for England (HEFCE), Local education authorities (LEAs) and research councils (Bain, 1993: 15, 16, Table 4.1, Diagram 1). The Dearing Report on higher education (Dearing, 1997) puts the 20 year figure of increase in expenditure to 1996 at 45 per cent. Peter Scott interprets these developments in a relatively favourable light (Scott, 1995: 25), pointing out that the former polytechnics are funded more favourably today than elite universities were a generation ago. However, though public expenditure on higher education has continued to grow faster than inflation, its growth has not been fast enough to match growing student numbers.

The purposes of higher education

The Robbins Report (Committee on Higher Education, 1963) defined the purposes of higher education as including: instruction in occupational skills (to develop the nation's economy); promotion of the powers of the mind (to develop the intellect of the person); the advancement of learning (to develop knowledge); and the transmission of a common culture and common standards of citizenship (to develop society). These were somewhat amended by the 1997 Dearing Report (Dearing, 1997), which stated that the purposes were:

- To inspire and enable individuals to develop their capabilities to the highest potential throughout life, so that they grow intellectually, are well-equipped for work, can contribute effectively to society and achieve personal fulfilment.
- To increase knowledge and understanding for their own sake and to foster their application to the benefit of the economy and society.
- To serve the needs of an adaptable, sustainable, knowledge-based economy at local, regional and national levels.
- To play a major role in shaping a democratic, civilized, inclusive society.

Such purposes are not the only ones possible, as Bligh (1990: 11) notes. However, the formulations of Robbins and Dearing demonstrate at least some of the numerous expectations that government and society have of higher education. Emphasis on the purposes of higher education tends to shift depending on the economic and political situation of the time. The OECD (1987) has long argued that it is appropriate that the chartered universities should adopt the same policy directions as the polytechnics, particularly their emphasis on: 'career-oriented courses of study . . . applied research and development . . . [which should result in] effective technology transfer and knowledge diffusion . . . greater government involvement and more responsiveness and accountability . . . [with increased] efficiency and productivity (OECD, 1987: 99–104).

These are all themes which were first heard and then reprised in various UK higher education Green and White Papers, beginning with the 1985 Green Paper *The Development of Higher Education into the 1990s* (DES, 1985) which emphasized higher education contributing 'more effectively to the improvement of the performance of the economy'. The 1987 White Paper *Higher Education: Meeting the Challenge* (DES, 1987) nodded at Robbins' view of the purposes of higher education but plainly stated the government's priorities:

> Meeting the needs of the economy is not the sole purpose of higher education nor can higher education alone achieve what is needed. But this aim, with its implications for the scale and quality of higher education, must be vigorously pursued . . . The Government and its central funding agencies will do all they can to encourage and reward approaches by higher education institutions which bring them closer to the world of business.
>
> (DES, 1987: 2)

The 1991 White Paper *Higher Education: A New Framework* (DES, 1991c) set out many of the structural and other reforms introduced by the 1992 Further and Higher Education Act and articulated even more strongly the need for economy, efficiency and a clear sense of purpose (focused on the needs of the economy) for higher education: 'the general need to contain public spending, the pattern of relative costs in higher education, and the demands for capital investment, all mean that a continuing drive for greater efficiency will need to be secured' (DES, 1991c: 10–12).

Barnett (1994) notes with critical concern the nature of the move from propositional knowledge ('knowing that'), towards performativity ('knowing how'), in the university sector. Whatever one's opinion of it, however, there is no doubt that this view of the key role of universities has left its mark on them, structurally and culturally, as a result of the carrots and sticks used by the government to achieve the desired outcomes. The incentives included, for example, generous funding for enterprise in higher education (EHE) (Keat and Abercrombie, 1991) and National Vocational Qualifications (NVQs) (NCVQ, 1995), while the sanctions involved reduced funding for humanities students and a focusing of the available research funding on applied research, as outlined (for science) in the 1993 White Paper *Realising our Potential* (DfE, 1993b). This change in the government's view of the appropriate functions of higher education over the years has led to what Elzinga (1985) refers to as 'epistemic drift' in research: the erosion of internalist criteria and the increasing predominance of externalist criteria such as economic relevance.

The system close-up

The discussion so far has focused mainly on what Becher and Kogan (1992: 9) call the 'central level'. Restricting the focus to this level risks losing sight of the variety and richness that exists at the level of the individual institution. Indeed, there is such great diversity at this level that the characterization of the British higher education scene as a 'system' at all is questionable. In 1994 there were 119 universities and 50 colleges of higher education in England alone (HEFCE, 1994: xvii). These ranged from the top ten (the so-called 'Russell Group'), with Oxbridge at the pinnacle topping most league tables (Cannon, 1995), to a group of unchartered universities at the bottom of the league tables, usually including the University of Luton (though that university is most successful in terms of graduate recruitment to permanent jobs). In the early 1990s student-staff ratios ranged from 10:1 (Cambridge) to 21:1 (Brunel); library spending per student ranged from over £1000 (Oxford) to just over one-tenth of that (Derby); numbers of units of research assessment ranged from over 90 (Cambridge) to 1 (North East Wales Institute); and the percentage of research active staff (as defined for the purposes of the HEFCE's research assessment exercise) from 100 per cent (several research-based institutions) to 8.1 per cent (Nene College). The percentage of graduate students varied between 40 per cent (City) and 7 per cent (Liverpool John Moores) (Cannon, 1995; *Times Higher Educational Supplement*, 1992). Many less-easily quantifiable differences exist also, including the mission and cultural make-up of the various institutions as a number of descriptive accounts demonstrate (Tapper and Salter, 1992; Smith *et al.*, 1993; Ainley, 1994; Brown and Scase, 1994; HEFCE, 1994; Burgess, 1995). Sir Christopher Ball (1990: 28) notes that institutions with the longest traditions and the highest prestige have understandably found the greatest difficulties in adapting to the changing nature of higher education, a point confirmed by Geoffrey Skelsey, assistant registrar of Cambridge university, who has said that it is 'wildly improbable' that the university will adopt a modular degree or join a credit transfer scheme. 'There is definitely no enthusiasm for such ideas here' he reports (Heron, 1991: 25). As I argue in the next section, trying to characterize such institutional differences in terms of just four unitary culture types (as, for example, Berquist, 1992 does) although heuristically valuable, is to grossly misrepresent the diversity that exists within higher education.

Characterizing the HE system

It is clear that the 1980s and 1990s has been a period of intense and, especially towards the end, accelerating change in higher education. Of course, these developments were saltatory rather than smooth and several commentators have discerned discrete phases during the period discussed. Fulton (1991b) suggests it is possible to identify three periods: 1945 to

1970, 1970 to 1987 (with a subdivision of 1983 to 1987) and 1987 to 1991. The first is characterized by post-war consolidation, growth and consensus, the second by stagnation and political hostility initially and then by a move towards mass higher education, and the last by a more determined move towards mass higher education. Scott (1995: 16–21) discerns five phases but essentially interprets events in the same way, concluding that 'Britain, in a fit of absent mindedness, has acquired a mass system of universities and colleges' (Scott, 1995: 22), though Fulton (drawing on Yeats) characterizes Britain as 'slouching' towards a mass system (Fulton, 1991b: 589).

The notion of 'mass' higher education is popularly used in the literature and draws on Trow's classic (1970) formulation of 'elite' (up to 15 per cent of the age grade in higher education), 'mass' (up to 40 per cent) and 'universal' (more than 40 per cent) systems of higher education. The British system became a 'mass' one in 1988 when the API reached 15.1 per cent (DES, 1991c). Despite their heuristic power there are a number of conceptual and technical problems with Trow's models[1] and they are not universally accepted. Other theorists would see the British system in different ways. Robertson, for example, declares it to be a 'crowded elite' system (1996: 350), apparently in agreement with Neave's (1985) view that '. . . mass higher education in Britain [is] elite higher education written a little larger'. However the adjective 'elite' seems misplaced when applied to some institutions. Richard Winter (1991) suggests the term 'new higher education' (NHE), and this has gained some currency in more critical circles. Its characteristics include a modular curriculum structure in a CAT framework with learning outcomes clearly specified and learners constructing their own sequences of study, the accreditation of work-based learning and 'quality' defined in terms of added value. NHE is founded on new epistemological assumptions too, according to Winter, particularly in terms of the value now placed on experiential and non-propositional forms of knowledge.

Winter's account is descriptively rich but confines its attention to the curricular aspects of higher education found in parts of the higher education system. Teichler by contrast is helpful in conceptualizing the system as a whole. He suggests that the UK higher education system is becoming a 'diversified' one, characterized by a large number of quite permeable institutions whose functions overlap, while at the same time each has distinctive mission and different academic standards (Teichler, 1988: 36).

In this account there is a certain amount of instability in the rank orders of institutions and there are very different types of institutions: some offering short degrees; some with strong postgraduate provision; different types of student body; different sorts of course programme, etc. We can add, too,

---

[1] These include the rather strange use of the API as a measure for a system which, by definition, increasingly involves students outside the 18–21 age group, the use of the term 'mass' for a system which includes only between 15 and 40 per cent of that age group, the determinism (subsequently retracted by Trow but still evident) that is inherent in the model, the 'modernist' and essentially uninformative nature of the concept 'mass higher education', the fact that 'elite' systems contain 'mass' elements and vice versa and so on.

that some have the characteristics of the NHE while others do not. While in the late 1980s there was still room for disagreement over the accuracy of Teichler's view of the changing shape of the system, with Levinson (1989) claiming to discern a process of 'isomorphism' for example, there are few who would now regard it as contentious.

This is quite different from the previous 'integrated' system in which qualitative differences between institutions are relatively limited, effectively comprising what Trow (1987: 273) has called the 'separate campuses of the University of the United Kingdom'. As in Trow's model, the differences are both structural and attitudinal: in diversified systems there is an assumption that students' abilities are to some extent dynamic and that differences of educational achievement can be kept within bounds if appropriate educational provisions are made. Under the integrated model students with different prerequisites and abilities are admitted to the same institution, even to a certain extent to common courses of study.

Teichler (1988) also argues that in addition to becoming more diversified, the British higher education system is becoming more diffused. Here, prerequisites for higher education become very varied, secondary education can give credit towards higher education, higher education moves intellectually 'downwards' in places, the borderline between higher education and further education blurs, credit for work or life experience further blurs the distinction between academic learning (formal learning) and any other kind of cognitive stimulation. However Teichler cautions against interpreting such characteristics as core elements of the system. So far at least they have remained rather peripheral, even bolt-on characteristics. While this is still true, they have become rather less peripheral in the late 1980s and 1990s and this trend seems sure to continue post-Dearing.

The model adopted in this book assumes there to be an British higher education 'system', that is a dynamically interlocked group of individual components at different levels. The nature of the linkage is both cultural and structural: universities and colleges of higher education share a common and unique language, and disciplinary links strengthen this at a lower level of analysis. Academics in the system attend the same sorts of meetings, read common newspapers and journals and react to common issues. Structurally there are common institutions operating across the system, examples being the external examiner system, the Quality Assurance Agency, and its predecessors. These common characteristics give British higher education a particular character, different from that found in the school system, for example. The system has certainly been increasing in size and it does seem accurate to describe it as a 'mass' one, though the quotation marks are necessary to acknowledge the existence of the numerically small but symbolically very significant exceptions. It is also one that is in the process of diversification and diffusion, a process apparently enhanced by government and HEFCE policy (for example the 'Mathew Principle' of 'to him who hath shall be given' on which the research assessment exercise is based). However these twin processes should not be overstated: the progressive inclusion of distinctive but previously excluded institutions should not be mistaken for internal change, and characteristics that are still mainly on the periphery of the higher education system should not be considered fundamental to it. I would characterize the system, then, as a slowly diversifying and diffusing 'mass' one which incorporates important elite elements.

Future developments in the higher education system

As this book was being completed, the Dearing Report (1997) was published. It recommended the expansion of higher education with an increasing proportion of the gross domestic product (GDP) spent on it and a more stable planning regime than existed during the Conservative years of government. It also recommended that students should bear part of the cost of their higher education, greater selectivity in funding for research, more collaboration between institutions, the establishment of regional centres of excellence, a new qualifications framework, greater provision for lifelong learning and more staff development in and emphasis on high quality teaching in higher education, including the better use of information technology in teaching. As expected, Dearing recommended the rationalization and clarification of higher education objectives, structures and qualifications to improve their transparency for employers, students and others. The then new Labour government amended some of the proposals on funding but accepted the principle that the student should pay some of the costs and, at the time of writing, a White Paper is being prepared in readiness for important new legislation.

At the time of writing the effects are difficult to predict, but it seems that there will be a greater diversification of the system with at least 'Ivy League' departments if not institutions being publicly acknowledged with, at the same time, a more comprehensive and nationally integrated CAT system. The American experience suggests that these two features are inherently incompatible, the effect of which is likely to be that the CAT system does not extend fully into the 'top' universities. The new emphasis on teaching and the establishment of a Teaching and Learning Institute should improve the quality of provision throughout the system. How far the shifting of the burden of higher education onto the student will suppress demand for it, however, remains to be seen. Meanwhile the system looks set to become more diffused as collaboration between further and higher education is extended and as such components of the credit framework as the accreditation of prior and work-based learning are extended across the system and further integrated into it.

The primary focus of the research project on which this book is based is not on the system level though but on the level of the individual and, to a lesser extent, the departmental level, what Becher and Kogan (1992) call the 'basic unit'. Its main aim is to shed light on the processes involved in interpreting and implementing policy at that level. As Fulton says: '. . . in looking at responses to environmental change at any level within higher education we must not neglect the individuals and basic units where a residue of autonomy always lies' (Fulton, 1991b: 604).

I move, now, therefore to the site of the research itself.

NewU: a brief description

Like many unchartered universities, NewU's origins lie in a nineteenth-century institution set up for the education of the working class. Various name changes over the decades culminated in the granting of polytechnic status in the early 1970s and finally to university status in 1992 following the Further and Higher Education Act of that year. It lies near a busy town centre and has a mixture of buildings the ages of which reflect the development of the university itself. In the early 1990s there was a sustained effort to provide accommodation in residential halls for the increasing number of students and this has led to the university acquiring a campus-like feel, with the main teaching and administrative blocks in the centre and large, new, residential areas on the periphery.

Today, the university could be considered a medium-to-large one. Indeed, growth in student numbers over the years is the most obvious change which has occurred at the institution, as it is in the system as a whole. Student numbers doubled (to almost 17,000) between 1988 and 1993 and reached nearly 20,000 in 1996-7, with the plan being to sustain that level subsequently. Meanwhile the composition of the student body was also changing, with more students from minority ethnic groups, more women and more mature students than had been the case in the early 1980s for example (NewU, 1993d, 1995d).

In 1994 the curriculum provision was dominated by the business and management area with around 20 per cent of students enrolled. This was followed by science, health-related studies, social sciences and maths/IT with around 10 per cent each. Other areas had a somewhat lower percentage of enrolled students, though combined honours had 9 per cent, a decline from a figure of 11 per cent in 1990-1. The majority of students graduating in 1993-4 had been studying on undergraduate degree or sub-degree programmes: there were 2261 degrees awarded, 1655 diplomas and certificates and only 356 higher or research degrees (NewU, 1995a: 16).

In relative terms the resources available to NewU have not matched this increase in numbers. The university's income from various sources rose from £41 million in 1991-2 to £58.7 million in 1994-5. The increase in staff numbers, too, has failed to match that in student numbers and as a result there has been an increase in the student-staff ratio. During the 1970s the SSR had ranged between 5:1 and 8:1, but by the early 1990s this was somewhere between 17:1 (the university's figure) and 24:1 (a league-table figure).

Though overall numbers of academic staff have not changed a great deal since 1988 there had been significant changes in the gender balance since an internal report on the issue in that year. By 1991 30 per cent of the teaching staff were female and women comprised 16 per cent of principal lecturers, 14 per cent of heads of department and 40 per cent of deans of faculty. While not good, these figures compared favourably with the national situation at the time (Bagilhole, 1993: 262).

However, NewU was not in the dire financial straits that some universities came to be by the end of the research period in the mid-1990s. A combination of relatively tight financial controls at the centre, prudent financial management and an apparently prescient reading of the vagaries of higher education funding policy had resulted in a reasonable balance of income and expenditure underpinned by a planning regime which had fostered expansion when it was profitable to do so and planned for a halt to growth at the very moment when funding of student numbers was capped.

During much of the period of this research the university's academic organizational structure was centred on a traditional faculty/department model with five faculties and a total of 26 departments or centres. The administration and academic leadership of the combined honours provision was subject to a number of changes during the research period partly as a result of the difficulties its administration were presenting to the institution. The university's management and committee structure was changed in 1992–3 in line with the provisions of the 1992 Further and Higher Education Act. The titles of the senior management structure were changed to conform more closely to university traditions and the top tier of management was slimmed while a new layer of pro-vice chancellors was introduced.

The credit framework at NewU

The university began its move to an institution-wide credit accumulation system in 1989, with full implementation of 'CATS II' in the academic year 1990–1 (CATS I had been a more limited scheme). This built on the flexible, modular base which had existed first within combined studies programme, set up in 1983, and moving to a CAT system in 1987. The two-year period between September 1989 and 1991 was one of rapid change: the existing provision had to be revalidated under the new regulations, and a large number of new courses were also validated. At the same time student numbers were increasing rapidly. Resources, especially new academic staff, were slow to follow the funding these students brought and the combined effect of all this on staff during this period included considerable stress and overwork. As I recount in Chapter 5, respondent 32 among others describes this period as a particularly damaging one for her and a critical period during which she was forced to reflect on and change her attitudes and behaviour in her work. The university-wide scheme was in place by September 1991. In 1994 the scheme was again changed with the stated intention of simplifying it. The new scheme, referred to here as NEWCATS, was modular in form as opposed to the previous unitized version which was widely regarded as too complex and difficult to manage.

A further change was to the university's academic year. The first semester scheme, introduced with university-wide CAT scheme, sat rather awkwardly on the term and holiday structure of the year. LEAs still operated a termly system of grants and the Christmas and Easter holidays interrupted semesters one and two respectively, causing significant problems for both staff and students. Respondent 31 sums up the views of many staff I spoke to on this:

> It's an artificial kind of semesterization . . . If we had real semesterization . . . that might be easier, but it is very hard to maintain the continuity and coherence when in both semesters there's a three-week break . . . I feel they've adopted a very American system and imposed it on a very British system. (31)

There was subsequently an attempt to resolve this. From 1996–7 the academic year began in early September and semester one finished before Christmas. Semester two ran from January to May. The stated intention was to resolve the semester/term problems and to provide a continuous period in the summer for staff to do research. However, many staff took the more cynical view that the new temporal structure conveniently made room for a third teaching semester over the summer period, to be introduced at some future date.

The university's changes to its internal curriculum structure were simultaneously being reflected in its wider links. The mission of the university stated its intention to 'encourage and enable those in the region of the University to participate in and benefit from higher education in general and the University's provisions in particular' (NewU, 1996b). In pursuit of this it had, since the mid-1980s, developed close links with 22 colleges in the region. The first steps were taken in 1984–5 when an experimental franchise was set up with a local college, offering education studies and economics at first year level towards a degree in combined studies. Eleven students were enrolled. Five further colleges quickly gained validation for a range of Subjects* at level one so that by 1986–7 400 students were enrolled. In the six years between its inception in 1984 and 1990 over 4000 students had embarked on franchised courses. By 1991–2 there were just over 1000 students enrolled in 13 colleges, putting NewU firmly among the top five franchising HEIs in the country at that time. By 1995 there were around 2500 NewU students studying in franchised colleges.

In addition to franchising, the credit-based system facilitates (but is not a prerequisite for) APL and APEL and these were also important at NewU. A snapshot of this activity was taken there in February 1994 (NewU CXT, 1994). A total of 401 claims had been received, split evenly between the combined honours degree and various defined fields, more traditional courses

---

* 'Subject' (capital 'S'): used at NewU to refer to a discipline or domain of study offered as part of the combined honours programme. A Subject must always be studied in combination with one or two others and cannot in itself lead to the award of a degree. The word 'subject' (with a small 's') is used here in Evans' (1995) sense: the institutional enactment of disciplines in the shape of departments.

with identified cohorts moving together through a single discipline or domain. Of these the majority (82 per cent) were for prior certificated learning, and only 12 per cent were claims relying on experiential learning alone. The three forms of qualification for which accreditation was most frequently claimed were nursing qualifications (20 per cent of the total), higher national diploma/higher national certificate (HND/HNC) and previous degree study (18 per cent each), though a large category (39 per cent) was not classified, appearing as 'miscellaneous other'. A quarter (98) of the claims came from students studying under a franchise arrangement at a local college and the bulk of these (56 per cent, 55 in number) came from only two colleges. A less detailed analysis was produced for 1994–5 and this demonstrated a similar pattern, though the overall numbers had increased to 574, excluding admission with advanced standing (NewU CXT, 1995).

The aims of these developments were, at least front-of-stage, articulated in terms of the university's mission statement, which had been in place without substantial change since 1987. This stressed the regional, collaborative character of the institution and its aim to provide access to previously excluded student groups. With regard to the credit framework, the university's statement of academic policy was explicit about its (at least rhetorical) aims:

> The University is committed to structuring the delivery of its courses to enable students and prospective students to develop their full potential . . . [to this end it] delivers its curriculum on a credit accumulation and transfer basis . . . [offering] courses in locations, in modes and at times which will facilitate access . . . The University acknowledges learning wherever it occurs.
>
> (NewU, 1994b: 2–3)

This message is reinforced by particular policy statements, especially those on admissions, partnership with regional colleges, and flexibility of course delivery (NewU, 1994e), while the summary of NEWCATS declares that 'the ethos of the scheme is student centred' (NewU, 1993e: 2).

However the institution's 'brief overview' for students of the then new CAT scheme contained a lexicon of neo-liberal, humanist and managerialist discourse: the words 'freedom', 'choice', 'personal benefit', 'responsive', 'flexible', 'efficient', 'student-centred' and 'relevant' all appeared at least once within the first 120 words. A broader summary of its aims than that contained in the 'brief overview' was offered by NewU's academic registrar in 1995:

> The move to student choice and flexibility is born of educational and economic principles. The desire of both government and institutions to introduce mass higher education and to encourage the concept of lifelong learning [in an environment where there is] an ever decreasing unit of resource and an increasingly fragile financial support system

for students gives impetus to the development of modularity across the
university sector.

(NewU academic registrar, 1995a: 1)

A desire to shift towards the new paradigm was evident throughout the
front-of-stage discourse at NewU, both in terms of the preferred nature and
role of higher education in general and the special contribution of the
credit framework in particular. With regard to the former, in the year in
which the binary divide was abolished the vice-chancellor of NewU commented that: 'The special contribution which the former polytechnics made
to the development of an accessible higher education system will be lost if
they seek to ape the traditional universities . . . there can be no doubt that
recent changes will reconstruct reality. The interesting question is, whose
reality is to be reconstructed?' (NewU vice-chancellor, 1992: 24).

This position was entirely in line with the university's mission statement
with its stress on 'the widest possible access' to and progression through the
educational system, providing the 'widest possible scope, choice and flexibility' in its educational activities as well as developing a 'positive relationship
with industry, commerce, public and private sector bodies and the professions' (NewU, 1996b). Such statements are reflected elsewhere, for example
in the briefing document for the Higher Education Quality Council's (HEQC)
1994 visit (NewU, 1994d: 3, 19) and in the institution's prospectuses (NewU,
1995e: 1).

Implementing the credit framework at NewU

Allen and Layer (1995) distinguish between 'big bang' and incrementalist
models of CATS implementation. The former was characteristic of Liverpool John Moores University as well as NewU while Greenwich, Northum-
bria and Sheffield Hallam adopted the latter. In the words of the director of
the Liverpool scheme, the big bang approach was an attempt to: '. . . embark
upon a sustained and radical programme of institutional transformation
which would bring the institution quickly forward on a broad front of sector
innovations' (Robertson, 1994a: 66).

Both approaches have their advantages and problems. The incrementalist
approach, as at Sheffield, attempts to garner understanding, support and
ownership of change among staff or, as at Greenwich, attempts to persuade
them to change. However, this can lead to problems for students and resistance from staff (Allen and Layer, 1995: 66). On the other hand the big
bang approach requires, as at Liverpool, the rapid introduction of 'highly
centralised and sophisticated management and administrative functions,
well supported through mainstream funding . . . bringing together registry,
management information, and guidance functions' (Allen and Layer, 1995:
47). This is not easy to do, particularly at a time of resource constraint.
Comparing the two approaches Allen declares his view that ' "big-bang"

models, which appeared to be increasingly the vogue, [can] never work'
(Allen and Layer, 1995: 47). Certainly at NewU there was considerable
resistance to the imposition of CATS and the attempt to impose change
from the top contributed to the features of the organization's cultural characteristics which I describe below. There the implementation of the credit
framework was more like an extended firework display than a big bang,
with systems being introduced and then quickly changed. The HMI Report
(1991) on the built environment department noted with concern the rapid
pace of change on many fronts in the institution and suggested that a
period of consolidation would be of benefit to all concerned. Many of my
respondents reported their frustration at these continual changes:

> I feel like I've never got to grips with CATS and it's been changed.
> We've got progression next week and at the moment I haven't got a
> clue what I'm going to say to the students. (39)

> In this place there's a change every five minutes . . . it leaves you in a
> whirl . . . [Tom] Peters [the author of *Thriving on Chaos*] has got a lot
> to answer for. (15)

Organizational culture at NewU

Because this project was centrally concerned with the values, attitudes and
practices of academic staff working in an institution of higher education it
necessitated a fully theorized account of the nature of organizational culture: the taken-for-granted values, attitudes and ways of behaving which are
articulated through and reinforced by recurrent practices in a given context.

A review of the literature revealed essentially four ways of conceptualizing
and analysing this: the nomothetic; the functionalist; the inductively-derived
categorizing; and the phenomenological approaches. The nomothetic approach to organizational culture is probably the best known, popularized in
work of Charles Handy (1976) through his development of Harrison's work
(1972). Here, organizations are categorized according to whether they have
a 'power', 'role', 'task' or 'person' culture. Berquist (1992) also applies the
approach of slotting institutions into pre-defined categories, discerning 'collegial', 'managerial', 'negotiating' and 'developmental' cultural types in the
higher education system. Several other researchers have attempted to do the
same thing in the HE context (Becher, 1988; Cameron and Ettington, 1988).

The functionalist approach, often allied to this, sees culture as playing
an important role in the survival and development of the institution. Sharing the nomothetic approach's notion of a unitary culture, functionalist
understandings of organizational culture see it as giving members a sense
of meaning and identity. Where culture is strong the organization is seen as
particularly able to succeed in its environment; it has a clear understanding
of itself and its mission. Its members share a common purpose and for the
most part can agree about the means to achieve it. Such a perspective, as

applied to higher education, is seen in the work of Barber (1984), Masland (1985), Schein (1985), Smart and Hamm (1993) and McNay (1995).

The inductively-derived categorizing approach is in essence a more sophisticated version of the nomothetic approach. Instead of pre-defining categories of organizational culture and then attempting to slot specific institutions into the categories, this approach studies the institution first, attempts to draw out the main characteristics of the culture found there and then describe it. Occasionally inventories are used as a way of doing this, as in the case of Whitcomb and Deshler's study (1983). Sometimes, however, the approach is more intuitive, as it is in Tierney's 1988 study.

The phenomenological approach sees culture as created uniquely in each social setting and considers this to be in a constant state of flux. Understanding and values develop into recurrent practices but are relatively insubstantial, and as they change so do behaviours. The analyst faces the task of arriving at an empathetic understanding of the nature of the culture at a particular site, then describing and analysing it. An example of this approach applied to higher education is Kempner's (1991) study of Hill College.

While each has its strengths and some have a certain heuristic appeal, my conclusion was that none accurately captured the nature of the cultural context as I had come to understand it at NewU. The following points summarize the inherent weaknesses in these four models as revealed by the attempt to apply them to NewU.

Culture is (partly) constructed as well as enacted

With the exception of the phenomenological approach, the approaches to culture outlined above portray organisational culture as *enacted*; that is, they consider individuals within organizations to be simply adopting a set of pre-existent values and attitudes which they encounter there and performing sets of behaviours which have come to be considered 'the way we do things round here' by members of the organization. In this view, organizations have consistent 'personalities', largely formed by founders (Martin *et al.*, 1985), and are therefore 'birth-marked' (Grieco, 1988). This view contrasts with an understanding of organizational cultures which sees them at least partly *constructed* on an on-going basis by individuals and groups.

My data revealed several examples of cultural construction occurring, both deliberate and unconscious. An interesting discussion about this took place at the quinquennial review of a department which I attended (fieldnote 17.5.96.). In the context of answering a question about staff workload the head of department reported a discussion with a former member of staff who had recently left to work in another university. During their conversation that person had reflected on the very different way in which students behaved at his new institution. There, students did not act in the 'dependent' way they had at NewU, treating academic staff as always ready and able to deal with trivial problems. Instead they respected their expertise and were aware of their varied professional roles, only some of which concerned dealing with students directly. Thus students there tended to confine discussion to academic issues and, for example, to allow the lecturer to walk away from the lecture room without approaching him or her with sometimes trivial non-academic matters.

This account was received by nods around the table and anecdotes from the members of the panel, drawn from across the university, confirming this account of NewU students' attitudes and behaviour. Those participating expressed puzzlement, however, about why this should be the case. What was at issue here was an aspect of the culture at NewU, some of the sources of which are clear. The university had recently emerged from a long period during which staff were appointed as teachers, not researchers; indeed research-oriented staff were rarely shortlisted for interview: 'The fact that they didn't want to do research was regarded as a positive factor in new appointees in the past. That's completely somersaulted now. We've reached the position where unless someone's got a PhD and a long string of publications we really don't want them' (33).

Since 1987 there had been a policy of discouraging staff from using academic titles (New Polytechnic, 1987) and this (and the anti-elitist philosophy behind it) had become reflected to some extent in staff practices: for example student handbooks in the departments usually made no reference to academic titles, publications or other academic output and only fleeting and largely inaccurate reference to specialist interests. A further illustration of this is in the ambivalence demonstrated in public arenas about academic and epistemological hierarchies. This existed at NewU because of an elitism inherent in such hierarchies which ran counter to the institution's proclaimed access mission. For example, during a discussion about the assessment of APEL portfolios at a university steering group meeting, an associate college staff member's view about the impossibility of assessing even academic essays with any degree of rigour went unchallenged. This illustrated the kind of relativist viewpoint sometimes used to justify highly permeable higher education boundaries and to attack any 'elitist' defence of those boundaries.

These observations constitute examples of the recursive instantiation of attitudes and values in recurrent practices which comprise organizational and other forms of culture; their articulation in behaviour which itself serves to strengthen them. The invisibility of this to the participants is perhaps not surprising given the way in which these norms and values become taken for granted over time, though these practices and values were becoming less opaque as the university increasingly engaged in debate about its role in a changing higher education system. The fact that members of the review panel recognized the description of NewU and saw it as a problem is significant. Some of my respondents had gone further than this and had begun to take action to change the culture at the ground level, as the discussion of reprofessionalization strategies (pp. 132–5) illustrates.

The 'stages' of cultural articulation

The four approaches to organizational culture outlined above generally fail to take into account the different 'stages' of articulation of organizational culture (Goffman, 1959: 114–15; Bailey, 1977; Becher, 1988). Tony Becher alerts us to the way in which organizational cultures operate in three arenas: front-of-stage (the public arena); back-stage (where deals are done); and under-the-stage (where gossip is purveyed). Models of organizational culture which fail to take this into account, perhaps accepting the front-of-stage articulation as 'the' culture, miss much that is important in understanding the cultural life of an institution.

The differences between the various 'stages' of organizational culture is well illustrated by the discussion of the university's sexual harassment policy. Front-of-stage discourse was found in various policy documents (for example, NewU, 1996d) and in the public utterances of the vice-chancellor on the issue (for example, NewU, 1993c), which identified a serious problem at the university in this area and supported the work of the sexual harassment officer (SHO), a full-time post since 1992, who reported directly to him. Under-the-stage, however, there was mounting concern about the escalating number of sexual harassment complaints being taken up by the SHO (35 in 1990–1, 89 in 1992–3) and about the procedures for dealing with them which some felt to be over-secretive and contravening natural justice. In private there was talk of McCarthyism, thought-police and witchhunts (fieldnote 12.5.93.). Some of these comments were personally directed at the SHO. In public more moderate versions of these ideas were articulated in the pages of the *New Guardian*, an unofficial staff newspaper and an under-the-stage counterpart to the front-of-stage university papers *New Diary* and *Newlook*. Back-stage, no doubt, deals were being done which subsequently led to the abolition of the post of SHO and different procedures for dealing with harassment, though I had no access to this aspect.

Organizational cultures as open and pluralistic

The four approaches to organizational culture tend to see it as unitary and as relatively insulated from its environment. At NewU, however, it was clear that there were numerous cultures in operation simultaneously and that the organization was open to and affected by the cultural contexts in which it was operating. The very language of credit, with its continual reference to the discourse of banking and commerce (franchising, credit-rating, credit exchange, the 'banking of credit' etc.) was clearly influenced by values and attitudes which had become predominant in the wider political culture of the 1980s as was the discourse of management (line-managers, senior management teams etc.). Moreover, values and attitudes derived from individuals' positioning with regard to gender, ethnicity and social class were also important in structuring their response to the cultural characteristics they found at NewU. On pages 86–7 for example I show how students' behaviour regarding academic counsellors was affected by wider notions about gender roles. Imported into the academy, too, were attitudes and values deriving from religious and political beliefs as well as cultural characteristics deriving from other contexts: for example, the worlds of fashion, journalism and commerce. These differences were most obviously, but not exclusively, expressed in cultural differences between departments and disciplines, though within these, different 'social fields' were in existence, each with their own cultural characteristics.

At the same time, organizational cultures operate differently at different levels in the organization, again undermining the attempt to assign a single label of set of characteristics to the organization as a whole. The level of analysis one adopts therefore structures one's understanding of the cultures operating within an organization. This issue is illustrated by the difficulty of attempting to determine whether NewU has a 'managerial' or a 'collegial' culture. Evidence from a number of sources for its 'managerial' nature seems strong. Some examples are as follows:

Staff are frightened to complain and feel under pressure because of the risk of losing their jobs.

(Female campus services staff member)

In order to carry the University through the period of change, it has developed and used strong central controls. This centralisation has helped the University to meet its statutory requirements and has undoubtedly been of value in the period of growth but it has also inhibited local initiatives and has helped to make the University more bureaucratic than many would wish.

(NewU, 1996a: 9)

I think that over all [what] . . . irritates the hell out of me [is that] we have not got a decent management. They spout forth about corporate identity but they do not understand that you've got a committed, excellent resource: your people actually doing the job. [T]hey have no respect for them, and the problem is that when it comes to it an organization is only as good as the people in it. I mean this is such a trite statement but it's true. (47)

Other data indicated that at the local level within the institution there was a considerable amount of 'collegiality' or aspects of 'clan' culture: '[There is in existence] . . . an informal supportive staff network . . . based upon the values of collaboration and communication . . . mutual respect and trust inherent within an informal community network' (Henry *et al.*, 1992: 6).

Both respondents in the Department of Journalism at NewU noted its collegial atmosphere. One said: 'This department . . . is one of the best departments in terms of atmosphere that I've ever worked in. Its a very pleasant atmosphere to be in . . . we work very well together . . . we're all pushing together . . .' (journalism).

The need for a theoretical elaboration of organizational culture

The phenomenological approach, while having considerable merit, lacks a developed theory of the nature of organizational culture. For a researcher interested in developing an ethnographic account of an organization this has serious implications. In particular it means that she or he is left at sea without a 'compass' by which to navigate during the fieldwork stage or the analysis of the data. Rather, he or she is left to cast anchor at spots that seem interesting but whose position and relationship to other land masses is unknown – a characteristic of Kempner's (1991) study, for example.

Moreover, the links between organizational culture and the implementation of change have been under-theorized. Analysts such as Robertson (1994a: 314–15) have thought only in terms of how organizational culture can be changed by management to facilitate their strategic vision. In this view culture is simply another lever available for management to pull. However it was clear from the data I collected at NewU that the cultural configuration there was also acting in the other direction, filtering academics' perceptions of and reactions to policies, conditioning the ways in which they 'implemented' them (effectively changing the policies in the process of their implementation) and often placing academic staff in dilemmas as they struggled to resolve competing expectations, interests and sets of values. Theorized in this way the relationship between cultures and change becomes altogether more complex, the manager's job much harder, and the process of change much more uneven as change is interpreted and reacted to in different ways within the organization.

Finally, most accounts of organizational culture have adopted a one-dimensional approach, concentrating in practice on *corporate* culture: the ways in which work is organized, decisions are taken, power is distributed and the nature of values and attitudes about the institution, its 'product', the market (or, in education, quasi-market) and 'consumers'. It seems clear that such a perspective when applied to higher education institutions (and almost certainly any organization) simply misses all of the other recurrent practices, values and attitudes which go on in any social institution and which, from an individual's perspective, help constitute personal identity. In short, cultures in organizations are as multi-dimensional in nature as they are elsewhere, but this has been missed by most organizational cultural theorists.

NewU's multiple cultural configuration

Given these weaknesses in previous theories about culture it was necessary to develop a theory which fitted more closely the situation as it was at NewU. Such a theoretical approach has been developed by Alvesson (1993) among others and is illustrated in the case studies in Sackmann (1997).

The approach posits that any large organization is characterized by a unique multiple cultural configuration – not a unitary whole but a set of cultures of different levels and kinds, manifested in different ways. Within the organization are local versions of cultural characteristics prevalent at the national level. There are also locally developed cultural characteristics which overlay and mix with these. Individuals within the organization may identify primarily with the organization as a whole, with some sub-unit of it, or with their wider profession (the so-called 'invisible college': Crane, 1972). Moreover, individuals bring with them cultural characteristics related to gender, class, ethnic group and so on. Thus organizations are very much 'open' institutions, permeable to cultural influences from outside but usually mixing and changing them as they interact with local culture. A number of examples of this theoretical framework applied in non-educational institutions are available in Sackmann (1997).

The study of organizational culture relies very heavily on metaphor (Alvesson, 1993: Chapter 1). Perhaps the best metaphor for the multiple cultural configuration view of an organization is to picture it as a major road. Smaller and larger roads feed traffic into it (wider political cultures, gender cultures, the aspects of the dominant culture of the wider society, or 'great culture'). These change its character but are also themselves absorbed into it. The resultant traffic patterns are altered, however, as they meet obstacles: roundabouts or road junctions (contentious issues such as what the 'mission' of the university should be). In this case the configuration lines up in particular ways according to the nature of the obstacle. For some traffic streams the issue is not particularly relevant and is barely noticed. For others it is extremely pertinent and results in a new environment to navigate, a new traffic configuration to negotiate. Some fellow travellers will be competitive, others cooperative. The concept of cultural 'stages' can also be applied in this metaphor. The highway code represents the front-of-stage version of how things are done while the actual behaviour of drivers, the interaction between each other and between them and their passengers (comments about other drivers and other cars) stands for the behind-the-stage and under-the-stage realities of cultural manifestations.

This vision of cultures within organizations is also a dynamic one in the twin sense that it is itself in constant movement and shows how cultural characteristics may be configured in ways which will impede or facilitate change. This is in marked contrast to the static nature of the models of organizational culture reviewed earlier in this chapter. This understanding to organizational cultures also has important implications for approaches to organizational change and policy implementation based on 'changing the culture' of higher education institutions.

2

The Credit Framework

The credit framework and managerialism

The introduction of the credit framework into the UK system of higher education can be interpreted as the application of either a 'soft' or a 'hard' form of managerialism. Soft managerialism sees the framework as providing a solution for the economic crisis in higher education which has resulted from under-resourced expansion; a solution with limited or no ill-effects and limited impact on the power and role of the academic community. The hard managerialist position, by contrast, seeks to rationalize and reshape higher education, making fundamental changes to it that are largely to the detriment of the academic community themselves. Hard managerialism elevates the role of management and the goals of economy, efficiency and effectiveness to a paramount position. Neo-Marxist and Foucauldian writers (for example, Jary and Parker, 1994) and others (Trow, 1994) adopt a highly critical perspective on hard managerialism. For the neo-Marxists the introduction of the credit framework is symptomatic of a form of exploitative Fordist managerialism which has severely deleterious effects on the provision of higher education in general and the academic profession in particular. I will review and evaluate the rationale for the credit framework put forward by those who cast themselves as soft managerialists before discussing analytically the work of those critics who interpret the framework in hard managerial terms.

Soft managerialism

Governments have increasingly come to portray the credit framework in managerialist terms. While the 1987 White Paper welcomed the development of the credit framework in higher education for the opportunities it provided for a wider range of entrants 'to pursue programmes of study tailored to their particular needs but within established academic standards'

(DES, 1987: 11), the 1991 White Paper declared that: 'The Government sees scope both for more extensive use of credit accumulation and transfer and for providing courses on a more intensive basis, making more effective use of existing buildings and equipment' (DES, 1991c: 12).

This White Paper is littered with references to 'effectiveness and efficiency' and 'cost effective expansion' and articulates a view of the credit framework that had already become prevalent among some commentators on higher education by the time it was published. Raban (1990: 27), for example, combines the managerial and progressivist rationales: 'CAT, in effect, attacks the blockages and restrictive practices that, in the past, have caused "inelasticities" in the supply of appropriately trained social workers [and others]. APEL, franchising, accreditation and credit transfer agreements can reduce the economic and geographical barriers to access.'

However it is among senior higher education managers that the managerialist arguments are articulated in their most unalloyed form. David Watson, now vice-chancellor of the University of Brighton, and his co-authors (1989) provide the already classic statement of this line of thinking. We learn (and are expected to applaud the fact) that sharpening thinking about course and institutional goals can permit the use of performance indicators (Lindsay in Watson, 1989: 100), that evaluation becomes much easier and 'scientific' (p. 98) and can involve employers (p. 101), that administrative systems can be unified, centralized and made more efficient (Coghill in Watson, 1989: 118), and that teaching is more efficient as the teaching of mixed groups of students takes place in common modules (Watson *et al.*, 1989: 5). Peter Toyne, vice-chancellor of Liverpool John Moores University argues strongly for 'customer orientation', for 'corporate aims' to be 'customer led', and for the right of managers to manage (Toyne, 1991: 61). Roger King, vice-chancellor and chief executive of the University of Humberside, finds it 'remarkable' that 'the core of the academic enterprise (the course or programme as 'product') lies largely outside corporate control', but notes with approval that things are changing so that:

> the product encompasses structure, delivery, explicable learning outcomes, flexibility, availability, resourcing and relationship to other products (including a medium or currency of exchange). And the quality of the product is likely to rest more clearly on judgements made by customers and consumers than producers. The search for growth, efficiency and quality are essential organisational requirements that will take senior managers more directly to the heart of the academic domain.
>
> (King, 1994: 71)

Each of these managers, though, see themselves as advocating a soft form of managerialism, one that will be to the benefit of all concerned. Each rejects any interpretation that they are in any way advocating 'hard' managerialism. Watson accuses those who interpret his views in this way of collapsing 'bundles of fears, resentments and concerns at the nature and direction of change into [this] . . . simple, single, emotionally satisfying charge' (Watson, 1995: 7), and says that creating a polarity between the managers and academics is 'myth-making' (Watson, 1994: 78–81). King calls for a 'compact' between senior managers and academics and Toyne argues that traditional decision-making models are simply unworkable in the present context (Toyne, 1991: 60). The vice-chancellor at NewU concurs that the inhospitable climate calls for clear management: 'Now is not the time to operate in an unfocused way', he says (fieldnote 22.9.95.).

It is hardly surprising that the government's managerialism resonated with some managers. Higher education institutions have always presented a particular problem for their managers, even, or perhaps especially, those in the more hierarchical polytechnic sector (David, 1989: 209). Even more than other organizations, universities were unlikely to be characterized by the four assumptions of the rational, top-down model of management of change identified by Elmore (1978):

1. Organizations act as coordinated units.
2. Policy is clearly and precisely expressed.
3. There is a shared understanding of policy.
4. There is hierarchic control in the implementation process.

As Cohen and March (1974: 206) put it in a much-quoted paragraph:

[In universities] anything that requires the co-ordinated effort of the organization in order to start is unlikely to be started. Anything that requires a co-ordinated effort of the organization in order to be stopped is unlikely to be stopped. The leading false expectation in academic reform is that large results can be obtained by top-down manipulation.

From a management perspective there was a clear need for change away from the 'organized anarchy' or 'garbage can' (Cohen and March, 1974) model of the management of change which universities apparently exemplified so well. The Jarratt Committee, set up by the CVCP, made recommendations to this effect in proposing that university councils should reassert control over academic senates, that the vice-chancellor be explicitly seen as both management and academic head, that academic and resource allocation decisions should be considered together in a single top-level body, and that academic departments should have more budgetary control (CVCP, 1985). Although the Jarratt Report received a cool reception from many senior administrators at the time, its recommendations were already being put in hand in many chartered universities, galvanized by government funding cuts.

From a managerialist perspective the credit framework offers the potential of being less resource-intensive and more amenable to control than previous 'curriculum delivery systems' (NewU, 1997: 3). As Becher (1994b: 233) notes, when student numbers are increasing and resources are scarce there is a pressure to increase staff-student ratios. One apparently simple way to do this is to rationalize the curriculum so that a single set of lectures in a subject common to students in a variety of disciplines is delivered in a combined group. This quickly leads managers towards thinking of knowledge as packageable into standard, self-contained units, available to any student who wishes to access it. This also has the advantage of being administratively neat: a unit of knowledge is delivered and assessed in a defined period of time. The student's profile is amended and the transaction is complete. In addition, treating learning as a commodity like any other makes it amenable to rationalistic management practices such as management by objectives and total quality management (Eriksen, 1995).

Although APL and APEL can be and have been practised independently of the credit framework, the contemporary notion of accrediting prior learning by closely matching learning outcomes derived from experience to the aims and objectives of particular modules and giving credit for them is a further example of processes rooted in a behaviourist epistemology which portrays knowledge and skill acquisition as objectively measurable, aggregative, context-independent (hence the notion of 'transferable skills') and imperishable. This view of learning discounts situationally dependent or transient factors such as the personal motivation to actually use skills that have been learned. Squires (1979, 1986, 1987) points out that modular schemes are based on this form of 'aggregative paradigm', which is so sharply different from an alternative 'holistic' paradigm of learning that the arguments put forward by the various protagonists 'simply miss each other completely' (Squires, 1986: 13). The arguments around these principles and propositions are outside the scope and aims of this book, and will not be discussed here, though a debate is taking place about the notion of 'transferability' (Melton, 1994) and the problems of converting non-propositional into propositional knowledge (Eraut, 1985; Trowler, 1996a).

Moreover, though Theodossin (1986: 12) has described CATS as 'a market mechanism to promote consumer control' with the student acting as the consumer, it seems more likely that its main beneficiary will be employers, as franchising, the accreditation of in-house training schemes and the introduction of learning contracts result in a shift in the location and control of vocational training in particular. From a managerial perspective this offers the attractive prospect of bringing private money into the institution, essential in a time of constraint in public funding.

Duke (1992) notes that along with this type of managerialist idea has come a change in the discursive practices of higher education. The 'new discourse' of higher education with its 'cost centres', 'funding allocations', 'programmes' and 'missions' has replaced the old with its 'grants', 'courses' and 'collegiality'. Words and phrases become emotionally loaded and are used tendentiously, so that 'embedding' is good while its opposite, 'bolt-on', is bad. This is noticeable in the language of supporters of the credit framework as the quote from King on page 32 illustrates. Theodossin describes credit accumulation schemes as simply a device for 'curricular accounting' (1986: 8) and the very title of his work, *The Modular Market* is indicative. Likewise, Toyne, even in the 1970s, referred to credit transfer as maximizing 'accumulated educational capital' (Toyne, 1979: 35). Students 'bank' their capital until they have gained sufficient to 'cash it in' for an academic award. They can 'trade' capital between courses and institutions and search for a 'good deal' with regard to advanced standing through APL/APEL, 'shopping around' between various institutions for the best offer. Meanwhile, universities themselves can franchise their product lines.

Eccles and Nohria (1992: 9) claim that managers live in a rhetorical universe where discourse is appropriated and mobilized to structure definitions of reality as much as to communicate. It seems that this is happening in parts of the higher education system; the new managerial reality and the discourse which reflects and helps sustain it is already well entrenched in places. Stuart Hall notes of the Open University that: '. . . good, social democratic souls [there] . . . have learned to speak a brand of metallic new entrepreneurialism, a new managerialism of a horrendously closed nature' (Hall, 1993: 15). Though he suggests that they have not changed 'for a minute what is in their hearts and minds' (p. 15) one wonders, with Eccles and Nohria, whether discourse and perception of reality can remain so insulated from each other. As Fairclough notes (1992: 153), what at first feels like rhetoric used in the interests of getting things done quickly can easily become a component of one's professional identity.

At NewU the 'market' discourse was found among middle and senior managers. One large departmental head spoke publicly to staff about APL removing the need for 'time serving', equating studying on a fixed-length course with serving a prison sentence. He aimed to set up an educational currency unit, the 'academic ecu', and wanted consortia set up in which the HEI could act as a 'leading broker using credit as an academic ecu' (fieldnote 27.11.92.). The university's strategic training and development plan concentrated on 'corporate priorities', and the needs of 'the internal customer' (NewU, 1994g: 1–2) while the vice-chancellor discussed the 'core business' of the university (fieldnote 22.9.95.) and the need to ensure 'student/ customer/market focused provision' (NewU, 1996a: 21–2).

The mechanistic epistemological assumptions inherent in this discursive repertoire were found at NewU also, at least in front-of-stage discourse:

> All courses and units should have clearly stated aims and learning outcomes . . . The university recognises prior learning wherever it occurs and will offer students the means to gain credit for such learning wherever it aligns with course learning outcomes . . . Assessments should test only pre-defined learning outcomes and offer student feedback in a variety of ways.
>
> (NewU, 1994b)

Managerialists rarely rest their case on the claimed economy, efficiency and effectiveness of the credit framework, however. As noted above, the managerialist perspective suggests that the credit framework offers a much-needed revolution in higher education. The shift of responsibility from the academic to the student (Watson, 1989: 5) makes higher education more relevant and meaningful; specifying clearly what is to be taught and how it is to be assessed can lead to exciting innovations in teaching, learning and assessing (Scurry in Watson, 1989: 77); regular and rapid feedback on their performance empowers students (Watson, 1989: 6); and the credit framework as a whole delivers flexibility, choice and a 'culture of negotiation' (Watson, 1989: 134). Thus soft managerialism is usually found buttressed by the rhetoric of progressivist student-centred approaches.

Some problems with the soft managerialist claims

Administrative fallout

'Administrative fallout' is defined here as any increase in the administrative load on academics resulting from aspects of the credit framework either directly – for example an increased amount of paperwork or the number of assessment boards and committees – or indirectly, for example the work involved in updating and correcting data held centrally. Administrative fallout has been one important repercussion of the move to a centralized CAT system at NewU. There is no doubt at all that the centre, given institutional form in the programmes office and subsequently the registry, having taken responsibility for the maintenance of student records, class lists and so on, did not have the capacity to fulfil this function effectively. This is apparent from the interviews I conducted and from official documents. Although only six of the respondents cited administrative fallout as the worst part of their job, 37 of them talked about it at some length and with some bitterness. Recurrent themes were the constant demands for information from the centre without discernible result, the inadequacy of the computer system to cope, the frequent errors in data supplied by the centre and the apparent powerlessness of academics to correct them. Many told anecdotes of sending in data about students' results which mysteriously became corrupted or simply disappeared. Respondent 30 put the point quite mildly compared to some: 'We don't feel that anything a centralized facility can provide is ... in any way beneficial to us. It actually involves us in as much if not more admin work than if we were actually doing it ourselves.'

Frustration with inefficient bureaucratic procedures can have real effects on academics' working practices. Respondent 24 reported a new reluctance to be involved with APL/APEL after the centre began to take responsibility for this area of work:

> The daft system now ... [is] this enormous great credit accumulation and transfer process that you have to go through ... I said [to a student who applied for APEL] 'fine ... I can give you credit for that but ... unfortunately you've got to go through this whole rigmarole. You've got to provide all this evidence which then goes off ... and it comes back to me and I just tick a form and it goes back again' ... A complete and utter waste of time and effort [for everyone].

However, perhaps the most telling confirmation of the problems of administrative fallout came from the head of academic registry who talked about the 'painful visibility' of the poor information systems at assessment boards (NewU's academic registrar, 1995b: 1). Indeed the phrase 'academic fallout' comes from a respondent (4) who was seconded to help administer the CAT system from the centre and in carrying out this responsibility had become only too aware of the 'fallout' issue. The vice-chancellor had also been made aware of it (if he had not been before) through the responses to a consultation exercise (*Towards the 21st Century:* NewU vice-chancellor, 1995a). He noted that one response summed up the views of many received by saying that 'the role of services should move from being one of information demand to one of information support' (NewU, 1995b).

Following this consultation exercise there was an attempt to tackle the issue. There was a major reorganization in the administration of the CAT system which, among other things, involved the excision of inter-faculty studies and the setting up of a combined honours department. Indeed, one of the main motives behind the move to NEWCATS in 1993–4 was the desire to simplify the system and thus promote its smoother working (NewU, 1993e: 8). Later there was an attempt to give students 'ownership' of responsibility for ensuring that their own records were correct and up-to-date as another angle on the issue (NewU, 1995f, 1995g).

It is clear that these problems are not peculiar to NewU, indeed they have been interpreted as endemic to managerialism, deriving from its assumptions and practices (Pollitt, 1990; Fairley and Patterson, 1995). Even at Oxford Brookes University, where the credit framework has been in place for much longer, academic staff found that personal counselling actually tended to be about mechanistic issues concerned with finding legitimate programmes of study. Moreover, while staff there had read-only access to student records and the system had worked very smoothly in the past (as described by Coghill in Watson, 1989), a new computer system was introduced in 1994–5 and this led to similar information-management problems to those experienced at NewU (fieldnote 1.4.95.). Very similar problems are also reported at the University of Westminster (Billing, 1996: 11) and by some respondents of a survey conducted for the journal *Management in Higher Education* (Warner, 1996).

Blau's 1973 study suggests that though large universities tend to be less bureaucratic than small ones, bureaucratic organization (including the administrative fallout resulting from multi-level hierarchies) 'does come into conflict with scholarship' (Blau, 1973: 280). Blau regards this as disturbing given that bureaucratic procedures are the 'easiest and cheapest way to give a resemblance of higher education to large numbers' (p. 280). However, administrative fallout is not an inevitable consequence of the introduction of the credit framework. Oxford Brookes' experience and that of colleges in the USA (fieldnote 2.8.93.) show that it *is* possible for the centre to cope with the information and administrative demands without placing a great administrative burden on academic staff, at least within large organizations.

However, it is a real issue for many institutions and one which derives from the demands simultaneously presented by the numerous requirements of a newly-introduced curriculum structure, staff and student fallibility and rapidly increasing student numbers in a context of resource depletion.

Modules and semesters

Beyond these remediable general problems, however, it seems clear from the data that there are a number of more intractable issues relating to the claimed efficiency gains of the credit framework. The notion that efficiency savings can be gained from students sharing 'generic' modules is a case in point.

There are numerous examples at NewU where this notion has been successfully applied. For example, engineering shared a number of modules across its HND, HNC, BSc and BEng programmes. Likewise, a department of applied science had responded creatively to a changing political and economic environment which saw an increase in their student numbers from 332 in 1989–90 to 477 in 1993–4 and a simultaneous reduction in both revenue and capital allocation, with new staff having been appointed only latterly. Their response was to move away from the traditional laboratory-intensive education, cutting laboratory sessions by around half over the last ten years (fieldnote 28.4.95. and applied science respondents), and to rationalize modular provision by increasing the number of shared modules as well as moving towards a concern with generic skills rather than disciplinary content – a move 'from dependence to independence' in student learning (NewU, 1994a: 1; fieldnote 28.4.95.).

This department was quite unusual in its adoption of a coherent strategy, one which seemed to find unanimity among its members. It has been successful, but this success has derived from the cognate nature of the streams which lead to the common modular pool. Such efficiency gains begin to break down once module sharing moves away from strictly cognate areas. The department found its students consistently met difficulties when sharing maths modules with maths students, the content being inappropriate to them and their need. So much was this the case that one external adviser to the review panel suggested in robust, neo-Liberal terms that 'if you don't like the product, don't buy it' while the other said 'if you can't teach it yourselves you don't need it' (fieldnote 28.4.95.).

Respondents from other disciplines, for example audio-visual media studies, business economics, engineering, design history and applied science 2 also reported difficulties of one sort or another experienced by students with different backgrounds sharing the same unit. These concerned both the different levels of preparation and cultural differences:

> You need all the work that precedes it, and when you've got people in your class that come from a variety of different sources you find that the students don't have the background. (Applied science 2)

Art and design students often feel very intimidated by the academic students, but what they don't realize is the academic students are often intimidated by them as well but for different reasons. (Design history)

This can be frustrating for academics:

I taught an instrumentation course in which . . . most students on the degree did OK but it was mixed in with people who were on our HND, our four-year degree, who weren't at the same level and they all did very, very badly, and that's where the whole system falls down, you see. If I was teaching that group of people as HND students . . . I would adjust my teaching, I would adjust the material, the level of it, everything to suit those people. But because they all took it together in one class it's very difficult to pitch it right, and you can get it wrong. And I did. (Applied science 2)

Moreover, the context of large modules consisting of people who do not know each other is a completely inappropriate environment for some areas of study. A respondent in nursing studies made this point about the discussion of bereavement, for example. Again, considerations of timing within one discipline or department can limit the extent of flexibility; art and design had an end of year and end of degree show and so wanted modules to run in semester one not two. A respondent in midwifery made the telling point that if they extended the concept of generic modules further than they had (common modules delivered to BA midwifery and BSc post-registration midwifery), for example to the diploma course, 'that means you would have three sets of students coming out of the clinical area at the same time. There would not be anybody left'.

The effect of all this is that the efficiency gains never really happen if the concept is pushed too far. Respondent 4, who had held a university-wide responsibility for the administration of CATS had clearly reflected in depth on this issue:

Having seen from programmes management the really remarkable duplication or multiplication of similar modules across the university . . . partly through mismanagement but partly because, when it comes to it, you can't actually have the same module that is maths for psychologists and maths for chemists [etc.] . . . you do actually need some element of tailor-making the particular module . . . Apart from anything else the administrative implications of record-keeping within a structure of that kind actually have resource implications attached to them and there are potential problems about intellectual coherence . . . It's all just a bit more complicated than people suggest when they imply . . . as a sort of given truth that CAT schemes improve flexibility and efficiency.

The semester system, too, brought with it a number of problems for many academic staff. These primarily related to pedagogical issues, especially the limited time available for assimilation of knowledge, understanding and skill, and for the introduction and use of student-centred methods. Other pedagogical concerns included the uniformity the semester system imposed on heterogeneous areas of study, the lack of time for formative assessment, the instrumental attitudes that students can develop when presented with a high assessment load in a limited period of time with no follow-up, and the 'surface learning' (Marton *et al.*, 1984) that this engendered. Other issues raised during interviews concerned the administrative fallout from semesters (double the number of assessment points and assessment boards), fears about the planned introduction of a third semester, and the very disruptive nature of a semester system imposed on a term-based holiday year.

In total, 27 of the 50 staff interviewed were highly critical of the semester system for one or more of these reasons, indicating the seriousness of the issue for them. Similar problems have been reported in other institutions, suggesting that the problem is not peculiar to NewU (University of Nottingham Union, 1993), though as with modularization some of the issues described here are not intractable. The problem about the interruption of semesters by holidays was resolved at NewU in 1995 by changing the length and start dates of the semesters, for example, as I described in Chapter 1.

Franchising

As with semesters and modules, academics' experience and perception of franchising was mixed. Many had operated franchise provision over an extended period and were supportive of the principles involved. Often this was done at considerable personal cost in terms of workload, however, as respondent 6 showed:

> I'm quite committed to [franchising] . . . I've worked very closely with colleges and got good working relationships and got a lot of trust in the course teams . . . But that's taken quite a lot of work. You know that's where quite a high proportion of that administration time goes in making sure that they're delivering properly and I go out to the colleges quite regularly so that the students, if they've got a problem, know me and can identify me . . . I do occasionally get students ringing up and saying there is a problem. So I see it as quite positive but . . . it takes my time to build those relationships.

Even the supporters of franchising recognized that there were a number of problems associated with it. These can be grouped under a number of (prioritized) categories. First is the administrative fallout from franchising. In some cases this led to withdrawal from involvement in it: '. . . once you've got franchise courses you get stage-two entry. It's actually quite a lot of extra administrative work as well. It's the kind of thing I think is desirable but I haven't time to create work for myself' (42).

A second, related point is the liaison difficulties involved in franchised partnerships: 'Where I have concerns they are about communications rather than the principles . . . particularly since our communications within aren't good . . . extending the lines, as it were, it could be like Napoleon's march on Moscow – cut off in the blizzard' (11).

Third is the issue of the sometimes fraught relationship between the two institutions and their staff:

> The staff [in colleges] feel that they must teach them by A level methods . . . spoon feeding the students . . . We just felt over the years that we should not alter things in order to accommodate that nervousness on their part because we are then moving down to a level which would be sub-degree level. (32)

> Also there is a political problem in the way they perceive the university . . . there's a kind of Oedipal attitude towards the university, a sense that it has not treated the colleges fairly. (4)

Fourth is the sharp contrast in the student experience, brought out particularly well in Bocock and Scott's report on further/higher education partnerships (1995: especially 37–46). One of my respondents said:

> [In franchised colleges] there's been particularly good staff-student relationships which have been a function of small groups and responsiveness to adults' needs as against 18-year-olds' needs . . . Here . . . we've got bigger groups and we don't know our students as well – and I think it's very difficult if they come here for the second year. They are doubly disadvantaged because all the friendship groups are sorted out. They are the outsiders, they don't know the computer network. (6)

Fifth is the issue of the maintenance of academic standards:

> I work on, or have worked on, the year zero combined honours access programme and we have worked with [college X and college Y], with members of staff from those colleges . . . I don't think we have sufficiently rigorous procedures for ensuring comparability and compatibility. We do franchise courses and we accredit courses held at other institutions in the name of this institution but I am not tremendously happy that we are sufficiently rigorous enough in the way that we either help or assess that work. (50)

Finally is the related question of the limited resources available in franchised colleges:

> They expect us to teach the first year of a degree in business on a 22-hour-a-week timetable. You just can't do it to the same standard as you do here at the university. (Fieldnote 13.12.94., college lecturer)

> I think franchising is a good idea for people who cannot come here, especially women. I think it's a positive programme expanding higher education . . . The only problem is that those institutions tend to be deficient [particularly in their library provision]. (6)

As in the other structural components of the credit framework, specific disciplines raise particular problems in the context of franchised provision:

Race and ethnic studies is not an easy subject to teach or to structure because it can be an area that raises emotive issues. You have to be conscious not just of the subject matter and how you treat it but also of the kind of chemistry of the group you are teaching it to and the chemistry as also caused by the ethnic origin and gender of the member of staff in the room. [Therefore I am unhappy about franchising the subject] unless the aims and objectives and ethos are shared by the other college. (Race and ethnic studies)

It's quite a practically-oriented subject in many ways and I think that a lot of the time they just don't have the facilities in the colleges to teach the practicals. (Physiology/pharmacology)

[Journalism as a discipline] can be diluted in [a number of ways]. You can call this media studies but it isn't, it's journalism and we pride ourselves on it being journalism. Media studies is something quite different, but of course lots of [further education] colleges now offer media studies . . . We do get our students into jobs . . . a hundred per cent within eight weeks of the end of the course last year. It's good and we're proud of it. But we all work hard here. It's a team effort: the students; us and the industry. (Journalism)

Despite these reservations most of the academics I interviewed were supportive of the underpinning philosophy of franchising and most thought its advantages outweighed any disadvantages they identified, a finding confirmed by the HEQC 1996 report on the NewU's collaborative provision: 'Staff from both the University and its partner institutions were clearly and enthusiastically committed to the delivery of the collaborative programmes and to their contribution to the realization of the University's mission' (HEQC, 1996a: 22).

Only 6 of the interviewees were explicitly against the idea, either for their own discipline in particular or in general terms, while 24 were clearly in favour, with 3 of these seeing no particular problems with it.

Despite this apparent success, franchised provision of higher education has seen a retrenchment at NewU in recent years due to the changes in the funding regime and the pressures for accurate planning of student intakes.

The credit framework: issues at the system level

While there are a number of reservations to be made about the claims made by proponents of the credit framework at the component level, there is also an issue at the system level. A number of respondents with experience of both credit and non-credit systems noted what they considered to be an inherent contradiction between the aspiration towards flexibility inherent in the framework and the administrative centralization which the framework tends to bring. They suggested the possibility, in other words, that far from being compatible, the ideological and the managerial aspects of the rationale behind the framework may conflict.

Respondents in the nursing, journalism, education, and statistics fields respectively noted with regret that aspects of the credit framework had meant that it was more difficult to achieve disciplinary integration than it had been. Primarily implicated in this was the centralization of the system, the consequent separation of departments and faculties who interact with the centre rather than each other, and the devolution of budgets. Together these meant that there were difficulties and penalties, both financial and in terms of administrative fallout, involved in any attempt to give the student an inter-disciplinary as opposed to a multi-disciplinary experience. Respondent 26 summed this up: 'I think that we had more vibrant course committees, course teams [before the introduction of CATS]. Even though we were across faculties and departments we got together regularly and decided how we were going to do things. It wasn't as formal, possibly, as the CAT system is now but it was more effective.' In fact the credit framework is designed to provide a multi-disciplinary rather than an inter-disciplinary experience. However, the point is that such an objective is considered a laudable one by these academics, and they see the credit framework as obstructing its achievement.

A second system issue concerns the rate of change to the credit framework initiated from the centre. The CAT scheme at NewU moved through three versions in five years, each an attempt to improve on the last. Liverpool John Moores University vice-chancellor and credit enthusiast Peter Toyne argues that: '. . . the best structures last about a year and you revise them every other year . . .' (Toyne, 1991: 63).

While this theory and the experience at NewU may accord with the precepts propounded in Tom Peters' (1988) book *Thriving on Chaos*, it was extremely poorly received by very many of my respondents; indeed this theme was one that constantly recurred in the interviews. Respondents clearly felt that constant changes to the credit system had undermined their ability to do their job properly. Respondent 17's comments stand for many:

> They change the system every year. Every year we have a different system for doing the same thing. What happens is that staff . . . suffer from . . . innovation fatigue . . . That means they say 'oh well I won't bother with the change this year because it will be different next year'. We never, ever, have a system that lasts. There's always something they have to change on it. Why they do it I don't know. (17)

As Ball points out when analysing management as moral technology from a Foucauldian perspective: 'the costs involved for workers in achieving greater efficiency . . . are rarely considered' (Ball, 1990c: 154).

In the next section we move on to use the data to evaluate the arguments put forward by the critics of what they perceive as hard managerialism.

The critique of 'hard' managerialism and the credit framework

A crucial distinction between soft and hard managerialism is that the latter stresses the primacy of the managerial role in the pursuit of efficiency and economy and makes no claims for the commonality of the interests of the various stakeholders. In the language of sociological structuralism, it is founded on a conflict rather than consensus model of social behaviour. My particular interest here is the effects of the application of hard managerialism on the academic profession. There are two positions on this. The first argues that the academic labour process is being de-skilled and degraded in the same way as working-class occupations have been according to writers such as Braverman (1974). Michael Apple (1989) has made this argument in relation to schoolteachers, suggesting that their work has been 'intensified' and degraded, while at the same time there has been de-skilling, most apparent in the separation of conception from execution: the decline in the (professional) cognitive work of teachers, leaving them the function of simply delivering a product. Those who use this argument often approach it from a neo-Marxist perspective, though Foucauldian and even Weberian perspectives also inform such work. The application of this kind of argument to the academic profession is not as new as it might appear. Tyler used it, for example, in his 1972 study *The Faculty Joins the Proletariat*.

The second position derives from a Weberian perspective and argues not so much that there has been degrading and de-skilling of academic work processes but that the status, class and power position of the academic profession has declined over recent years. This position is articulated by Halsey (1992) and Trow (1994) for example. Here, however, the emphasis will be on the first perspective because the arguments it makes implicate the credit framework (as opposed to, say, declining pay and external threats and competition to universities) much more centrally, incorporating and extending the arguments made in this respect by the second perspective. This emphasis should not be taken to imply that the first is seen as having more merit than the second, merely that the arguments it puts forward are more relevant to the current discussion and more fully elaborated. It is worth noting initially, though, that both positions exhibit the characteristics of 'gender blindness' (Wormald, 1985). The phenomena they discuss and the general consequences of the increasingly post-Fordist character of higher education in the UK are highly gendered issues (Acker, 1992a: 60, 67), yet (with the notable exception of Pollitt) this aspect of them is rarely raised in this literature.

I will begin by examining the general arguments put by labour process theorists and then focus specifically on those writers who implicate the credit framework most directly.

For Christopher Pollitt (1990: 1) managerialism is a 'set of beliefs and practices, at the core of which burns the seldom-tested assumption that better management will prove an effective solvent for a wide range of economic and social ills'. It is a theoretically developed form of Fordism with well worked-out policy imperatives. He ties managerialism in the public services closely to the new-right agenda. Where privatization is politically or economically unfeasible, managerialism is believed to be an alternative route to increased efficiency and productivity.

Found throughout the public sector, and latterly even in the 'professionalized' services which had previously been immune (Pollitt, 1990: 27) the application of managerialist ideology has involved the attempt to control activity through its quantification and measurement. This has involved techniques such as activity costing, the devolution of budgeting to 'line managers', the use of performance indicators, staff appraisal schemes, merit pay, objective-setting and so on.

Applying similar arguments to higher education from a classic neo-Marxist labour process perspective, Wilson argues that the term 'proletarianization' is a useful one to describe a situation in which the academic labour process is becoming degraded and de-skilled. There is: '. . . less trust and discretion; a growing division of labour; stronger hierarchies of management control; greater conflict; growing routinization; bureaucratization; worse conditions and facilities; above all a steep decline in relative pay' (Wilson, 1991: 251).

Presenting a classic neo-Marxist labour process argument, Wilson has little to say about the credit framework, simply suggesting that: 'Modularity is implicated in this because of the standard, pre-packaged nature of modular provision' (Wilson, 1991: 257). Wilson usefully distinguishes between two key processes implicated in the application of hard managerialism: degrading and de-skilling, noting that: 'University academics themselves seem to broadly disagree with the de-skilling hypothesis . . . the academics who benefit by losing routine work [by displacing it to non-academic staff] may gain new skills or may be freed to do more interesting or challenging work (Wilson, 1991: 257–8).

He maintains, though, that proletarianization, if only in the sense of work degradation, is occurring both objectively (labour process) and subjectively (class and status situation). Henry Miller agrees with this position, noting the process of degradation without necessarily wholesale de-skilling in the 20 universities in three countries which he studied (Miller, 1995a: 157).

Jary and Parker specifically implicate the credit framework in the deterioration of academic work. They argue that the development of the NHE has led to greater managerial control and a reduction in professional autonomy bordering on proletarianization. These changes 'are both reflected and reinforced by administrative [sic] structures like modularity' (1994: 2) which, while being grounded in the progressivist rhetoric of student choice are actually centrally involved in the erosion of 'responsible autonomy' that academics have historically exercised over their own labour process.

Jary and Parker are concerned with the implications of the change to a NHE. Central to this discussion are aspects of the credit framework, especially modularity, semesterization and franchising, but they also track the effects of, for example, the 'marketization' of higher education (emphasized also by McMurty, 1991), the 'quality' movement, the research assessment exercise, and research funding regimes with their stress on 'useful' knowledge and hence on 'performativity' (Lyotard, 1984), and the use of student feedback as a surrogate surveillance device (Jary and Parker, 1994: 8).

Jary and Parker consider the credit framework to be crucial in the changes they detect. The subtitle of their paper indicates a key argument: 'any colour you like as long as it is [multi-coloured]', suggesting that the move away from single honours towards combined honours degrees has resulted in the 'de-differentiation' of disciplines (Lash, 1990) so that, for example, sociology in one university is indistinguishable from sociology in another. It is perhaps not surprising to find Jary and Parker making this point: Christine King, the vice-chancellor of Jary's university, Staffordshire, has applauded the fact that modularity 'deconstructs academic tribes and territories' (King, C., 1994: 1). The import of this is to downgrade the academic from a producer of distinctive knowledge who engages in informed debate with colleagues to a mere 'worker' who delivers a package.

The notion of the decline of the distinctive discipline, and with it the deprofessionalization of academic work, is found elaborated in the works of authors writing from other perspectives also. Bernstein points to the demise of the traditional discipline and the rise of domains of study in universities, arguing that a process of 'regionalization' is occurring which weakens the disciplinary discourse and leads to the 'formation of less specialised professional identities whose practices are technological' (Bernstein, 1990: 156). Similar arguments are found in Lyotard's work (1984: especially 39). Richard Winter (1995) develops a similar argument, suggesting that in allowing students to construct their own 'customized' courses the university applies a kind of ideological pressure, the culmination of which, if successful, will be to disempower academic staff because they will no longer be able to shape student identities by designing a sequence of learning activities for them. In this scenario academic staff will become 'purveyors of commodities within a knowledge "supermarket", which may or may not be selected by the student-as-customer' (Winter, 1995: 134). Modularity is central to this potential for the commodification of higher education, according to Winter.

According to the critics, then, change in the 'shape' of knowledge in universities is one of the processes by which academic life and academic disciplines become less 'framed' both in the Bernsteinian sense and physically in terms of loss of 'gown's' and separation from the 'town' (Jary and Parker, 1994: 11; Rustin, 1994: 180). However this point is almost certainly being made too strongly by these critics. There are countervailing forces which act to *preserve* the dominance of disciplines as they are traditionally perceived: the persistence of discipline-based A levels as the 'gold-standard', the strong disciplinary underpinning of the HEFCE research assessment exercise and teaching quality assessment discipline networks are only a few examples. Burton Clark (1987) also shows how disciplines seem to reproduce prolifically in different ways.

These critics argue too that modularity is the perfect managerial tool for driving down costs and increasing surveillance (Jary and Parker, 1994: 8), through its ability to provide detailed information on academics' performance. Moreover, franchising and modularity permit the casualization of academic labour, the use of part-timers, postgraduates and further education lecturers, each of whom lack the job security, pay levels, autonomy and time associated with the higher education professional. These post-Fordist characteristics are intimately tied into the deprofessionalization that is a central part of the Jary and Parker thesis. Many of the characteristics of modularity 'open up to view the secrets of the profession and . . . ensure that internal motivations become external and hence manipulable' (Jary and Parker, 1994: 9). Thus, for example, the stress on writing aims and objectives for modules and the development of distance learning materials to support modular delivery in franchised colleges and internally (for post-Fordist 'delivery' by postgraduates and others) have this effect. The credit framework as a whole is part of the mechanism by which higher education becomes rationalized and instrumental, subject to evaluation through quantitative performance indicators: 'Credit accumulation, modularization and semesterization are intended to ensure rationalization and comparability of units . . . Each task is separated from the other, analysed for its costs and benefits to the institution and controlled by . . . forms of audit' (Jary and Parker, 1994: 3, 10).

Jary and Parker agree with Pollitt that there is an over-simple (Taylorist) model of motivation involved in the application of hard managerialism which involves a lack of understanding of multiple and conflicting goals and loyalties of staff (for example to their discipline rather than to the organization). Management's failure to understand this leads to demoralization in the workforce and associated problems. These authors are critical of the inappropriate application of entrepreneurialism and the market model to the public services and to higher education. Pollitt usefully supplements Jary and Parker's critique with an analysis of the impact of managerialism on equality of opportunity in organizations subjected to it, an aspect which Jary and Parker mention only in passing. He argues that managerialism creates a workaholic 'macho' ethos which permeates organizations exposed to it. This leads to the exclusion of those who have domestic responsibilities. Many posts now have stress and long working hours written into the job description. Rather than seeing more women move into management with a greater variety of possible management styles and role models, we are witnessing a creeping 'hard' managerialism in the public sector which associates managerial competency with masculinity, according to Pollitt.

Many other writers echo the spirit and refine the detail of the critique of hard managerialist Fordism and the way the credit framework is implicated in it. Rustin, for example, argues that: '. . . The ideology of "flexibility" in higher education is at the leading edge of [the] transformation of hitherto closed and bounded systems into more open ones' (1994: 182).

The requirement for explicitness within the modular curriculum has the same effect as the development of computerized 'expert systems': the alienation of the worker from his or her knowledge and expertise: 'One of the attractions of "flexibility" and "modularisation" for new academic managers is precisely that it does undercut or circumvent the power of the subject departments and their hierarchies. It, in effect, attacks their monopoly of supply of "psychology" or "sociology" to students and to the institution of which they are a part' (Rustin, 1994: 192).

Shore and Roberts (1993: 9) are critical of the uses to which a rationalistic epistemology can be put:

> The value of the curriculum is measured in terms of finite, transferable and above all marketable skills; modularization and CATS lead to the quantification of student work hours; constant assessment and auditing mean that course objectives and teaching methods have to be reoriented to suit Management Teams' mission statements. In short, unpredictability and personal growth are seen as liberal concepts of a bygone era and are being replaced by a new form of populism whereby the availability of courses and the way in which they are structured is dependent upon the extent of the consumer demand.

It is worth highlighting the isomorphism between the situation in higher education, as described by the writers discussed here, and in the school system, particularly with regard to the introduction of the national curriculum. Goodson argues that the introduction of the national curriculum was rooted in new-right concerns about the decline of the nation and the need for national regeneration. Rhetorical, financial and political structures were recruited to support the national curriculum, and an explicit agenda about state power over the school curriculum by implication involved an attack on the professional position of teachers and a diminution of their power (Goodson, 1990: 228, 230). Calls for greater accountability, vocationalism, clearer objectives, greater responsiveness to markets and better work habits which are now being made in the NHE as a result of a moral panic about lack of competitiveness with other countries have all been presaged in the school (and further education) systems. There too, according to Goodson and others (Maclure, 1988; Jones, 1989; Ball, 1990), the hidden agenda concerns the power of the state, disguised as 'the market', just as it does now in higher education.

Looking generally at the system as a whole, it is not difficult to interpret aspects of the credit framework as confirming the Fordism thesis. The Open University provides a good example of the points these writers make. Organized along post-Fordist lines, the Open University costs roughly half as much per student as a conventional one. With its army of local tutor-counsellors on part-time, short-term contracts, the central core is very small. The irrelevance of the particular academic to module delivery is ensured by the development of multi-media materials and the limited nature of tutorial contact. Techniques of surveillance are well developed, ranging from statistical comparison of marking across the country to observation of tutorials by regional staff tutors, scrutiny of and commentary on tutors' feedback on assignment and evaluations from 'customers' (fieldnote 22.2.96.). Regional staff tutors act as elements of the 'panopticon' (Foucault, 1977a; Shore and Roberts, 1995), being sent the results of analyses of tutors' performance from the centre and being required to take action where necessary. Their powers to take managerial action are much greater than those of a conventional head of department because of the nature of the Open University tutorial contract.

Tall *et al.* (1994) unwittingly demonstrate the way in which modularity can facilitate managerial control. Their use of quantitative measures to identify abnormalities in the moderation within and between modules on their courses for teachers (and hence implicitly to 'normalize' the situation) illustrates very well the point that Shore and Roberts are making. It also demonstrates how these innovations can be interpreted differently according to where you sit. For Tall *et al.* their modular system is designed 'to support students . . . [and is] demonstrably fairer to [them]' (Tall *et al.*, 1994: 92–3). For Shore and Roberts (1995: 14) it would be symptomatic of the 'control and audit' of higher education, or what Kickert calls 'steering at a distance' (Kickert, 1991: 1).

Some detailed empirical academic labour process studies lend weight to the thesis too. Selway provides evidence in support of the Fordism account in her study of the implementation of the move to the NHE at the University of Portsmouth (Selway, 1995). She abstracts a number of 'key themes' from the 'narratives' offered to her by academic staff whom she interviewed at that institution. These comprise: intensification of tasks; loss of control over the work process and hence loss of job satisfaction; reduced control over the use of time; loss of autonomy; and de-skilling. In the face of this proletarianizing Fordist onslaught 'there is a high degree of passivity and reactivity in academics' (Selway, 1995: 31) whose job role suffers accordingly. Such findings appear to validate the application of general accounts of managerialism and proletarianization such as Pollitt's (1990) to the higher education context.

In a similar vein Puxty *et al.* (1994) argue that changes to the labour process of academic accountants like themselves is best understood in terms of the process of commodification: the shaping and intensification of the work through the operation of mechanisms that stimulate market control and weaken academic control over the content and organization of teaching and research activities (1994: 164). While Puxty *et al.* make no explicit reference to the credit framework (though like Rustin they make the point about flexibility) their argument easily incorporates it. Again, details of empirical data collection and analysis strategies are thin, though the argument is clearly grounded in some of the authors' own experience and the analysis of secondary data.

Slaughter writes from a North American perspective and uses a case study of the State University of New York (SUNY). She argues that academic department managers are essentially colluding in the managerialist thrust in that country and shifting the purposes of higher education towards a human capital approach (Slaughter, 1985: 52). She sees faculty as essentially working harder but falling behind in the attempt to meet these demands: '... faculty are confronted with the same assaults on their job security and their work life as their blue-collar brethren: speed-ups, give-backs and lay-offs ... managers are trying to take charge of an academic reward system long controlled by faculty' (1985: 52, 54).

Like Selway she reports no identifiable resistance to this from academic staff themselves in any form, the only threat to managerial success being the fact that 'managers may be expecting the impossible, asking faculty for higher performance while providing fewer resources and reduced services' (1985: 54).

However, being based on a content analysis of planning documents from the state and SUNY itself, Slaughter's study has accessed only the front-of-stage policy output. There is no access to back-stage or under-the-stage responses to that output, nor is there any attempt to access the implementation of policy or identify the nature of any 'implementation gap'.

'Hard' managerialism: discussion

I turn now to an evaluation of the critics of Fordist consequences of the credit framework and other aspects of the NHE. Here, portions of my interview data in particular suggest that the arguments outlined in the previous section have merit. I deal with these portions under a series of headings which derive from the work of those critics and from the data.

Work intensification and degradation

The message from the interviews on work intensification was loud and clear: it was occurring and it was hurting. Several respondents used factory analogies to describe the situation: 'It's like a factory. It's awful' (18); 'almost like processing peas' (29); 'processing students through a system ... People use factory analogies, don't they?' (10).

Many reflected on the consequences of work intensification for the quality of what they do: 'research, teaching and administration ... I do all of them badly' (13); 'nowadays I rely on what I did last year' (22); 'so overworked you don't have time to even think about new avenues of research, never mind actually carrying them out' (31).

Even for 'star' researchers such as respondents 21 and 31 with teaching loads which were 'very light indeed' (21), the ability to do the research was impaired by obligatory involvement in assessment boards, departmental meetings, reassessments, invigilating resit exams in September and then marking them. Such duties 'have pock-marked the summer ... I found it very much more disruptive than I had been used to before' (21).

Respondent 13 confirmed the point made by Slaughter (1985) that the combined effects of work intensification and degradation meant that there would come a point at which what was expected simply could not be achieved: 'I don't want someone telling me "you should be able to turn out a book a year". That's bullshit, not the way things are now' (13). A respondent in languages agreed, pointing to the special demands of her discipline:

> Students . . . will normally do six or seven pieces of assessed coursework through the year for their one course, and that would be quite a heavy amount of marking given the attention to detail that language marking involves. So I would say it's close to being an impossible marking load, which comes at a time of the year when you are not able to do it. (Languages)

There was worry among others, too, about the future, especially the idea of three semesters: '. . . people are saying we are now going to move to tri-semester and perhaps this is a back door way into the two-year degree programme. So there's all that sense of insecurity and worry that we all share' (9).

Certainly, for some, the personal consequences of work intensification were considerable: '. . . I used to [work] . . . [in a busy hospital] and it feels like [that was] a holiday compared to the work levels [here] . . . It's all a bit of a nightmare' (14).

Bureaucratization

There was a very clear sense, too, that work intensification had been compounded by what at least appear to be inefficient and unnecessary administrative structures and processes; 'bureaucratization' in its pejorative sense. There was very widespread concern about this:

> [The CAT system] is far too complex to operate . . . you spend more time filling in the necessary forms and it becomes an absolute nightmare. And it's not necessary. (24)

> The fact is that you're having to get bogged down in doing bloody petty things which you shouldn't have to do. But the reason you have to do them is because of inadequacies of the system elsewhere. (19)

> Yes I do feel disempowered in that . . . the . . . bureaucracy of the institution sometimes lets you down so that you don't have the information you need when you need it. (39)

The APL/APEL system provides an interesting case study with regard to bureaucratization. In the early years of NewU, course leaders simply made decisions about credit exemption and transfer themselves, without the quality controls in place for taught courses, examinations and other forms of assessment. In 1992 procedures and structures began to be put in place to normalize this situation: the creation of a credit exemption and transfer panel, the appointment of a credit exemption and transfer officer, the progressive development of administrative procedures and regulations for the operation of APL/APEL, staff training days and so on. Academic staff interpreted these developments in terms of the general feeling of bureaucracy and disempowerment described above. While it is clear that the demands of HEQC quality audits and HEFCE quality assessments require the sorts of measures put in place, and that they could be argued to be necessary on the grounds of natural justice, the effect seems to have been that the procedures at NewU became, as Griffin predicted such procedures would, so 'complicated and time-consuming as to present a barrier to anxious students and hard-pressed staff' (Griffin, 1987: 9).

Power shifts

The sense of pressure on academic staff that the interviews gave was compounded by a feeling among many of them that power had shifted away from them – a 'decline of donnish dominion'. Asked about this, respondent 2, a senior administrator with a cross-university role and contacts, summed up the feeling of many respondents: 'It's a more managed institution than it ever was . . . the academic delivery etc. is driven by management objectives so that's where the shift is. It's not in the administration.'

For one academic the feeling of disempowerment had hastened her decision to retire:

The inability to manage my time [is] very pernicious and it's very difficult to get back. It's one of the reasons I'm going . . . I don't think I would ever be able to function as, say, a course leader again. I have lost something, now I'm trying very hard to recover it, which is being in control, [I feel] . . . like being a feather in the wind and I'm finding that very difficult. (11)

For respondent 13 the fault lay with the adoption of industrial production models by the management at NewU: 'How many other universities have a rector who is chief executive officer? What is this – General Motors?'

Many too felt that the demands of 'the computer', the prime system which was the key to the university's information systems, was reducing their power as academics: '. . . in some cases the computer refuses to accept the name change of a course. So I changed the name of a course three years ago and we've still got the old name. The computer will not accept the name change' (31).

Blau's study of the influence of the administrative organization on academic work concluded that 'the administrative use of computers tends to centralize authority in academic institutions' (Blau, 1973: 279) and indeed at NewU the vagaries of 'the computer' was a tacit metaphor for academic disempowerment. This goes far beyond its (clearly documented) inadequacies in dealing with large amounts of rapidly changing data as the following account shows.

Fieldnotes and secondary data collected during the first nine months of 1992 document a very heated debate about the issue of assignment of grades to students' performance on an in-service part-time professional course. This programme had been developed along competence-based lines and the course leader was adamant that students' performance in such programmes should not be graded: students should instead be regarded as either competent or not yet competent in specific areas. The issue came to a head at the summer assessment board in 1992 when the board had to confirm results. Ungraded module results for each student were minuted (represented by an S or a U, for satisfactory and unsatisfactory) but after the meeting the secretary reported that the computer would not accept these letters, only the official CAT grading scheme; numbers at that time. This immediately foregrounded an issue which had up to that point remained back-stage. A series of meetings and memos followed between members of the department concerned, its head, the head and deputy head of programmes and a member of the rectorate. The department itself was divided on the issue of grading and several of its members were relieved that the rectorate's decision was that 'any unit without a grade cannot be fitted into our system' (memo 27.7.92.) and this programme must conform (though there were to be subsequent revisions of this decision).

During this time 'the computer' tended to be seen by the 'non-graders' as the villain of the piece: reprogramming would solve the problem. Even those in favour of grading resented the fact that its demands were part of the debate and had introduced participants into that debate from outside the department. For them the issues were about pedagogy and the principles of an integrated CAT system, particularly progression for students within it. For those above head of department level the issue was about maintaining a coherent university-wide integrated system. The computer programme was simply an external articulation of this; to change the programme would be to change the system. From the ground level, then, 'the computer' became a symbol of hard managerialist use of the credit framework: systems above people; procedure above process; numbers above personal development.

Not all the academic staff whom I interviewed and had contact with focused on power shifts resulting from managerialism within the institution, however. A minority blamed national higher education policy, particularly funding policy, for their plight. Respondent 6 is an example: 'At the end of the day what happens to the funding council affects how the institution moves and what I think is neither here nor there. So I don't have a strong position on it. We're the pawns in that way, aren't we?'

Surveillance

A few respondents raised the issue of their sense of increased surveillance. Respondent 31, for example, felt the burden of:

. . . an extremely high level of accountability which . . . was in many cases unnecessary, very intrusive and did constrain you in terms of what you were free to do within your own courses . . . So many people now see your syllabus and see your reading list that if you did try to get away with it I'm sure it would be noticed and probably something would be said about it.

However, for most the issue was not so much about oppressive surveillance of their work and professional lives as about the burden of work that the processes of surveillance involve. Respondent 27 summed up the views of many on this:

[We are] under far too much scrutiny, more scrutiny than it is reasonable for anyone to bear. Where you've got teaching quality assessment and . . . RAEs and you've got the internal quality assurance mechanisms, the external ones, and a whole panoply of things . . . you're producing fairly similar sets of documentation in rapid succession for a whole succession of bodies.

Conclusion

The picture of the credit framework painted by its supporters portrays it as increasing the accessibility of higher education in an economical, efficient and effective way. While its flexibility does increase accessibility, the data presented here suggest that there are some important costs to this, including costs to students, though this is not the focus here. The costs to academic staff in terms of what they perceive to be the problems associated with the credit framework are vividly demonstrated in the data, though it is difficult to untangle the multiple and interlinked causative strands: more students; rapid growth; managerial style; bureaucratic surveillance mechanisms and limited resources, as well as the credit framework (Schuller, 1990). Even the claims for the efficiency and effectiveness of the framework are questionable; this part of the picture at least has been painted with too broad a brush by the credit proselytizers.

One could conclude from all this, as Selway (1995) does at the University of Portsmouth, that the combined effect of these factors is the proletarianization of academic staff who passively collude in implementing policies which are detrimental to them: classic examples of 'docile bodies' discussed by Foucault (1977b). Certainly it would be easy to interpret the impact of the credit framework, and other aspects of the NHE, as meaning that the particular claims to professionalism that academics make become less tenable as disciplines lose their distinctiveness in the combined honours system and as epistemic drift occurs with the rise of vocational 'transferable skills' and the demise of disciplinary content. Without doubt academic work *has* been intensified, degraded and bureaucratized over the last ten years, partly as a result of the credit framework, though the declining unit of resource and other factors are implicated too. Yet such a conclusion about academic professionalism is not justified on the basis of my data taken as a whole. Unravelling the various elements of 'Fordism', taken as a synonym for hard managerialism by the critics of the NHE, highlights issues on which my data bring doubts about this interpretation of developments in higher education and the role of the credit framework in them.

Two issues are key in qualifying the 'Fordism' account. The first is the fact that de-skilling, perhaps the most important aspect of Fordism, did not appear to be occurring, at least to academics in posts with full-time and long-term contracts – many individual academics had maintained their professional identity and autonomy in the face of these various pressures. The second is the fact that the Fordism thesis sees academics as passively accepting their own proletarianization. Though some were indeed suffering badly under the combined weight of the various aspects of the NHE, including the credit framework, and did not feel able to respond in ways which would alleviate their pain, others were coping in ways not accounted for in the Fordism thesis while still others were thriving in the new environment and actively shaping it from the ground level. Huw Beynon showed in his landmark ethnographic study *Working for Ford* (1973) that even assembly-line workers have room for manoeuvre, that their behaviour creates an 'implementation gap' between managers' aims and actual outcomes even in the 'pure' Fordist case. In the university context the importance of how ground-level actors think and behave is heightened. Jary and Parker characterize academics' strategies in Mertonian terms: they conform, retreat or behave ritualistically (Jary and Parker, 1995: 330). They do not yet rebel or innovate according to these authors (1995: 335). McMurty, too, says that academics 'mutely accept' (1991: 216) the changes to their professional practices. My data show, however, that this conclusion would be to misrepresent the position. Academics are clever people. Rebellion and innovation are their forte and they frequently stand in strategic locations on the 'implementation staircase' (Reynolds and Saunders, 1987). Later chapters explore and illustrate these ideas, using a fine brush to apply some colour to the broad-brush monochromatic pictures painted so far by the supporters and detractors of the credit framework.

3

Responding to Change

The essentialist paradigm

Stephen Ball (1994) makes the point that policy is not passively received and automatically implemented, rather it is actively interpreted, decoded, and responded to in complex social and cultural contexts. However, in the study of higher education the paradigmatic approach to understanding the forces that condition academics' values, attitudes and behaviour, including the ways they perceive curriculum policy and put it into practice, roots them firmly and simply in the knowledge structures of academic disciplines. This chapter sets out that epistemological essentialist viewpoint, takes issue with it, and puts an alternative point of view.

This position of epistemological essentialism is reflected in, for example, Tony Becher's classic text *Academic Tribes and Territories* (1989) and Burton Clark's work *The Academic Life* (1987) as well as many less well-known texts (Lodhal and Gordon, 1972; Shinn, 1982; Ruscio, 1987; Davidson, 1994a; Gregg, 1996). It means that any attempt to understand academics' responses to change, including the development of the credit framework, must primarily be informed by an understanding of the nature of the discipline in which they specialize. This will strongly affect their professional cultures and hence responses to any innovation. Burton Clark, for example, says the following:

> As knowledge is newly created by research, and is reformulated and repeatedly transmitted in teaching and service, its force continuously bubbles up from within daily operations, right in the palm of the professional hand. The logic, the identity, the very rationality of the academic profession is thereby rooted in the evolving organisation of those categories of knowledge that disciplines and professional fields of study have established historically and carried to the present, producing an inertia that powerfully prefigures the future.

> (Clark, 1987a: 268)

For Tony Becher too the way groups of academics organize their professional lives and the nature of the professional task on which they are engaged 'would seem to be inseparably intertwined' (Becher, 1989: 1). Their offices are bedecked with artefacts which symbolize their disciplinary allegiance. The very language they use is structured by their discipline, conditioning the modes in which arguments are 'generated, developed, expressed and reported' (p. 23). Beyond these, though, are the more explicit aspects of culture: the customs and practices, traditions, values and beliefs, and rules of conduct which are so obvious to those who share them as to be invisible. These include the disciplinary analogue of the organizational culture's 'saga': the 'heroic myth' involving the key figures in the discipline. The academic's *modus operandi* is conditioned too by epistemology at both the disciplinary and sub-disciplinary level: '. . . the close-knit epistemological structure of high energy physics research is mirrored by the fast-moving, competitive, densely populated – one might say urban – research community associated with that field' (Becher, 1994a: 153).

The influence of the discipline permeates personal life too: physicists relax from their frenetic professional lifestyle through theatre, art and music, while engineers prefer aviation, deep-sea diving and boating for their relaxation (Becher, 1989: 106). Academics in modern languages, meanwhile, inhabit a more laid-back 'rural' world (p. 153). So strong is the link between disciplinary epistemological characteristics and academic professional cultures that academics who become cut off from their discipline (such as higher education researchers) are even said to 'lack a culture' (Becher, 1994a: 160).

Epistemological essentialism and the credit framework

Davidson (1994a, 1994b) and Gregg (1996) both operate within this epistemological essentialist paradigm in their analysis of academics' reactions to and implementation of modular curriculum policy. Davidson, on the basis of a three-year study of CAT largely within chartered universities, suggests that 'linear' disciplines such as the natural sciences, computing and languages are most suited to the adoption of modularity. Hierarchical and cumulative in nature (having what Bernstein, 1971: 49 calls a 'collection code'), these have an inherently modular structure: 'packets' of knowledge are taught sequentially and lead the student through a pyramidal structure from a broad foundation to increasing specialization in later years of study. Such disciplines tend to be strongly classified, that is their contents are strongly bounded as against other disciplines (p. 49); in fact it is their strong classification which gives rise to their collection code (p. 51).

Disciplines and domains with 'non-linear' knowledge structures, however, do not fit the modular structure according to Davidson. Progression here is more to do with the development of skills and understanding rather than increasingly arcane knowledge built on a solid foundation. The most obvious examples are domains such as education studies, women's studies and race and ethnic studies as well as disciplines in the social sciences and humanities. Here knowledge is agglomerative rather than cumulative, horizontally rather than vertically structured. These areas of knowledge are loosely classified and there is rarely agreement among specialists about what should be considered 'core' knowledge (Davidson, 1994a: 43). Other areas of study such as economics, sociology and anthropology occupy intermediate positions between these poles.

Davidson does recognize that in some cases the strong conditioning influence of epistemological characteristics is influenced by cultural factors, ethical codes and practices and, where they are weakly framed (i.e. open to influences from outside the academic profession), by the requirements of external bodies (Davidson, 1994a: 44). However, such influences are relatively weak:

> The structure of knowledge dictates students' flexibility to select units and to combine them in novel forms. It is influenced by the degree to which subjects require previous specific knowledge in order to progress, the contemporary nature of information, the degree of maturation required, the volume of study which will enable students to best perform, the amount of practice an area demands, the constraints of external bodies, and the awards students hope to receive.
>
> (Davidson, 1994a: 51)

Staff attitudes then, will also be conditioned by these factors: a finding apparently confirmed by Patti Gregg's study (Gregg, 1996). Gregg studied a total of 14 higher education institutions in the UK and, while she found some concerns which ranged across the disciplines, her results appear to indicate that epistemological factors shape academics' responses, particularly their view that modularity inhibits students' ability to develop skills and cognitive characteristics as well as to integrate knowledge. Art and design and humanities staff in particular were strongly resistant to modularity while maths and science staff and (particularly) those in business and management studies were less resistant or even in some cases in favour of modularity and other aspects of the credit framework. Social scientists tended to fall somewhere between these positions. Law exhibited a more complex pattern with law staff in unchartered universities being more positive about modularity than their colleagues in the chartered ones. Gregg attributes this difference to the lower classification strength of the discipline in the former polytechnics (p. 15).

Some problems with epistemological essentialism

The focus on elite institutions, disciplines and academics

Much of the empirical work which has adopted epistemological essentialism has been conducted in elite institutions of higher education, often concentrating on high-status individuals within the disciplines concerned. The rationale for this has been an implicit or explicit 'trickle-down' model of culture, articulated by Parsons and Platt in 1968 and frequently replicated since. As Becher (1989: 3) says:

> I confined my attention to members of those departments which were viewed as reasonably prestigious within their disciplinary communities . . . The disciplinary values with which [most academics] are first inculcated are . . . the values of the leading departments in their fields . . . So it seemed sensible to concentrate on the pacemakers rather than those that follow behind them.

As long ago as 1974 Donald Light was questioning this approach and suggesting that academic staff in different structural locations (in terms of the institution they work in, the nature of their employment and their own characteristics) develop different cultures. The continuing lack of attention to lower-status institutions, disciplines and individuals has had a number of effects. First, because of this concentration on leading academics, whose primary concern is usually research, the literature on academic professional cultures based in this tradition has usually concentrated on this rather than, for example, on the implications of culture for pedagogy, curriculum policy, administrative work and so on.

The second effect is that the special factors which operate in the newer, lower-status disciplines and domains of knowledge, for example women's studies, fashion and media studies, have up to now received very limited attention in this strand of research. The same is true of the factors operating on and within the lower-status institutions. The literature provides little direct theory or evidence in this area, a particularly serious omission since factors are foregrounded in non-elite settings that are usually only implicit in more advantaged contexts.

Confusing theory and 'reality'

The model of academic cultures in the literature based on epistemological essentialism is predicated on a view of 'academic man' which is close to Dahrendorf's notion of 'homo sociologicus' (1968), the individual as the player of predetermined roles. In this literature the roles are highly prescribed, epistemologically conditioned, received from cultural leaders and relatively context-independent. Dahrendorf argues that other images, particularly that of the 'free' individual, are possible and (consciously adopting the relativism of Kantian dualism) that each has equal validity. The individual as free and the individual as constrained by roles are 'simply different ways of comprehending the same subject' and are not contradictory (pp. 61–3). Homo sociologicus is, however, a 'tool for rationalising and explaining certain aspects of the world we live in' (p. 49). With it, Dahrendorf argues in a postscript to the essay that the sociologist can 'reach much further . . . than with statements that aim at an accurate description of man's [sic] nature' (p. 77). Effectively he is arguing for using homo sociologicus as an ideal type in the Weberian sense. However Dahrendorf rightly notes (p. 77) that the notion of homo sociologicus can do damage when applied to the empirical domain if the abstract conceptualization is mistaken for empirical reality. One of the strengths of Becher's work is his outline of the academic tribes and their respective territories, but in my view these should be seen as ideal types not (as Becher suggests they are) descriptions of empirical 'reality'. In practice, individuals have considerable freedom to depart from the models depicted and they do so, as I will now demonstrate.

Over-emphasis on the ideational

Authors whose theoretical position is rooted in epistemological essential-ism fail in general to demonstrate convincingly the mechanisms by which knowledge structures become translated into attitudes on, for example, the credit framework, the direction which higher education is taking, pedagogy or many other aspects of academic life and work. The focus is firmly on the ideational: rites, rituals and the symbolic dimensions of daily life, perhaps because these are more easily linked to the characteristics of disciplinary knowledge. An appreciation of, as Clark puts it, the 'characteristics imported into the academic profession by individual members from their personal background and prior experiences', which he considers to be 'the least important components of academic culture' (Clark, 1987a: 107) can, together with other factors, help to draw the links between professional culture and such issues.

The absence of an account of power

A further area of concern with this approach to understanding academic professional cultures is its omission of the role of power in academic con-texts. Power is normally thought to be exclusively concerned with the dis-tribution of resources. However, Giddens notes that meanings, norms and power are logically implicated both in the notion of intentional action and that of structure: every cultural milieu is a system of power, involving a 'horizon of legitimacy' (1976: 161). Any attempt to understand how aca-demics reproduce, and produce, social reality must take power into consid-eration as must any account of culturally-bounded policy implementation. One of the deficiencies of epistemological essentialism is that it assumes that academics are almost completely autonomous and that power lies in their own hands in disciplinary and in most other matters. While this may be true for high-status individuals in high-status disciplines in elite settings, it is not so in other contexts and certainly not at the site of this study. A sociologist in my sample noted how attitudes towards his discipline among those in senior positions in the institution had led to an unarticulated conscious or unconscious policy of disciplinary dispersal so that while today sociologists could be found in such areas as organizational studies and race relations, there was no disciplinary identity among them: 'To use Thomas Kuhn's phrase, they walk along the corridor not talking to each other. Not because of paradigm crisis, but because of not knowing each other' (sociology).

On the other hand most top-down studies of policy implementation have seen the academic as powerless, as I argue in Chapter 4. What is needed is a view of power which does not see it as a one-sided phenomenon, for example the one espoused (but not actually put into practice) by Foucault: 'Power must be analysed as something which circulates . . . Power is employed and exercised through a net-like organisation' (Foucault, 1980: 98).

The complexity of epistemological characteristics

The conception of the nature of disciplines which underpins the essentialist viewpoint is an over-simple one: disciplines have multi-dimensional characteristics ignored in the simple linear/non-linear model which Davidson in particular puts forward. She is not alone in this. Squires (1992: 202) and Lattuca and Stark (1994: 403, citing the work of Dressel and Marcus, 1982) point out that many discussions of disciplines (e.g. Lodahl and Gordon, 1972) fail to take into account their multi-dimensional nature. While this critique applies less to, for example, Becher (1989) or Donald (1986), it is certainly the case in Davidson's discussion. Davidson's prime concern is with disciplinary content or object and fails to take account of what Squires calls their 'stance', by which he broadly means their ontological standpoint and related methodology, and the discipline's 'mode' or approach to itself, for example 'normal' in the Kuhnian sense, or reflexive (Squires, 1990, 1992). Adopting this more complex model of disciplines means that simple disciplinary 'maps' like Davidson's begin to fragment and what seemed a simple set of distinctions breaks up into an apparently chaotic series of multi-layered overlapping fields. Any unity that exists may variously lie in the object of study, the methodology, professional organization and so on, though some strong disciplines maintain internal sub-disciplinary commonality along a number of dimensions (for example, physics). Even here, however, the 'strength' may be conditional and short lived. Law, which Squires describes as 'strong and self-contained' (1992: 203), has recently begun to suffer internal schism around the issue of the application of postmodernist theory to law as a discipline.

The situation becomes more complex still if one makes a distinction between *discipline* and *subject*, where subject is understood as the organizational structures and patterns into which disciplines are translated (Evans, 1995: 253–4). Institutional context will both reflect and pattern the forms that a discipline takes as well as the particular understandings of it that inhere among academic staff and students. Thus, for example, the design history input to an art and design course may be perceived as 'merely' servicing from another discipline and art and design itself be seen as a relatively highly classified discipline if the design historians are located in another academic department.

However, the social construction of disciplines goes much deeper than this. Talking of practical subjects only Davidson says that: '... the "shape" of knowledge fitted into a modular format reflects the manner in which a community of practitioners operates within a culture at a particular historic time ...' (1994a: 44).

This is true, though, of *all* disciplines and domains. Bernstein (1971, 1990) takes a view of curriculum structure as conditioned by social structures and the distribution of power. He argues that the distribution of power and the principles of social control condition how educational knowledge is selected, classified, distributed and evaluated (1971: 47). While Bernstein would agree with Davidson's point that highly classified disciplines with strong collection codes are particularly suitable for modular curricular structures, he parts company with her on the issue of whether there is something intrinsic to the field of study which gives it those characteristics. Indeed, for Bernstein, changes in authority structures and social identities are reflected in changing knowledge structures, and, at the same time, disturbance in the classification of knowledge will lead to disturbance of power relationships and social alignments (p. 59).

Bernstein overstates the paradigmatic nature of disciplinary culture, however. Frequently one finds internal schisms within disciplines conditioned by educational ideology. Thus, for example, whether an academic subscribes to the linearity 'story' about their discipline or not is essentially conditioned by educational ideology:

> ... at Bristol University the [important question] was ... 'how on earth can you possibly teach the late nineteenth-century novel in the second year if the students haven't done their early nineteenth-century novel course in the first year? You just can't do it.' I think that attitude is very strong when you are coming from that ethos that you are producing specialists. But ... I ... think ... a third year literature module is not just [about] doing different literature than ... you did in the second year, it's actually looking into things at another level and I think that the ability to read novels and to read poetry is something that deepens ... It's this question of not wanting to prevent students joining your courses because they haven't got pre-requisites. (49)

Colin Evans gives a detailed account of how the discipline of English is fundamentally split between the Leavisites and the critical theorists. The former essentially subscribe to what I refer to below as the traditionalist educational ideology, viewing the English canon as central in the transmission of the discipline. It is the approach of the academics at Bristol that respondent 49 is describing. As one of Evans' (1993: 131) respondents said of this tradition: 'There was an understanding that if you hadn't studied figures like Chaucer, Shakespeare and Spenser, you hadn't studied the subject'.

Critical theorists on the other hand are committed to the deconstruction of the canon, injecting theory derived from sociology and feminist writing among other sources. Describing this tradition, one of Evans' (1993: 143) respondents said:

> Theory is staked inevitably on the idea of a good argument. The trouble is that those who are against theory [Leavisites] wouldn't accept that there is such a thing as having their ideas knocked down. They are appealing to values which claim to stand beyond any sort of theoretical dismissal. So there's an awful lot of mutual bafflement and ill-will generated by the fact that we are talking on different wavelengths.

In its moderate form the critical theorists' position is founded in the educational ideology which I call progressivism, while its more radical form is based in social reconstructionism. These ideologically-based disciplinary splits were found among English lecturers at NewU too. Critical theory is dominant there, though there are internal dissenters, while Leavisites are preponderant in the franchised colleges:

> The first year is a kind of skills-based course . . . it deals with the whole idea of how literature is . . . a way of imbuing notions of Englishness and social control . . . ideas about the middle-class culture and the way English became a professional subject in universities . . . It's a way of asking students to reflect on what they are doing. And it's this kind of thing that the franchised colleges find difficult . . . The deconstruction of the canon has been one of the most important influences on the way that literature is taught . . . One or two colleagues don't agree with that kind of approach, but most agree that it's a good thing that it's come to be questioned. (English)

In the same way, a respondent from engineering in talking about his discipline echoes the debate about 'subjects' or 'topics' in schools, reflecting the 'traditionalist'–'progressivist' divide there:

> There are two ways . . . of looking at it; you can either look at the subjects that are the basic engineering subjects . . . and teach mathematics, thermo-dynamics, electronics, all as discrete chunks. The problem with doing that is that you then very artificially have to put applications on them . . . you need an assignment to investigate mechanics only . . . Or at the other extreme you can break it down into complete project areas and for example look at a car . . . which involves a whole lot of mechanical and electrical engineering principles . . . The former makes teaching very straightforward but makes the subject very dry with not very much reality in it. The latter makes the teaching extremely difficult because generally staff are specialists in one area. (Engineering)

Bernstein and Evans are not alone, of course, in demonstrating that disciplines and domains are historically and socially situated. Mary Henkel (1988) shows how social and cultural values influence epistemological characteristics as well as the reverse. Using the techniques of discourse analysis, Gilbert and Mulkay (1984) have shown that natural scientists construe their actions and beliefs in a context-dependent way using, alternately, empiricist and contingent repertoires. Thus to Squires' (1992) already sophisticated model of disciplines and sub-disciplines must be added the further layers of discursive context and interpretative form. This is not to say, though, that disciplines are completely social products, a relativist position which Becher rightly criticizes (Becher, 1995: 397), only that knowledge structures are mediated by social processes; a view which Becher himself comes to acknowledge (p. 398). The metaphor of an epistemological landscape seems appropriate here. Land exists without an observer, but landscape does not: the 'scape' is the projection of human consciousness – the way the land is perceived (Bowe *et al.*, 1994).

The data presented in the next section demonstrate that in the minds of some respondents the perceived epistemological characteristics of their discipline are important in conditioning their view of the credit framework. Whether this has a basis in 'reality' as the essentialist position suggests, or whether it is simply a disciplinary 'story', as some postmodernist positions would maintain, need not detain us. The important thing is the academics' belief in its importance, and it is this which leads me not to discount it completely as a factor in the study of change in higher education. Colin Evans' discussion of Tony Becher's essentialist position is helpful in conceptualizing the importance of epistemology in change. As I implied above, Becher is aware of the extremely complex nature of disciplines and sub-disciplines and the difficulty of classifying them (1989: 179, 1990: 334). Yet as Evans points out (1993: 162) the difference of opinion between Becher and Huber in the special issue of the *European Journal of Education* on disciplinary cultures (1990) essentially revolves around an anthropological (Huber, 1990) and an essentialist (Becher, 1990) view of culture. Evans aligns himself with Huber (Evans, 1990: 275) but adds the important rider that members of groups are also in a kind of dialogue with a hypothetical world of coherent, bounded entities, placing themselves in a relationship of perceived consonance or dissonance with them. Thus Becher's 'academic tribes and territories' are important in a 'virtual' sense. This restricts to some extent the parameters within which the social construction of the discipline can take place, and its rate of change (Evans, 1993: 163). Academics position themselves against a 'story' about their disciplinary culture and, I argue, similarly relate (sometimes in different ways within the same discipline) to a story about the demands of their discipline in terms of how its content can, and cannot, be sequenced and presented when it is taught in the university context.

In this sense the (perceived) epistemological characteristics of the discipline are important in conditioning responses to change, but they should be

seen as only one important factor. Other factors are discussed in the following section.

Conditioning structures

The data from the study at NewU suggest that the factors conditioning
attitudes and behaviour are multiple and more complex than is suggested
by epistemological essentialism. There are two senses in which this is the
case. First, as I have already indicated, if we use the word 'structure' to
mean properties which lend coherence and relative permanence to social
practices in different times and locales, then confining attention to only
one structural influence, disciplinary epistemological characteristics, ignores
a number of other important influences. Second, the model of structure
or structures strongly conditioning behaviour in a unidirectional way is also
a limited one because it ignores the importance of social actors' power
to influence structure. Giddens' work is important in taking forward our
understanding on both these points. With regard to the first he suggests
that structures have the characteristics of rules and resources. The former
consist of normative elements and codes of signification while the latter
comprise both authoritative and allocative aspects (Giddens, 1984: xxxi, 17).
An understanding of the influence of structure should take into account
each of these aspects where they are relevant. With regard to the latter, his
account of the processes involved in structuration takes us beyond the model
of structural determination inherent in epistemological essentialism. I elaborate on the first of these points below and return to the second in Chapter 6:
this chapter concentrates on structural factors while Chapter 6 considers in
greater detail the interaction between action and structure.

Multiple structural conditioning

The set of conditioning structures I found important at NewU is indicated
in Figure 3.1. I deal below with each of its components in turn.

Educational ideologies at NewU

Curriculum decisions are always highly value-laden. Perceptions of and responses to them and to the environments they create are conditioned not
only by cultural contexts but, more narrowly, by the patterns of the educational ideologies found among the individuals involved. Ideology is understood here as a framework of values and beliefs about social arrangements
and the distribution and ordering of resources which provides a guide and
justification for behaviour (Hartley, 1983: 26–7). Educational ideology, specifically, refers to those aspects of ideology which relate to the nature and
purposes of education (Skilbeck, 1976: 10).

Figure 3.1   Structural factors conditioning compatibility of academic staff with the credit framework

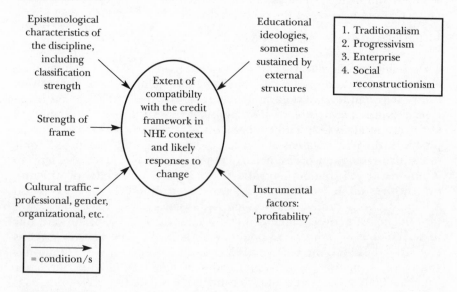

Figure 3.2   Key Axes of educational ideology at NewU

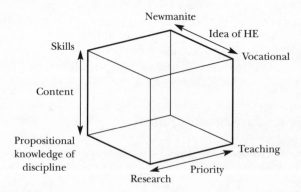

Analysis of the interview data in particular demonstrated that at a general level educational ideologies primarily revolve around three axes: the **aim** of higher education (Newmanite or vocational); the important **content** (discipline-based propositional knowledge or general transferable skills); and the important **functions** taking place within it (research or teaching). At their most fundamental level, then, they answer the three essential questions about education: 'what exactly should we do?', 'why should we do this?', and 'how should we do it?'. Figure 3.2 represents this diagrammatically.

Within this matrix it is possible to identify four ideological positions, though these are subject to the qualifying comments below. They are, in summary: traditionalism; progressivism; enterprise; and social reconstructionism.

At a second, more specific level, these ideologies reflect a co. of values and beliefs which, in the contemporary British highe context, relate to views of the following areas:

- The nature of disciplinary knowledge (for example, whethei covered' or 'created').
- Academic 'standards' and changes in them.
- The relevance and importance of different types of skills.
- The preferred level of permeability of the boundary to higher education.
- The nature of society (for example, conflict/consensus).
- The use of IT in teaching and learning.
- The distribution of talent in society.
- The nature of the typical student.
- The role of the student in higher education.
- Most importantly for this study, the credit framework.

In some cases these views will be identical, or virtually so, in two or even three of the ideological types identified. Taken as a whole, however, the ideologies are distinctively different.

Traditionalism

Found in the recent literature articulated as Ainley's (1994) 'hard' position, Skilbeck's 'classical humanism' (Skilbeck, 1976) and Collier's 'academic' ideology (Collier, 1982), this is rooted in a belief in the value of cultural and disciplinary heritage, of which academics are custodians, and hence in the 'autonomous tradition' (Burgess, 1977). It is usually characterized by a form of elitism, justified in terms of the inherent difficulties of higher education study and the limited distribution of talent in society. Implicit in this position is a mass-minority view of society, therefore, and elements of sociological structural-functionalism. This educational ideology can be found articulated in the works of Plato (1955), Arnold (Super, 1964), Leavis and Thompson (1933), Bantock (1968) and Minogue (1973). In terms of the three axes shown in Fig. 3.2, the traditionalist favours research, disciplinary content and a Newmanite idea of higher education.

Traditionalists tend to be worried about epistemic drift: the dilution of their own disciplines by transferable skills and other features. Respondent 36 is an example: 'That material has disappeared because we've got things like IT in there and things called common skills . . . they gobble up a lot of time, so do group studies and time management and electives'.

In the higher education context the mass-elite dichotomy revolves around the possession of 'intelligence', which is perceived as existing in a fixed and limited amount and distributed in a highly uneven way: 'If they basically don't have the intelligence, if they don't have the good minds to actually cope with the problems that [my discipline] poses then they will never make a good [scientist] however much you add on to the course' (44).

The corollary of this characterization of the nature and distribution of intelligence is a concern about measures designed to increase access on the grounds that this will open the boundaries of the academy to weaker minds:

> We have taken people on who have come through these franchise courses and so on, open access and all that, and we've had a mixed bag, and some have been OK and some have not. Some have been absolutely terrible . . . I favour straightforward A level entry . . . I can't see the point in these open access courses at all. The only reason they're there is because the people that are doing them are basically not able or not willing to do A levels . . . What we're doing is we're giving people an easy ride into a university course. (44)

Or, from within another discipline:

> [With applicants for APL] what you often get . . . [is] a lot of idle lay-abouts. [Some of these have been in danger of being thrown out of other institutions or felt they deserved to get a degree in one year. On being frustrated in their hopes for APL they] . . . burst into tears and go off and see the rector or anybody else and eventually they often man-age to end up getting a degree . . . It's just pushing the system. (29)

These two respondents represent classic examples of an unalloyed tradi-tionalist perspective. However the position was found among other academics who qualified their position, possibly in deference to its currently being out of fashion: 'I think access is great but I think sometimes students . . . may do an access course and then expect to get onto a degree course and get a degree at the end . . . In the terms of what we're doing and what we're expecting of our students, I think they're not always the right people to be on degree courses' (39).

Traditionalists usually expressed a concern, too, about the measures the institution was taking to protect these new, 'weaker', students:

> I think there's an [institutional] agenda about students passing, that it's almost impossible for them to fail in a way. They can redo work and so on and I think they make it a bit easy for them sometimes. (39)

> [CATS is] . . . also going to reduce the amount of material that students will come across. That is also difficult for [my discipline] because there is a lot of material . . . [to cover] and we are already not doing every-thing we ought to be doing. (48)

Traditionalists view with suspicion the motives that the institution has for introducing the credit framework:

> . . . the purpose of it being done here, I think, partly has been in order to maybe just jack up the numbers, rather than being simply a device to achieve and to recognize learning. (41)

> There's the impression that if they breathe on the mirror then we'll take them . . . [Franchising too is being pursued] . . . a bit too greedily:

[imitates an upper class English accent] please, this is a university after all don't you know? (13)

For the traditionalist the credit framework has been almost uniformly deleterious in its impact on the effectiveness of higher education. Respondent 37 encapsulated a number of the criticisms:

> This is the third credit accumulation, supposedly credit accumulation scheme, that we've had and prior to the idea of implementing a credit accumulation scheme there was this whole emphasis on integration with previous courses . . . A lot of that goes out, it just disappears . . . [When CATS was introduced] people stopped talking about integration . . . and started talking about flexibility . . . I think educationally it isn't such a good idea . . . the lack of integration I think is a problem and I think also for the students a problem of identity as to where they belong . . . I think if you felt you were doing a well-specified course that had been outlined for you, you knew where you were and knew where you belonged . . . The psychology now is very much more 'well I've got to pick up some credits so how can I do it?' I think a really worrying thing about the whole structure . . . is that if you define a course then students have to pick up the various components whereas the growing philosophy at the moment amongst the students is not necessarily what's sensible to take but (through the grapevine) what's easy to take . . . [T]here's a real implication there for standards because quite obviously the motivating factor for them is to do as well as they can in these various modules and so, just extending that argument, they try and look for modules they think are going to be easy enough to pick up, to get reasonable grades in.

The data from the interviews tend in some ways to confirm and in others to refute stereotypes about the association between discipline and traditionalist ideologies in university contexts. The physical sciences and 'hard professional' disciplines (Clark, 1987a) are often said to be bastions of traditionalism, not least by respondent 28 who described staff in one hard professional discipline at NewU as 'old gits'. While it is true that the majority of traditionalists in my sample came from these disciplines, traditionalists were also found in others, for example in the humanities. Moreover, some of the respondents from the physical sciences and 'hard professional' disciplines were represented among the very clear examples of other educational ideologies. The respondent who was course leader of an engineering 'flagship' course heavily stereotyped in this way fell into the progressive category, as did another respondent from the same discipline. It seems likely that age is at least as important as discipline in this. I defined 50 per cent of the traditionalists as 'older', compared to 33 per cent of progressivists and 0 per cent of the other two categories, while 41 per cent of progressivists, 25 per cent of social reconstructionists and 71 per cent of enterprise academics were 'younger' compared to 17 per cent of traditionalists. The rest were coded as 'middle aged'. Discipline and current age profile are not unrelated, of course, somewhat muddying causality.

In general, the shaping influence of professional and disciplinary culture on educational ideology seems more limited at NewU than previous studies like Becher's (1989) would suggest. Disciplinary background and the articulation of a particular ideological strand bear a loose but not coterminous relationship to each other. For example two lawyers strongly articulated very different ideologies. Commitment to the research function was, though, strongly linked to a traditionalist ideology by its very nature. However, far from all of those espousing a traditionalist viewpoint were active researchers in practice. Respondents 13, 21, and 37 were strongly active researchers, 23, 29, 36, and 48 weakly so. Respondent 12 fell firmly into the traditionalist category but, though she was postgraduate research tutor for the department, had 'no time' for research herself. The category 'researcher' is not something which is fixed, of course. The significance of research can ebb and flow at different stages of an individual's professional life in much the same way as relative poverty can become significant at particular stages of one's personal life cycle. While most traditionalist academics interviewed had a PhD, some of the respondents were on the up wave in terms of research (for example, 39) and some on the down (for example, 24, 44).

Progressivism

In the literature on ideology this roughly equates to Ainley's 'soft' position, Skilbeck's 'progressivism', Collier's 'soft' version of the ideology of economic renewal and some aspects of his 'ideology of consensus'. It claims to be 'student-centred' in the sense of valuing students' participation in planning, delivering, assessing and evaluating courses. Partly as a consequence of this, disciplinary knowledge and traditions are considered to be relatively unimportant: students' freedom of choice and personal development take priority over propositional knowledge and experiential learning is valued at least as highly as other types. This ideology rejects elitism and favours mass access. Where there is a concern about social inequality the role of education is to give a 'step up' to disadvantaged individuals and groups in the largest numbers possible, not to reconstruct society. Academic standards are relatively unimportant; what counts is the possibility for the individual to benefit as far as possible and in their own way from higher education. This educational ideology can be found articulated in the works of Heafford (1967), Robinson (1969), and Duke (1992). It is also to be found in the pages of *The New Academic*, the journal of the Staff and Educational Development Association. In terms of the three axes in Fig. 3.2, progressivism in the higher education context favours teaching over research, personal skills over disciplinary content, and a Newmanite idea of higher education.

It is largely from this group and the next that the CATS gurus or fundamentalists are drawn. These people represent extreme examples of this ideology and often have achieved positions of relative seniority at NewU: the climate there has suited them and they have thrived, though one academic interviewed (45) once held a senior CATS-related administrative post but became disillusioned and returned to academic work.

The importance of the students to the work of the 'new academics' who subscribe to this ideology was stressed by many of them: 'We tend to get involved with our students . . . you can't separate the student from the subject . . . I find being involved with planning and having responsibility for the administrative side helps you keep in touch with students' (law).

The discipline was considered to be relatively unimportant to them: 'A lot of my colleagues would say that in a semester there isn't enough time and to some extent I would share that . . . [but instead of] trying to force too much in [to six modules] we need to give them the skills to look it up for themselves' (law).

So, while a traditionalist lawyer laments the lack of available time to deliver the content of a module on land law, a progressivist in the same discipline (above) is less concerned with content and more with 'transferable skills'. She or he might recognize the issue but does not see it as a problem.

Traditional pedagogical approaches in higher education need to be rethought according to most progressivists: '. . . people need to be doing something to learn rather than sitting and receiving information – it just doesn't go in' (34).

The new emphasis should be on active learning and the acquisition of generic skills: '. . . performing experiments or going away and researching some information and writing that as an assignment or doing some more project work using their initiative' (34).

A suspicion of the use of technology in education is characteristic of the progressivist, unlike the enterprise academic, discussed below. A respondent in languages is critical of the attempt to: '. . . direct students to our language learning centre and to encourage what's commonly referred to as resource-based learning, which basically means . . . a load of tapes and books and videos, one or two computer programmes. Off you go and get on with it . . . I think it's a substitute for face to face . . . dialogue' (languages).

This is indicative of the fact that the progressive new academic is, like the traditionalist, often critical of the university's implementation of policy in its attempt to conserve resources and in other ways:

> I don't like the sound of . . . people putting lectures onto video tapes and students going and keying into a terminal and watching me deliver a lecture about some aspect of journalism. I can't see the point. I mean why not let's post it all out to them. Let's close down the buildings. Let's really cut our costs and let's just have a video unit here so that . . . we can all work from home, and the students as well, we just set them all up with terminals. It would be a lot cheaper. (Journalism)

The CATS gurus in this category are particularly bitter on the issue of resource limitations undermining principle: 'The basic problem was the fundamental infrastructure was never in place and still is not in place. I think NEWCATS is a disaster. It has removed that necessary flexibility, and I think that's a great shame. It's not solved anything' (45).

The distinction between the progressivist ideology and enterprise ideology is clearest on the issue of the purposes of higher education. For the enterprise ideology the main function of higher education is the vocational one, but this is not the case for progressivism:

> [Higher education] . . . is not about preparing young people for the world of work, to improve the economy of the country . . . it's about producing critical, independent thinkers . . . Certainly, looking around my colleagues, my impression is that there is a strong desire to keep that, but . . . with the students themselves viewing university education more and more as a passport to a career, my suspicion is that we are going to lose it and I'm shocked already at the political passivity of students. I don't want to turn them all into revolutionaries but I think that they don't think critically and I think that is actually dangerous, to everyone, long term. (49)

> I . . . feel that [higher education] ought to have an unashamedly social function in terms of preparing citizens for participation in the community, in society. I think in a genuinely pluralistic society, education does have that very important function of preparing people for participation in democratic life. (50)

This leads to serious concern about those aspects of higher education concerned with 'knowing how' rather than a critical approach to 'knowing that' (Barnett, 1994). For example, competence-based approaches:

> The danger . . . is when attempts are made to interpret everything from the point of view of skills, competencies and . . . behavioural objectives to be fulfilled . . . it's almost like dismembering . . . It feels rather artificial to me . . . In my field there are language skills which people can genuinely develop and generally demonstrate. However . . . we have to retain a more holistic approach and I would be happy to see a mixture of competence-based and rather more holistic, for want of a better word, measures of achieving. (Languages)

Consequently there is a suspicion of those aspects of the credit framework that align with this among progressivists. Questioned about the very vague learning outcomes specified for new modules in the validation of a new humanities degree, the course leader designate said that they had deliberately been left open in order not to restrict the opportunity for negotiation and following students' own interests and concerns (fieldnote 24.3.94.).

Enterprise

The development of the view that the main role of higher education is to equip the student with the transferable and vocationally relevant skills necessary for a successful personal career and a contribution to the general social and economic good has been tracked by Tapper and Salter (1978). This view equates directly with Collier's (1982) 'ideology of economic renewal' and lies firmly in the 'service tradition' (Burgess, 1977) of higher education. Higher education is principally concerned, therefore, with the development of 'human capital' (Schultz, 1961) and it is seen primarily as an economic rather than positional good (Barnett, 1994: 4). Experiential learning is valued and a primarily utilitarian view is taken of propositional knowledge. New technology and new approaches to teaching and learning are valued as more efficient and effective tools, as a challenge to traditions in higher education and for their development of important skills in students. Enterprise ideology can be found articulated in the literature from the Enterprise in Higher Education initiative, the Employment Department (for example, 1992, 1994), TEED, the journal *Capability* and the work of Sir Christopher Ball (1990). In terms of the three axes in Fig. 3.2, the enterprise academic favours vocationalism over the Newmanite ideal, skills over content, and teaching above research.

For the enterprise academic the formal demise of the 'binary divide' represents a threat to the vocational mission of the polytechnics – a threat of academic drift:

> The good thing about polytechnics was . . . that they were much more down to earth, much more realistic about the skills they were teaching and they were spending a lot more time and work on their teaching and making their teaching excellent whilst university was much more interested in research . . . and that was fine. So I'm not sure where we are going here . . . and whether we are doing anyone a favour by trying to be an old university and really losing a whole market. (46)

The enterprise academics I spoke to usually enthused about the potential of information technology: 'I think that we are on the verge of this IT revolution and I think that we've got to try and exploit that and keep . . . the control as much as possible . . . through trying to be at the leading edge of IT . . . and learning . . . and teaching developments' (47).

Generally they were keen to innovate and undermine old practices and were relatively uncritical of managerialism or the 'erosion of collegiality': 'We've started a scheme of voluntary peer observation this year which is turning out to be quite stimulating' (43).

They were keen, too, on experiential learning: 'Students must do a presentation, must be on camera as well as behind the camera . . . They have to work in groups . . . and they're enjoying themselves' (audio-visual media studies).

For the enterprise academic the flexibility of the combined honours system is attuned to the variety of skills that are demanded in a modern economy. Modern jobs require a combination; for example languages and technical skills: 'People do strange jobs that require strange combinations of talents at the end of the day and I think people should be able to do what they are good at. If they're good at French and electronics then let them do French and electronics and go and be an electronics engineer in France' (audio-visual media studies). Another respondent in audio-visual media studies was keen that the field should meet the requirements of employment, and hence employers, quoting one as saying that graduates cannot write, work in teams and so on. These were important to this respondent and they were built into the programme, of which he was one of the primary initiators.

However, the enterprise academic usually has concerns about the partial implementation of the credit framework, which may undermine the advantages to the student and employer:

> What we are trying to produce here is a product that is marketable and sellable at the end, i.e. the student. The people out there have to understand what they are getting and I think for that reason the combined honours system doesn't actually lend itself to doing that very well . . . It would if we were using the profiling system and the sort of log system which I think it was ideally supposed to have . . . it would really give you a clear profile of what they have studied. (47)

Again, the reality does not conform to the enterprise academic's ideal in other ways too:

> I don't think the university really as a whole institution makes it clear what its expectations are of students, or what it is prepared to offer to students . . . I really don't think that there is any serious attempt . . . to engage students in finding the mission statement meaningful or in, for example, defining what their learning agreement or learning expectations are in relation to themselves in the institution . . . You have to go for the image of the students . . . being co-workers and not customers and that you have to try and create the atmosphere of a modern institution which is like a workplace. (43)

Social reconstructionism

Skilbeck argues that it is only in periods of great social upheaval or crisis that reconstructionist thinking finds a ready audience among educators and consequently it has rarely been seen in the schools context in Britain (Skilbeck, 1976: 34). While this may be true in schools, it is not so in higher education where the critical tradition found particularly in the social sciences fosters it. Collier (1982), for example, notes its presence with his 'hard' version of the 'egalitarian ideology'. In the higher education context social reconstructionism claims that education can be a force for ameliorative social change, including (and perhaps especially) for creating an improved individual who is able critically to address prevailing social norms and help change them for the better. Thus the social reconstructionist shares a change orientation with the enterprise academic, but the nature of the desired change is very different and more radical. The social reconstructionist shares with the progressivist a preference for active, problem-solving pedagogy. In this respect and others, however, the social reconstructionist can also see potential deleterious effects (Foster, 1994: 25). Social reconstructionism can be found articulated in the works of Lawton (1975), Williams (1980), Apple (1990), the journal *Living Marxism*, and in the publications of the Hillcole Group (for example, Ball, 1990b). The social reconstructionist favours the Newmanite philosophy over vocationalism, teaching over research (though 'emancipatory' action research is favoured: Kemmis, 1988; Weiner, 1989), and skills over disciplinary content (however, see below).

The social reconstructionist ideology generally takes a very distinctive approach towards the higher education context also. The neo-Marxist variant is generally critical of the credit framework, seeing it as undermining higher education's role in developing autonomous critical thinkers and as part of a general reorientation of the sector towards vocationalism. The increasing emphasis on 'knowing how' rather than 'knowing that' means that students lose the opportunity 'to study the beautiful, the irrelevant, the arcane, and can readily endorse a philistine attitude to abstract concepts' (Foster, 1994: 26). Flexible, multi-disciplinary courses replace in-depth specialism with superficial understanding derived from pick and mix modules. Epistemic drift is occurring as the emphasis shifts from disciplinary socialization towards 'transferable skills', both found in discrete 'skills' modules and infiltrating substantive ones. Here the rhetoric of student-centred learning masks an agenda concerned with conserving resources and responding rapidly to market demand (Robson, 1992: 20). The undermining of disciplinary knowledge, of the status of academics as experts and the power of their symbols (Rustin, 1994) has the effect of neutralizing a potential force for opposition to class rule. The result is 'an incoherent and inferior degree' delivered by proletarianized 'full-time teachers', mostly in 'underfunded, overcrowded FE colleges' (Robson, 1992: 20). Rather than being a mechanism for the enhancement of social mobility, higher education becomes highly polarized and class-based, with 'opportunity' existing only at the rhetorical level in those sectors of higher education available to the working class (Ainley, 1994). The effects of processes currently occurring in higher education under the guise of student-centredness have already been seen in the school sector, and been subjected to critical scrutiny by neo-Marxist scholars (Sharp and Green, 1975).

Curiously the logic of the argument places neo-Marxist reconstructionists like Foster on the same ground as traditionalists such as Minogue: 'the old system in this country may have been elitist. But at least it gave students something worthwhile in the way of education' (Foster, 1994: 26). Both positions see higher education as ideally concerned with the arcane, studied in a master-pupil relationship in a context which is as remote as possible from the world of work. From the social reconstructionist perspective of neo-Marxists, however, the desirability of traditional models of higher education lies in their potential for creating change.

While neo-Marxists stress the need to resist higher education becoming an aspect of cultural reproduction, class domination and social control, for Foucauldians like Shore and Roberts (1995) the concern is with the incorporation of universities into the system of state power. As I showed in Chapter 2, for Shore and Roberts the credit framework is one aspect of a general trend in higher education and elsewhere towards quantification of inputs and outputs, surveillance, and central control masked by an apparent and rhetorical devolution of responsibility. The credit framework facilitates the quantification of student work hours while course objectives and teaching methods are shaped by constant assessment and auditing to suit management teams' objectives. This creates, according to Shore and Roberts, a 'compliance culture' in which: '. . . emphasis is placed on form rather than content and where noncompliance with the management drive for normalisation and standardisation is to be punished' (Shore and Roberts, 1995: 14). This needs to be resisted if higher education is to play a reconstructive role.

Perhaps unsurprisingly, three social reconstructionists in my interview sample were sociologists and the fourth had a background in politics and history. Of all the respondents, number 10 was the most explicit about his social reconstructionist ideology. His aim as an educator was:

> . . . to get students to challenge and to be able to locate the knowledge that they are acquiring historically . . . socially and politically . . . with a view ultimately to that process being liberating or emancipatory. That in coming to understand more about how knowledge is produced in a particular field of domain . . . there'll be liberating experience for the student . . . Knowledge not dominating them is what I'm after . . . there's no reason for them to be afraid of the expert, no reason for them to be fearful of people who display this kind of knowledge. (10)

This had important consequences for his attitudes on aspects of the credit framework, for example semesters: 'I find that negotiated learning, student-centred learning is much more difficult when the period over which you are able to have contact with a student group is foreshortened to 14 weeks . . . and at the same time you only meet them for two hours a week'.

A women's studies respondent was similarly explicit about her ideological position:

> I feel that what sustains me in [my work] . . . is more to do with what's outside than what's inside [the academy]. That's partly because I am a committed feminist. I am also an activist . . . It's actually really important that the women's studies that is around is actually helping women to understand and to change their situation for the better. (Women's studies)

There is a Robbins trap-like issue for social reconstructionists. While they tend to be in favour of the access that the credit framework in a 'mass' higher education system can bring, they express worries about the resources allocated to it and the exploitative uses it can be put to in a managerialist context. This can be summed up in the question 'access to what?' Respondent 9 encapsulated this:

I think franchising is a good idea for people who cannot come here, especially women. I think it's a positive programme expanding higher education . . . The only problem is that [the colleges] tend to be, particularly library-wise, poorly resourced . . . [There is a] hidden agenda about the semester system [too] . . . people are saying we are now going to move to tri-semester and perhaps this is a back-door way into the two-year degree programme . . . (9)

There is an underlying concern too about the effects of moving away from a disciplinary base: 'I hear people say you empower students, you do this for students coming through non-traditional routes but I don't think so because . . . students become terribly instrumental, they simply come here, do the essay you ask them to do and stay away so they do not have an overall framework in terms of knowledge base' (9).

This has a potentially retrogressive effect, undermining the power of disciplines to create change. For a respondent in sociology, for example, the credit framework leads to 'major problems around the fragmentation of knowledge' so that the students 'don't have a clear identity of themselves as sociology students, even those ones who are doing joint or even major sociology. There isn't a clear sense of . . . class identity. The class themselves don't seem to gel' (sociology).

This is not only a pedagogical issue but a wider one related to social change: students do not attain an understanding of their class location, and so never become part of 'a class for itself':

[At Essex University] there were staff who had clear perspectives on their discipline and although staff obviously disagreed amongst themselves, as academics do . . . as a student you knew what your department stood for . . . you knew where it was coming from. The sociology department at Essex was radical, it was Marxist, largely. There was a very clear sense of belonging to that and that you fitted in with that. And I think that our structure here doesn't facilitate us developing that identity. (10)

This leads to another dilemma for social reconstructionists:

How much choice do you give to students and how much control do you take upon yourself for what they shall have to learn? (10)

I'm torn between being practical and what I would really like in an ideal world. (31)

Respondent 10 felt the need to take action against the progressive proletarianization happening to him, partly because one consequence of it was that he could no longer operate in the ways he felt he should in terms of his students' development. Similarly respondent 31 felt a need to fight against 'disempowerment', as she termed it:

One of the first things that hit me was my lack of autonomy as a lecturer in the system . . . In [another town] where I had done some teaching part-time for two years I had a very high level of autonomy about what I taught, how I taught it. I could change it around from year to year and really didn't have to tell anybody that I was doing this. (31)

Generally, the feeling was that recent developments had moved the credit framework more towards its negative, managerialist, than positive, expansionist, side: 'I feel that there was a particular epoch in this place when . . . [the institution] had that commitment to [access and equality of opportunity issues] . . . Some of us stuck our neck out and we fought for those issues and we saw changes in this institution. But right now I doubt it . . . Now it's a question of number crunching' (9).

Some qualifications about this form of typology
There are a number of good reasons to be cautious about the type of categorization developed above. Discourse analysts tell us that interview discourse represents a choice from alternatives rather than simply giving 'outer articulation to an inner world of thought' (Potter and Wetherell, 1987: 178–9). At a more basic level researchers need to distinguish between 'espoused theory' and 'theory in action' (Argyris and Schön, 1974). Moreover, individuals often do not fit easily into only one ideological 'slot': the discursive repertoire is wide and elements from a variety of ideological and political positions can be found, often in close proximity in a single 'text'.

However, such arguments do not mean that the categorization developed above and ones like it have no value. The ideological forms elaborated above are presented as ideal types, 'analytical instruments for the intellectual mastery of empirical data' (Shils and Finch, 1949: 106). This section clarifies the relationship between these constructs and empirical 'reality'. Respondent 3, for example, simultaneously stresses the progressivist access, personal development and social mobility themes and the enterprise critique of traditional practices and catering to employers' needs, while the transcript of the interview is littered with both enterprise and progressivist discourse. Similarly respondents 34 and 36 produce both traditionalist and progressivist discourse at various points during the interview. Others, by contrast, betray no strong allegiance to any educational ideology, perhaps because they have become disillusioned, interested mainly in self-preservation, winding down to retirement, or simply because the course the interview took did not give them a full opportunity to express any such allegiance. The picture of academics as ideologically 'fired' that typologies such as those above may paint would be an inaccurate one for some, though not very many, staff. Similarly it is probable that other, more weakly expressed and minority, ideological positions are in operation at NewU. The four discussed here are merely those which are most clearly discernible from the data available; searching for and identifying others would move the analysis into increasingly tenuous areas.

Interview data, then, need to be treated with caution and the ontological claims of ideological typologies should be modest. Ideological sets represent not categories but rather preferences which actors can to some extent choose or reject in any given social context. However, any enquiry into ideological viewpoints should not treat them as valueless for four main reasons. First, while ideologies are given expression in individuals' discourse, they operate within wider structural and ideological frameworks within which respondents form their attitudes. Thus it is possible to seek confirmation of representations of ideal types in the wider context. The four represented here are clearly found on the wider higher education stage as the references at the beginning of the description of each of them illustrate. Each, too, is supported by 'grounded' structures which sustain them (Parkin, 1972), most obviously represented by the journals and conferences which give the opportunity to articulate a viewpoint and to sustain otherwise isolated individuals (Allen and Layer, 1995: 16).

Second, not only the interview data but other types of data collected at NewU tend to validate this categorization of ideological sets. Thus, for example, during a portfolio-assessment moderation meeting of a work-based learning programme, the discussion turned from the merits of individual portfolios to the very essence of what was being assessed (fieldnote 1.6.94.). Traditionalist and enterprise viewpoints quickly clashed and resurfaced at the assessment board (June 1994) for that programme. Similarly, at an in-house training session discussion of the merits and demerits of a videoed maths lecture highlighted a progressivist/traditionalist clash in attitudes towards students, propositional knowledge, the role of the academic and pedagogy (fieldnote 31.1.95.). Numerous fieldnotes from observant participation of the university's CAT panel also highlight these different ideological sets.

Third, the interview data are not treated as self-explanatory, but are subject to careful analysis and interpretation. Labov (1969) has demonstrated that interview data must be analysed with an understanding of the meaning systems of participants. Insider research such as this project allows the researcher to construct a 'second record' (Stenhouse, 1979; Hull, 1985), an interpretation of what appears 'on the record' of the transcripts informed by knowledge of those meaning systems. Harman makes the same point (though studying a different university from her own) in relation to making judgements about respondents' practices from their statements about them: 'Useful inferences can still be drawn about behaviour by noting normative statements offered by informants about what constitutes expectations, and good and bad practice, in their respective fields of study' (Harman, 1988: 181).

Fourth, ideological perspectives are apparent not only in what is said but in the discursive medium used, as the comments about respondent 3 above indicate. To paraphrase McLuhan (1964), the medium is sometimes more reliable than the message, though one should maintain a wariness about 'reading off' ideology from discourse (Pritchard and Willmott, 1996). Of course, academics themselves are not unaware of the ideological significance of discourse. Both 13 and 50 commented on this:

When I came over here [from the USA] and saw all the institutionaliza-
tion of CATS as a word, as a description, I thought well why dignify it
that way, why bureaucratize it that way? . . . It struck me as very bizarre
. . . You know: every five year plan has an acronym . . . Calling it something like CATS makes it more alien. (13)

I am 'marketing' my modules and students 'accumulate' 'credit'. So
I think the language of the administration of HE gives us a very clear
indication of what's happening. (50)

Instrumental factors: 'profitability'

Levine (1980) suggests that the 'profitability' of an innovation is an important precondition for its successful implementation and this view is confirmed by my data which identify it as an important structural factor too. By
profitability he means whether or not the innovation can bring such things
as security, prestige, peer approval, growth, efficiency and improvement in
the quality of life. For academics and academic departments the profitability of the credit framework usually lies in its ability to attract students or to
'deliver' the curriculum in more cost-effective ways. Both these aspects were
evident in certain sites at NewU.

In the languages department for example the 'elective' element of the
modular system (in which students must choose two modules outside their
field of study to broaden their education) means that many students choose
to study a foreign language in addition to their core area of study. Without
this the department would be much less significant than it is at NewU: 'We
know our department is very heavily dependent on the electives programme.
Almost fifty percent of our FTE's at the moment come from electives . . .
structurally speaking the idea of modules is not a bad thing' (languages).

In a department of applied science there had been a creative response to
a changing political and economic environment which has seen an increase
in their student numbers from 332 in 1989–90 to 477 in 1993–4 and a
simultaneous reduction in both revenue and capital allocation with new
staff having been appointed only latterly. As a department they had moved
away from the traditional laboratory-intensive education, cutting laboratory
sessions by around half over the last ten years (applied science respondent;
fieldnote 28.4.95.). They had used the credit framework creatively too by
rationalizing modular provision through increasing the number of shared
modules as well as moving towards a concern with generic skills rather than
disciplinary content – a move 'from dependence to independence' in student learning (NewU, 1994a: 1; fieldnote 28.4.95.). They were successful in
this, but this success derived from the cognate nature of the streams which
lead to the common modular pool.

Others in a less fortunate position with regard to student recruitment
had been able to take advantage of elements of the credit framework to
recruit and to achieve efficiencies and economies in just the ways described

in Watson's 1989 text: using generic modules within the department, recruiting new types of student through more flexible delivery patterns and so on. Engineering is an example, sharing a number of modules across its HND, HNC, BSc and BEng programmes.

Again, the inherent flexibility of the credit framework has permitted alternative responses to a decline in student recruitment. The academics responsible for developing the new subject audio-visual media studies had done so after seeing engineering suffer a steady decline. They used the flexibility of the credit framework and the marketization of higher education to develop this new area of study and have been extraordinarily successful in attracting new resources and larger numbers of students. Similarly the design historians had also used the inherent flexibility of the credit framework to attract as many students as possible at minimum cost. New degrees in material culture, film and media studies and museum and heritage studies had been developed out of the base in design history. Each, however, drew heavily from a common pool of modules making it unnecessary to increase provision as significantly as the university prospectus might suggest.

The credit framework can be profitable for individual academics also. Individuals who have been able to take advantage of the credit framework to move their discipline 'up' from a few modules to a combined honours subject and then, perhaps, a whole degree, have often progressed with it. They have gained course leaderships, promotion and the prerogative of determining their own areas of teaching and research as they have moved their field up the module > subject > degree ladder. I return to this point in Chapter 5.

Cultural streams

In Chapter 1 I demonstrated how traditional concepts of organizational culture were essentially unfruitful for the study of institutions such as NewU, and pointed to Mats Alvesson's notion that higher education institutions were characterized by multiple cultural configurations, adding to this idea the concept of the multiple 'stages' of the articulation of culture. Organizational cultures in such contexts, I suggested, can be likened to traffic systems with traffic patterns, points of congestion, flows and movement forming and dissipating according to the obstacles and features encountered in the environment.

From this perspective academics import into the academy sets of values, attitudes and norms of behaviour from other contexts and these can have important implications for the way they approach given issues, including those which pertain to the credit framework. In the debate between Clark (1987a) and Becher (1989, 1990, 1995), on the one side, and Huber (1990), Evans (1993), Joseph (1978, 1980) and Greed (1991) on the other concerning whether the epistemological characteristics of disciplines or wider cultural practices and preferences are more important in shaping academic professional cultures, this perspective suggests the latter position has considerable validity.

The position on academic professional cultures proposed here sees their relationship to the environment as multi-causal and multi-directional. Adapting aspects of postmodernism it includes an appreciation of, but goes beyond reliance on, epistemological characteristics for explanatory power, seeing personal identity as fluid. As Hall says: '[Identity is] not an essence but a positioning. Hence there is always a politics of identity, a politics of position . . . Identity should be seen as a "production" which is never complete, always in process, and always constituted within, not outside, representation' (Hall, 1990: 226, 222). Such an understanding is one that attempts to develop an awareness of the impact of professional culture beyond the ideational level and to appreciate the influence of outside forces, including what Alvesson calls 'great culture', on professional identity.

In the next section I illustrate this approach with some examples from NewU, beginning with a discussion of female gender roles, one of the clearest examples of the import into the academy of wider norms and values: what Nieva and Gutek call 'sex role spillover' (Nieva and Gutek, 1981: 60; Gutek and Cohen, 1992: 134).

Women academics and 'role conflict'

The particular demands made on women in contemporary Britain, including women academics, do tend to give those with partners and children a distinctive location with respect to their discipline – the 'invisible college' issue (Crane, 1972) and others. As female respondent 15 notes: 'it's very strange trying to be the two things at once [a mother and an academic]'.

Female respondent 21 is perhaps an extreme example of the way in which the interaction between the social organization of work within disciplines and the wider aspects of the gendered nature of the division of labour has a differential impact upon male and female academics' professional lives. A natural scientist, she noted that the research she was engaged in requires large uninterrupted batches of time for data collection and analysis. With a background in research she was relatively new to teaching and estimated that she took between eight and ten hours to prepare for one lecture. Yet with two small children she got little assistance from her husband who alternately lived away during the week and stayed at home but commuted long distances each day. She described herself as: 'a one man band [sic], doing three jobs' with only half an hour to relax in the evening before beginning lecture preparation at 9.30 p.m., continuing to midnight. Unsurprisingly she complained about the 'sheer level of exhaustion: I've never been so tired as after that one semester of doing six hours lectures and preparation per week'.

Respondent 32 made similar points, noting that around 1990 when the institution was going through a period of change and expansion she suffered tremendously. The combined demands of a family, early starts, increased marking (student numbers in the first year suddenly tripled), new courses to teach and the administrative fallout of the new CAT system resulted in a health threat: 'I started to have dizziness and panic attacks and these sort of pinned themselves on certain events and I just thought it was me . . . thought I was just going nuts really'. She saw her GP about it but received frosty treatment. She gradually came to the realization that she needed to reduce her level of commitment to the institution and to stop feeling obliged to do things. This realization was confirmed for respondent 32 when a female member of staff who was widely recognized to work extremely hard and take on a huge range of commitments suddenly died shortly after going on study leave, an event many people subsequently connected with over-work (fieldnote 26.7.94.). Respondent 6 also illustrates this pattern in women academics of extreme commitment, detrimental effects on health, followed by selective defensive withdrawal. She reflected on the advantages of no longer being so driven: 'There's masses of advantages to being here now that I've learned to say no . . . I like the freedom to spend all day on work that I've defined . . . There's some really positive things about being able to follow your own research ideas and indulge your own interests . . .'.

This coping strategy of withdrawal into more controllable areas has also been identified among women in the further education context by Leonard (1996: 6). This is not to say that men do not suffer the health effects of stress, however. Male respondent 37 noted the pressures on staff during the period from September to December and admitted that: 'I personally feel that I was close to a nervous breakdown this Christmas. I was really stressed out.' However, this is the only example of a male respondent making this sort of comment.

Tokenism and lack of integration

Even women without families experience additional pressures where they are appointed in disciplines with a masculine gender identity (Thomas, 1990). Here they are likely to be in a very small minority, to be regarded (and perhaps regard themselves) as a 'token woman' and to suffer numerous personal and professional dilemmas raised by confronting traditional gender identities, both personally and as manifested in academic disciplines and in other areas (Measor, 1983; Thomas, 1990). Here their status as women puts them at a disadvantage. Respondent 6, for example, said that she had to work harder than men. The department's only female academic in a traditionally male discipline, she noted that she tended to be allocated more teaching, at lower levels, than other new members of staff and additionally felt both a level of commitment and a need to prove herself that impelled her to take on professional commitments and to become involved in women's access courses: 'I always like to say yes. I like to be involved. If someone were to say "Would you like to be on this committee? Would you like to be on this validation?" I would say "yes". I'd learn something from it but afterwards you realize that everything else is being squeezed, particularly your health and your sanity.'

That this kind of experience of giving more time to the institution is widespread among women academics was confirmed by the Carnegie Foundation for the Advancement of Teaching (1990), by Bagilhole's study of women academics in a higher education institution (Bagilhole, 1993: 267) and by Davies and Holloway's analysis of an Association of University Teachers (AUT) survey of working hours which found that women professors worked a 64.5-hour week compared to their male peers' 58.6, for example (Davies and Holloway, 1995: 16).

In discussing the importance of sex roles and the disadvantages they bring to women Janet Newman suggests that the problem lies '. . . with the cultural norms of the mainly male . . . group, and the isolation and visibility of women within it' (Newman, 1995: 24). Bagilhole, commenting on interviews with women academics, also reports that 'the experience of being in a minority with the accompanying lack of support systems and the difficulties of integrating into a male working environment . . . affects [women's] confidence and impairs their ability to perform professionally' (Bagilhole, 1994: 21–2). Some women in my sample and that of Bagilhole were made to feel that they did not really deserve their post, especially those in traditionally male disciplines. That was certainly the case for respondent 6:

> It was widely felt and it was actually said to me that my appointment was . . . you know I got into HE more because I was the right person at the right time rather than something that took a long time working through PhDs and all that business and so I feel lucky to be here . . . Sometimes I feel that someone is going to come and say 'that was your time; off you go' . . . I was perfectly adequately qualified and yet my appointment was seen as very political which had a very significant undermining effect on my self-esteem in the department . . . It was said to me by a number of different people at a number of different levels in a number of different ways, including people that appointed me.

This passage illustrates nicely the importance of differentiating back-stage and under-the-stage discursive contexts when thinking about cultural milieux. While front-of-stage there was an 'awareness and understanding of equality issues that permeated discussions and actions within the university' (as others studying NewU had noted in a 1995 text), back-stage and under-the-stage there was a different story. Fieldnotes record under-the-stage comments by staff about the institution's language policy concerning the use of sexist terms and derogatory comments, located in gender stereotypes, about women senior managers. More subtle back-stage and under-the-stage pressures on women academics than those recounted by respondent 6 are also revealed by my fieldnotes. Several studies have shown that women academics are more likely than males to suffer social and physical isolation (O'Leary and

Mitchell, 1990; Bagilhole, 1994). This was certainly the case in one department I observed: three female academics were placed together in a staff
room, physically isolated from others in the same department and from
the departmental office. While a group of males in that department met
informally each lunchtime for sandwiches and tea, the women were only
invited if they happened to be present when this was being organized each
day. They usually refused, presumably recognizing the token nature of the
invitation. While it was methodologically impossible for me to establish how
far this custom was replicated elsewhere in the institution, the recurrence
in the literature of the point about the isolation of women in the academy
suggests that similar practices occur elsewhere as a matter of routine. Commenting on this aspect of the problem, Acker notes: 'There is a sense . . . in
which being a woman academic in a male dominated institution brings . . .
forms of "sexual politics" – dilemmas of power, visibility, relationships – into
everyday life' (1992a: 69).

Many researchers note that the differential ability to network with other
academics has serious consequences for women's full integration into the
profession and career opportunities (Kaufman, 1978; O'Leary and Mitchell,
1990; Thomas, 1990; Bagilhole, 1994). In the NHE it seems likely to confirm their position in those regions of professional work characterized by
low status, lack of recognition and limited rewards.

Personal identity

The comments that many of the female respondents made appeared to
confirm the findings of studies such as Sutherland's extensive cross-cultural
survey (Sutherland, 1985) that, more than men in general, women enjoy
contact with students and are enthusiastic about teaching and education:
'Everything I do in the supervision session is to help the student' (21).

Likewise, respondent 26 talked about 'looking after' a course rather than
being course leader and the fact that she had 'twenty-five hungry mouths to
feed. Or brains', while respondent 14 sent me a note after the interview: 'I
had an interesting conversation with colleagues at a staff meeting after my
meeting with you. I commented that I'd received a disproportionately large
amount of marking this year, and one [male] colleague told me I had to
learn to disguise any trace of "niceness or approachability" because students
would harass me.'

The greater orientation of some women academics towards students was
apparent not only in their greater willingness to become involved in the
pastoral side of student contact but in other kinds of activities too. For
example, respondent 27 (a woman) and respondent 10 (a man) make the
same point about access for previously under-represented groups in higher
education being about not only getting into university but also about what
they experience there and what happens after university. However, only the
woman followed up the point by giving examples of how she tried to build
relationships with students and to improve their employment prospects.

Many of the female respondents demonstrated the lack of self-confidence and belief in their own worth which some studies suggest gender-role socialization produces:

> The research community is something that I'm a bit frightened of. (Electronic engineering)

> [Attending a conference in London] would ... mean almost a hundred pounds for the return ticket ... [I ask myself] should I be spending the department's money on this ? ... It's not just trivial money ... after about twenty or thirty pounds I begin to think hard about it. (21 – a very well-qualified woman researcher in a high-status discipline)

However, stressing this aspect of sex-role socialization risks pathologizing women academics. It was clear that in many cases women academics were confronted by situations which were not of their own making. The gendered nature of cultural flows into the academy, brought there by staff and students, males and females, have an important impact on women's work and the degree of their integration into academic professional cultures. This can place women in situations which they had no part in creating. If women are generally more concerned about students than men, students also seem more motivated to come to women than men with counselling issues, particularly personal ones:

> I do feel from talking to colleagues and students that women do get a disproportionate number ... it is women who get caught for a lot of that ... I frequently get students coming to see me and I'm not their academic counsellor at all but they may have an academic counsellor ... whom they don't know or don't get on with and so they tend to seek out women, I think, who they see as sympathetic ... [It] takes up a huge proportion of my time and is emotionally often draining ... but you're always left with a sense of 'I didn't do enough, I should have done more'. (31)

> It's very noticeable how many [students] have switched to being academically counselled within this [female-dominated] department and you suddenly find yourself with nearly the whole lot. (25)

> They usually want to talk to someone they know quite well as their first port of call, not necessarily their academic counsellor ... You've got the 'hand on the door syndrome' – they come and see you about something else and then on the way out they say 'oh by the way ...' (26)

> I have a lot of students who come to me and I say 'well who is your academic counsellor?', and they say 'Oh. Well my academic counsellor is in my other department ... [but] I've come to see you.' (49)

This may be because culturally-derived notions of women's nurturant role make it seem 'natural' to approach a woman or, as Gayle Letherby (writing autobiographically) suggests, a combination of this and the fact that: '. . . as a woman in a junior position rather than a man in a fairly senior one I was much easier to shout at and demand from' (Letherby, 1996: 7).

This latter interpretation lends weight to Cockburn's view that men 'get in the way of women by using various strategies to get and keep women in the "feminine" aspects of the organisation's work and then conferring lower value on it' (Cockburn, 1991: 63–4). Teaching, counselling and remaining a 'local' rather than a 'cosmopolitan' (Gouldner, 1957), like many other forms of work where women predominate (Gaskell, 1992), tend to be 'invisible' and unrecognized in terms of pay, promotion or even relief from other duties.

Other aspects of cultural flow

Social background was clearly an important influence on many of the academics I interviewed. Respondent 3 was explicit about this, identifying three important influences on his attitudes and values regarding higher education in general and the credit framework in particular. These were: his working-class background and subsequent social mobility achieved through education; the time he spent in the USA; and his socialization as an academic in his field of study. The first gave him a strongly-felt and genuinely expressed commitment to broadening access to higher education through flexible curricular provision, franchising, APL and the other manifestations of the credit framework. This has driven much of the work he had done in this area for the institution. The time he spent in the USA provided both the technical knowledge about the implementation of the credit framework and a particular habitus or set of values about what is acceptable or normal. Thus he reports returning to the institution with ideas about student-initiated credits and credit transfer, for example. His professional background gave him the motivation to become involved with the implementation of the credit framework for quite instrumental reasons as well. He had worked in a teacher-training college which was closed in 1977 and the setting up of combined studies was a means of redeploying staff like him.

However, his rather neat account is not the whole story. Flows from 'great culture' are also evident. Observant participation and data from the interview provide evidence of New Right ideology in his value set too. Anticorporatism or a rejection of what the right calls 'producer capture' and Dahrendorf calls sectoral hegemony (1979: 142) is found in the interview. For example:

3:     There is still something of the Oxbridge arrogance, to say you are empty vessels . . . [and] I am going to fill you . . . In fact most learning takes place outside of those four walls . . . [and] once you come clean [about that] you lose ownership and privacy and control.

PRT: So, basically academics are protecting privilege and their own position?

3:   Yes. Like lawyers. Like doctors.

Similarly, his discussion of the purposes of credit exemption and transfer demonstrates that notions of institutional competition, marketing and income generation form part of his value set regarding the nature and functions of higher education (fieldnote 27.11.92.). Such notions are apparent in his discourse too, littered as it is with such phrases as 'adapting your product to market forces' and 'bringing the product closer to the customer through franchising'.

Respondent 27, a member of a minority ethnic group, noted that:

As someone who comes from a working-class background and a minority ethnic background ... I feel particularly conscious about [access issues]. So I don't think access is just about who you let in through the front door ... I think it's also about what happens throughout and what happens particularly at the exit point ... I was let down by, unprepared by my own university for going out as a graduate with my particular background and experience.

This consciousness is translated into professional practice, and she went on to give examples of how she makes her students aware of potential careers and attempted to give them as rich an experience of higher education as possible.

The influence of cultural currents outside the institution and outside academia generally is found in other areas. Academics involved in fashion design and those in the journalism and public relations areas tend to come from and retain links with industry and commerce and this has important effects on their values, attitudes and behaviour. For example: '[Higher education] cannot stay like it is. I can see there being an enormous number of changes in the whole way that they have to look at themselves ... Coming out of industry I will probably relate to them more favourably than others might ... Things like looking at what you do and monitoring different people's input more carefully' (25).

A respondent in development studies eschewed the research community but was extremely involved in a non-governmental organization active in development issues while another lecturer came to NewU with a strong Christian background and continued to have links and do work with Christian charities for which he had done voluntary work earlier in his career. These examples illustrate both the importance of extra-institutional links not related directly to the discipline (the 'invisible college') and the flow into the institution of non-disciplinary cultural currents. Parkin's work (1972) is helpful here. He shows how external structures, such as the business world, charities, pressure groups and other types of organization can sustain sets of norms and values which do not accord with or even run counter to those which have established hegemony. This happens within organizations as well as within the wider social world.

Strength of frame

Frame strength – the boundary between what is and is not 'knowledge' – and the influence of non-academic forces on this, seemed to be high for most of the disciplines and domains studied in detail at NewU, and this proved to be less of an influence on attitudes and responses to change than I had assumed might be the case when setting up the sample. However, few (only nine) of the interviewees reported significant syllabus control by external bodies, three reported some control but qualified this in some way, and twenty-six reported no significant control. In general there was concordance between the two academics from the same discipline about the degree of control: only in midwifery and accounting was there any disagreement to any extent, though this was a question of degree. In Chapter 6 I raise again the issue of the control that external bodies have in the curriculum, suggesting that this is at least as much a 'story' constructed by respondents as a statement of 'fact'. The point I make here, however, is that whether 'real' or not, these respondents perceived these issues as 'problems' and in some cases changed their behaviour as a result, and hence they were real in their consequences.

Perceived to be real is real in consequences

I was correct to assume, however, that the most important perceived 'threat' to frame strength came from external professional bodies rather than, for example, the 'marketization' of higher education in the form of any greater exercise of choice by students. Where respondents did report external bodies having an influence on curriculum change (for example in the case of Institute of Mechanical Engineers on the BEng, on some computing courses, the Law Society on the LLB, the English National Board on nursing studies and the British Psychological Society on the psychology degree) this seems to have been operating in a 'conservative' direction. However, without detailed examination of exactly what each of these bodies require, and how rigorously they enforce their requirements, it is difficult to establish how far respondents' perceptions of influence accurately reflect the regulations. I have a suspicion, shared by more than one respondent, that the symbolic importance of professional bodies, particularly the weight they lend to an argument for a particular direction of change, is at least as important as the actual effect of their stipulations. Frame strength then, like disciplinary epistemological characteristics, appears to be more a constructed 'story' which individuals may or may not subscribe to, than a 'real' characteristic of disciplines in a given context.

(The perceived) epistemological characteristics of disciplines

I argued above that academics' understanding of the epistemological nature of their disciplines can have real effects on their responses to curriculum policy and other issues. Moreover the 'real' epistemological characteristics of some disciplines may be important in just the way that Davidson, Becher and Clark argue. Morris, for example, argues convincingly that the nature of art and design is such that only an integrated (i.e. non-modular) course can produce creative and innovative students (Morris, 1992: 333). Modularity loses the cohesion of history, theory and practice which is essential to this discipline but may be suitable for those not intending to graduate as professional artists or designers.

There is some evidence from my data to support the view that epistemological characteristics, or academics' understandings of them, represent a further factor in conditioning response to the credit framework. The issue of 'linearity' for example, though not put in those terms, was brought up by respondents in the physical sciences and the hard professions in particular: 'Now with physics being the kind of subject which actually builds up, then the thing is, before you can actually study one topic, say at level two or level three, you need all the work that precedes it . . .' (applied physics). Similar comments were made by respondents in accounting and statistics, in each case to support the idea that academics need to structure students' programmes very carefully.

Another point that came up from these disciplinary areas and others was the loss of a holistic understanding of the discipline among students when it was broken up into many small modules. An engineer, for example, noted that the 1977 Finniston Report into engineering education advocated integrated engineering courses but found that modularity: '. . . is not compatible with that kind of concept because . . . the modules have to stand by themselves as a valid mini-course and . . . it doesn't give you the flexibility . . . to do what . . . Finniston wanted us to do . . . We had to . . . jigsaw up our integrated course into what were called modules and it doesn't really work' (engineering). Similarly, respondent 31 said that: '[Modularity] creates major problems around the fragmentation of knowledge. Everything has to be bite-sized . . . They are finding it incredibly difficult to make connections between various modules that they've had over the past three years'. For these respondents, then, modularity has led to incoherence in the programmes of study.

A further point, made by an astronomer but emphasized by several respondents in the physical sciences was that a common modular structure is a Procrustean bed into which a discipline is expected to fit regardless of its (perceived) epistemological characteristics: 'Our subject does not come in tidy packages of modules and half modules . . . so we're having to put two of those together to approximate one module but that sometimes has produced some very strange marriages of subject material to do it' (astronomy). This respondent worried that: '. . . students seem to have many more things on the go at once . . . [It would be] much better to have the students concentrate their minds on fewer things and break the back of it'.

In this view modularity *per se* may not be problematic but an inappropriate structure imposed across the whole university does create difficulties, including placing potentially excessive demands on students because the impact on the student experience of the structure as a whole has not been considered.

A further point made by many respondents concerned the sheer bulk of their discipline and the limited time available in the semester system for assimilation of knowledge and/or skills:

> The main problem we've found with semesters, particularly with pro-gramming languages, is the students don't have time to analyse the information. (Computing)

> By the time they've done their practical work and they've done the practical report and it's marked and it's given back (that means usually the end of the semester) . . . they don't really have the chance to show they can improve on that with the next practical report. (Physiology)

The reduction in class contact time is another area of concern: 'Over the years we've lost time . . . The teaching has been drastically reduced and that's a major problem for us because there just is not enough time to do the work required' (physics).

That point was made by many respondents. The fact that loss of teaching time is happening elsewhere was confirmed in a study by Frank Webster and colleagues at Oxford Brookes University which found that the amount of contact time had reduced by as much as 50 per cent over the ten years between 1984 and 1994 at that institution (Webster, 1996).

While the loss of teaching time also results from declining resources and increasing student numbers, the way time is distributed is affected by the curriculum structured around the credit framework and this has serious implications given the (perceived) epistemological constraints of some dis-ciplines. For a respondent in design studies for example, semesterization and modularization are: 'just a complete waste of time . . . It's just a nonsense . . . It's just a hindrance to the smooth operation of the academic year'. This respondent complained that the Christmas and Easter holidays interrupt the semester's teaching, the reading weeks, and the assessment periods. Art and design courses usually end with the students presenting a public exhibi-tion, with students working hard on that until the end of their degree. But the respondent felt that semesterization has:

> . . . brought the date of our exhibition . . . forward . . . In the first year [of semesterization] we said to our students 'you can now polish up your project work and get it all together.' I suppose that worked reasonably well but . . . now what's happened is that the pressure's been put on us to bring the date forward all the time in the academic year so that the . . . mechanism of going to all the various [assessment] boards can be handled. So now they're . . . losing out on about six weeks' teaching . . .

Indeed, in arts subjects generally tutors believed that the very pedago-gical approach of this discipline requires an holistic approach and intensive contact between tutor and student: 'We're actually trying to force a square peg into a round hole . . . The atelier system of teaching which operated in art and design successfully for generations is very difficult to operate . . . with the increasing group sizes . . . The amount of contact time it needs isn't compatible with what the university wants or expect' (fashion).

For some respondents on the other hand epistemological considerations meant an affinity to one or more aspects of the credit framework. For example, an economist reported that the credit framework at NewU has: '. . . not created any great problems . . . the essence of economics is that it's a subject where you can in a sense pare it down to a few important concepts and if you've got those concepts you can build up from that to as much as you want' (business economics).

Likewise the linguists were comfortable in general with the framework, though for different epistemologically-related reasons: 'Language learning has always worked in kind of building blocks in terms of defining people's levels, assessing whether a student is a complete beginner or whether a student has a certain amount of experience and could be defined as inter- mediate or advanced' (languages).

For those staff who teach languages and another subject, for example marketing or literature, the modular structure also helps to demarcate the two (or more) areas. Thus 'fragmentation' rather than 'holism' can be an advantage in some areas: 'I don't have one big course where I do all sorts of things but I can actually teach marketing . . . as an option, as a half module or a module as the case might be and then I can do a straightforward lan- guage module . . . straightforward language only' (languages).

Davidson's point about the role of professional bodies constraining the 'fit' between discipline and credit framework is confirmed by a nursing studies respondent. She reported that the diploma is 'very much dictated by the ENB's guidelines'. These do create problems: students have to study for a total of 72 weeks and it is an integrated theory and practice course. They are salaried and they have to fit holidays in. Organizing placement is a problem too, with there potentially being: 'too many students in the same place at the same time' because of the relatively short semesters. The re- sponse was that: 'We are going to have to start the course some time in July in order to make it so that they can fit into the semesters and get the 72 weeks in' (nursing studies).

In psychology too, the British Psychological Society lays down require- ments and the reduction in contact time has meant that there isn't enough time in the semester structure to fulfil them, at least according to one respondent from that discipline.

The accreditation of prior learning (APL) and particularly of experien- tial learning (APEL) is a further area in which the interviews and fieldnotes suggest that (perceived) epistemological differences between disciplines con- dition the ways in which policy is implemented, thus lending support to Davidson's thesis. For staff working in computing, statistics, languages and some areas of the natural sciences the application of what Butterworth (1992) calls the 'credit exchange' model of APEL presented no problem at all. This was because parts at least of their courses involved the acquisition of easily demonstrable skills and/or knowledge which could also have been acquired experientially. One example is the use of statistical techniques in a research methods course, another is pattern cutting in fashion design courses (fieldnote 7.6.95.). It is also appropriate in those areas of enquiry where course aims can be or usually are stated in terms of clear and testable learning outcomes. Thus, for example, respondent 35 (commenting on experience on engineering courses) noted that: 'It [APEL] is . . . straightforward. You can . . . gauge how up to date the knowledge is . . . you can actually categorize them quite well'. Similarly, respondent 24 said that: '. . . the majority of part-time students will get some accreditation for prior learning. It's very easy to do with us . . . because we can easily see what they've done . . . Our competencies are very clearly based around certain techniques they've got. Learning how to programme computers, for example, is something we could easily test.'

The implementation of an APEL policy based on the credit exchange approach is facilitated where parts of a course meet the twin criteria of, first, the potential for the experiential acquisition of the knowledge and skills involved in it and, second, the ability to test simply for them (Trowler, 1996b). Alternatively, where an area of study is concerned partly with inculcating reflective practice (Kolb, 1984; Schön, 1987) Butterworth's 'developmental model' seems particularly appropriate, as her own work and that of others would indicate (Bloor and Butterworth, 1990; Collins, 1993; Newton, 1994). Conversely, where none of these conditions apply and the discipline is founded on 'pure' propositional knowledge then it seems unlikely that there will be enthusiastic implementation of APEL policy, as a development studies respondent indicated:

> We are reluctant [to get involved in APEL] . . . most people in the beginning of the course have views on development which are over-simplistic so most people's prior experience if anything wouldn't be that relevant . . . Development studies requires understanding of international economics, international politics and familiarity with the literature . . .

Conclusion

This chapter has demonstrated that the dominant unitary approach to the structural influences on academics' attitudes, values and behaviour with regard to the credit framework needs to be modified by a more complex model which takes the interaction between other structural features into account and which incorporates the influence of not only normative elements and codes of signification – the rule-giving aspect of structure – but the authoritative and allocative aspects also. However, the account given in this chapter has tended to accept the underlying structuralist perspective adopted by the traditional model, largely seeing individual academics as responding to forces beyond their influence. In the following chapters I present argument and evidence to support the view that social structure and the enacted aspects of culture have received too much attention in the literature on higher education to date, and suggest that Giddens' (1984) theory of structuration has much to commend it as one that allows us to conceptualize the interplay between individual action and structural constraint.

4

Policy and Practice at the Ground Level

Managerialist approaches to change in higher education

As I showed in Chapter 2, much of the writing on the credit framework in higher education comes from senior managers. Perhaps as a result of their position they adopt a top-down model of change with an under-theorized approach to the ground level – in short, a rationalistic, managerialist model of change. In the following sections I will seek to demonstrate that while this managerialist model was once paradigmatic in the broader study of policy implementation, theoretical development has since moved beyond this position, leaving the study of change in higher education in a theoretical dead end.

Early approaches to the implementation of change adopted what is usually known as a top-down perspective, sometimes also termed the 'forward mapping' (Elmore, 1982), 'unilateralist' (Fox, 1990) or 'fidelity' perspective (Fullan and Pomfret, 1977). This asked the question 'what characteristics of policy change from the top can ensure its successful implementation at ground level?' Essentially this assumed that, given a number of prerequisites, policy could be successfully implemented by direction from above. This is evident in the work of, for example, Pressman and Wildavsky (1984), Hood (1976), Mazmanian and Sabatier (1981) and Ham and Hill (1984). From this perspective it was important to identify the necessary and sufficient criteria for successful implementation by analysing the causes of any 'implementation gap' which appeared between policy objectives and policy outcomes. Examples of prerequisites that were identified in this work by Cerych and Sabatier (1986) are:

- The clarity and stability of policy objectives.
- How far objectives change over time.
- The relative priority of the innovation compared to others.

[handwritten marginal note: Top-down change]

- The degree of symbolism as against real expectation of outcomes inherent in the policy.
- The adequacy of the causal theory underlying the reform.
- The adequacy of financial resources.
- The degree of commitment of those involved.
- The stability of the environment within which policy is being implemented.

Thus, for example, poor policy formulation, lack of clarity in goals, inadequate resources, failure to create commitment among the workforce and so on can result in an implementation gap.

This top-down approach is evident in the managerialist writing on change, and specifically the credit framework in higher education, examples of which tend to have most or all of the following characteristics:

1. An emphasis on a clear rationale for change.
2. Manipulation of the cultural characteristics of the organization is seen as important.
3. There is limited development and theorization of ground level responses and reactions to and interests in change.
4. However a minority of staff are seen as important in that they are innovators or resisters.
5. Empirical studies concentrate on the top level.
6. There is a generally uncritical view of the credit framework (see Chapter 2).
7. There is a predominant model of the academic as passive in the process of social change.

David Robertson's work is a clear example of this type of approach. Robertson's discussion of the implementation of the credit framework also deserves special attention because of its official status as the report of the HEQC CAT development project and because Robertson has been so tireless in promoting it around the country. Robertson suggests that staff can be categorized as being one of the following in relation to the introduction of what he calls a 'credit culture': enthusiasts, pragmatists, sceptics (who are open to persuasion but need to be convinced) and antagonists. The credit culture itself consists of a set of principles (see Table 1.2, p. 8) and requires structural change for its realization, including fundamental 'adjustments' to academics' conventions and preconceptions about the nature and requirements of their own disciplines (Robertson, 1994a: 324). Clearly Robertson has very little time for epistemological essentialism. The way to bring about a credit culture within an institution is to change '*the essence* of the institution as it defines itself' (p. 313, emphasis Robertson's).

Citing Beckhard and Pritchard (1992) Robertson advocates institutional cultural change, a paradigm shift led by senior managers who establish an 'institutional commitment' to 'do things differently' (Robertson, 1994a: 314). In a telling paragraph (p. 315) Robertson alludes to the loosely coupled nature of universities and the potential of academic staff to subvert change, but dismisses these with the phrase 'there is no time here to unravel these aspects of the problem' and continues with his elaboration of an essentially top-down model. However 'these aspects of the problem' (as Robertson sees it) are in fact extremely important and should not be so lightly dismissed. Robertson's approach to change, then, lacks a developed theory of the crucial (to his model of change) and very ambiguous concept of culture beyond a simplistic list of characteristics. It relies on a top-down managerialist model of change (the shortcomings of which will be discussed below), and it summarily dismisses well-theorized and empirically well-supported reservations about the potential for success of the kind of strategies he is suggesting, particularly in universities, for example from Cohen and March (1974), Easterby-Smith (1987) and others.

Other writers adopting a managerialist model also under-theorize the role of academic staff. They tend to adopt a simple binary model of organizations, at least as far as the implementation of the credit framework is concerned. They see academic and administrative staff on the one hand and managers on the other. Robert Allen and Geoff Layer (1995), for example, position 'staff' on a continuum which ranges from 'resisters' (p. 60) through 'disciples' to 'gurus' (p. 16). In such a simple structure it becomes easy for Allen and Layer to make generalizations about 'staff' and the implementation of the credit framework: 'staff have little experience of supporting students within flexible curriculum models' (p. 60); '. . . staff may feel that their security and place within the organisation have been threatened . . .' (p. 59); thus essentially making invisible the individual actor.

David Watson's 1989 work sets out the rationale and appropriate systems and structures for the delivery of the 'modular course' as it was developed at Oxford Polytechnic, in many ways a test-bed for the credit framework in the UK. The contributors to that book are all centrally involved with the administration and evaluation of the course rather than being (any longer) ground-level actors. In one sense it is not surprising that the book as a whole is largely concerned with systems and structures, given that it is offered as providing 'an invaluable guide for all those policy makers considering or committed to "going modular"' (cover notes). However, the invisibility of the views and responses of ground-level staff in the book, even in the chapter on evaluation, is quite striking. What is being offered is a practical handbook for setting up and managing the credit curriculum founded on a top-down model.

A more recent book (Bocock and Watson, 1994) does include a three-chapter section on ground-level actors and two of these chapters (Haslum, and Bocock) move some way to examining the values and attitudes of academic staff and the implications of these for the management of change. Mary Haslum's chapter proposes the interesting thesis that 'many of the implementation costs of the changes in HE are . . . hidden as they fall . . . on the people who drive the system and deliver the courses' (p. 103). However, only just over two pages are devoted to articulating and substantiating this thesis and within them there is little in the way of empirical evidence to support it. Paradoxically the thesis itself lies within the managerialist model as it sees academics as passive victims of change rather than contributing towards it, albeit in ways unforeseen and perhaps unwanted by senior managers. Jean Bocock's chapter has similar characteristics: little empirical data and a passive model of the academic which makes an analogy between academics' attitude to change and bereavement and mourning, tellingly under the sub-heading 'loss and identity'. 'Many academics', writes Bocock, 'have felt dispirited, undervalued, diminished in their autonomy and have suffered an increasing lack of empathy for the goals of institutions' (pp. 124–5). Like Allen and Layer she makes generalizations about academics. Those in the former polytechnics are particularly disenchanted, she writes, because 'so many of the educational objectives with which [those institutions] . . . were identified, and to which many academics were personally committed, have come to fruition in circumstances they did not envisage' (p. 125). This more recent contribution from Watson and others has failed to move away from the top-down managerialist model of change although it is now recognized as requiring qualification.

Robin Middlehurst's contribution (1993) to this discussion is in some ways a disappointing one, given the empirical data she has at her disposal. While she sets out the limits to the applicability of the rational, top-down, model of management and leadership in the university context (for example, p. 59) and also discusses the importance of cultural characteristics of universities and the interpretations of policy made by ground-level actors (for example, pp. 36–7), this reads as a theoretical preamble which has a rather limited impact on the account of university leadership she develops in the latter part of the book. It is unclear, also, how far that account itself is informed by the data she collected during her empirical study of university leaders – very little of which is presented in the book. Certainly she attempts to draw general conclusions about leadership in the higher education system which is so diverse as to preclude such a level of generality, and in doing so she largely draws on a top-down model of change, not surprising perhaps given the subject of her study.

Two other contributions to the understanding of change in higher education are worth a brief commentary: Weil (1994) and Slowey (1995). It is not surprising that the text edited by Susan Weil predominantly adopts the managerialist model of change given its title (*Introducing Change From the Top*) and purpose (providing insights on the management of change from those 'at the top' for their peers). Weil's contribution is very much in the tradition of Watson's 1989 work and similarly makes invisible academics' values, attitudes and responses to change. What is surprising, though, is that this invisibility is maintained in a book which centres on the notion of producing 'cultural change'. There are references to this project throughout, for example on pages 37 and 59 and in Weil's concluding chapter which centrally addresses the issue. Yet the nature of culture (or cultures – there seems to be a difference of view among the contributors on this) and the question of whether 'managing culture' in this way is even possible are issues which are never problematized in the book except, to some extent, in Weil's concluding chapter. Here Weil does recognize some of the dangers and omissions inherent in the top-down managerialist model (for example, p. 151) and there is a very interesting discussion of the importance of 'hearing stories' within and without the institution and of recognizing that all those involved in change are both 'actors and audience', as she puts it. This interesting theme is left undeveloped in an empirical sense however. It is particularly disappointing, therefore, that the companion volume to Weil's, Slowey's *Implementing Change from Within* (1995) does not take up Weil's concluding theme. Despite the intention to 'render transparent a wide range of interior landscapes' (p. 13), what we are offered is another series of chapters from those 'at the top', with the exception of Lee Whitehead, president of a university Students' Union at the time of writing. Much of the book is concerned with leadership roles, developing appropriate structures for successful change and so on – the usual top-down concerns. The book is, effectively, part two of *Introducing Change From the Top*.

There is, of course, much of value in both books and these comments should not be taken to imply that they have no merit. My intention here is to indicate important aspects of the implementation of change that are missing from them and to demonstrate that they share a particular 'blindness' to them with other parts of the literature on higher education.

Many of the authors discussed in this section, including Slowey, Weil, and Robertson, cite Beckhard and Pritchard (1992) as an important influence on their thinking about policy implementation. The focus of this text is clearly upon the leader as the central agent in the implementation of change in private and public organizations, particularly in terms of his or her role in shaping the culture. Its authors are firmly situated in the top-down tradition, focusing as they do on leadership, culture and change. They look at 'the implications of change for leadership behaviour and at ways to create an appropriate organizational culture for achieving change' (p. xii). These two authors suggest that: 'In the past few years, many organization theorists and writers have paid increasing attention to leadership as a basic factor in the fully functioning organization . . .' (p. xi).

Many commentators on the introduction of the credit framework and other change-related issues in the field draw on the work of Beckhard and Pritchard, a classic 'top-down' approach to policy implementation through the management of cultural change. Robertson (1994a: 314–15), for example, says that (my emphasis):

> Much of the contemporary material emphasises the need to produce *cultural change* rather than merely structural change (Beckhard and Pritchard, 1992, for example). This involves committing the organisation to attitudinal readjustment . . . institutional leaders are encouraged to 'lead by example' in order *to commit others to their vision* . . . Our investigation has convinced us that strategic change is cultural change, and cultural change is related to institutional mission.

Because of this reliance on Beckhard and Pritchard's book by Robertson and others (for example Weil, 1994; Jones, 1995; Slowey, 1995) it is worth looking in a little more detail at what they have to say.

Beckhard and Pritchard (1992) attempt to give what they call an 'integrated approach' to the three factors of leadership, culture and change in the study of organizations. They give priority to the first of these, suggesting that 'vision driven' leaders can effect the changes they desire primarily through changing organizational culture. Their approach is an ideal-typical example of what I earlier called the managerialist model of change. Their model of change has four key stages: creating a vision of the future; communicating the vision; building commitment to the vision; and aligning people and what they do to the vision. They suggest that the 'leaders of the organization must have a clear vision of the desired end state of the entire system . . . [and] a clear commitment . . . to making significant personal investment in developing and building commitment [among staff] to an inspirational vision . . .' (p. 4).

Top leaders are advised to diagnose their current situation and to facilitate this diagnosis by switching into 'learning mode', a pre-requisite for change. After 'unfreezing' themselves from 'currently held beliefs, knowledge or attitudes' (p. 14), they should develop a plan by which other staff can do the same thing; in other words, change the culture of the organization: 'All of this requires conscious and explicit planning and managing . . . It cannot be left to chance or good intentions' (p. 15). The emphasis is on the top of the organization throughout: 'An effective vision will have a consensus among top management over the end state toward which management is moving the organization . . .' (p. 23).

Once this is achieved it is then possible to change the culture, by which these authors mean: 'The set of values . . . and assumptions . . . that distinguish a particular organization from others [and] norms . . . and artifacts . . . that guide actions in the organization' (p. 46).

The main levers in this are as follows: changing the behaviour or leaders in the direction of the vision (they act as models for others); cascading these changes down the management hierarchy and among 'key players'; rewarding desired behaviours; improving the flow of information within the organization so that feedback about behaviours improves; and changing recruitment policies and orienting staff development in the direction of the vision. The need to creatively destroy and remake the organization round new visions, to change its essence, is the heart of Beckhard and Pritchard's message about bringing about change.

Fullan rightly says of Beckhard and Pritchard's book and others like it that they are 'chronologically new, but paradigmatically old or wrong' (Fullan, 1993: ix). One wonders how different *Choosing to Change* (Robertson, 1994a), *Implementing Change from Within* (Slowey, 1995), and *Introducing Change From the Top* (Weil, 1994) would have been if their formative text had been, for example, that of Jermier *et al.* in *Resistance and Power in Organizations* (1994) or Michael Fullan's wise appraisal of the realities of educational change in *Change Forces* (1993). Beckhard and Pritchard's approach, though, has been the dominant one in the field of higher education, not only in the major texts reviewed above but in less well-known studies of and symposia on introducing aspects of the credit framework in specific higher education institutions, for example Jones (1995). Even some of those aspects of the literature which are critical of the managerialist approaches in general tacitly or explicitly share their assumptions about the passive nature of academics in the change process – what I have called elsewhere the 'quiet don' approach (Trowler, 1996c), and so I will now very briefly review some of these less well-known studies.

Many of the critics of the hard managerialist or Fordist outcomes of the move towards the NHE in general and the credit framework in particular adopt an under-theorized, 'over-socialized' (Wrong, 1966; Dahrendorf, 1968) and essentially passive conception of academics, even though they write from a variety of perspectives (Weberian, Foucauldian, neo-Marxist) and are looking specifically at changes to the status and labour process of academics on the ground. I noted in Chapter 2 that Jary and Parker (1994, 1995) suggest that academics adopt only three of the five Mertonian strategies when threatened with the proletarianization that the NHE brings: conformity, ritualism and retreatism. These authors call for innovation and rebellion, but claim they are not yet present. Likewise I showed that McMurty (1991) suggests that academics 'mutely accept' (p. 216) the application of market principles to education and calls for them to recognize their inherently antagonistic nature. Selway's interesting insider research project at the University of Portsmouth examines the effects of NHE on ground-level academics but concludes that 'there is a high degree of passivity and reactivity in academics' in the face of developments which are very damaging to them (Selway, 1995: 31). Indeed, the very notion of the Robbins trap itself, proposed by Martin Trow (1989) and believed to be operating not only by him but by Guy Neave (1985) and Leslie Wagner (Utley, 1995) hides a model of the academic as inactive; caught in the bright light of policy change from the top. The implication of the 'trap' metaphor is the powerlessness of those caught in it. Similarly A.H. Halsey (1992) tracks with 'an air of sadness' what he considers to be the decline of donnish dominion, a depressing and seemingly ineluctable decline in the power, status and rewards of the academic profession, even its proletarianization. The once mighty dons seem powerless in the face of change, doing little about it beyond 'ceas[ing] to recommend the academic succession to their own students' (p. 269). Becher and Kogan (1980: 146–7) also tend to see academics as strongly constrained by their institutional context, despite the fact that it is designed, at least in some cases, to operate in their interests:

> . . . many changes, including those generated from within, fail because they are unable to accommodate to existing structural constraints. Academic structures and regulations for the most part evolve to protect the legitimate interests of researchers and teachers. They help define,

and also defend, the main areas of professional concern within an institution. But once established, they can prove surprisingly intractable . . . The main constraints on change are social, not psychological: they depend more on the way the system operates than on the particular stand that its individual members choose to take.

Authors like these then would agree with C. Wright Mills who began his classic *The Sociological Imagination* (1970: 1), first published in 1959, with the words 'Nowadays most men [sic] feel their . . . lives are in a series of traps'.

Bottom-up approaches to change

This very passive model of academics is doubly strange. First, because general social theorizing has moved beyond the 'over-socialized' conception of man and woman discussed in Chapter 3 towards a stress on agency, and second because this theoretical move has shifted thinking in the study of various applied areas such as the study of organizational culture, the study of policy implementation, and generally in the study of the compulsory educational sector, both primary and secondary. I will explore these ideas next.

In general social theorizing about change, there has been a move away from the structuralist and over-determined view of the individual since Wrong's early paper (1966). Structural-functionalist and 'crude' Marxist thinking have yielded their former intellectual dominance to theoretical approaches based on phenomenology and interactionism, more indebted to Berger and Luckmann (1967), Mead (1934) and Gramsci (1971) than to Parsons (1960), Marx (1867) or Durkheim (1938). The latter's *Rules of Sociological Method* have been displaced by Giddens' *New Rules of Sociological Method* (1976). Giddensian structuration theory has helped us to understand that the actor is both constrained and free, operating within social structures yet able to change them to some extent. Thus Giddens (1984: 16) notes that:

> Power within social systems which enjoy some continuity over time and space presumes regularized relations of autonomy and dependence between actors or collectivities in contexts of social interaction. But all forms of dependence offer some resources whereby those who are subordinate can influence the activities of their superiors. This is what I call the *dialectic of control* in social systems.

The work of Foucault (1980, 1982), too, has stimulated a discussion about the relationship between subject and power and has led to a deeper understanding of subjectivity as distinct from the 'grand narratives' inherent in modernist structuralism. The formation and reformation of the self is pivotal in Foucault's account and this notion of identity can be seen as central to the notion of resistance at the ground level (Jermier *et al.*, 1994). Though some interpretations of Foucauldian theory, particularly from labour process and Marxist perspectives, argue that the omnipresent nature of power within it leaves almost no room for ground-level resistance, others clearly see his work as implying empowerment of the individual (Knights and Vurdubakis, 1994). Dwyer (1995) is probably right that there is a contradiction between Foucault's theoretical position (which recognizes the importance of the social actor) and his application of it (which tends not to). Others, however, have attempted to apply Foucauldian theory in a grounded way, showing that such a disjunction is not a necessary characteristic of Foucauldian theory (Austrin, 1994; McRobbie, 1994; Gillespie, 1995).

In the study of policy implementation there has also been a move from top-down towards 'bottom-up' models. This bottom-up approach (sometimes called 'backward mapping', 'mutual adaptation' or 'multilateralism') explores aspects of and changes in individual and group behaviours, processes and cultures as and after implementation is effected, showing how these affect the implementation process as well as being affected by it. It argues that to fully understand processes of change in any social context we need an understanding of the nature of the ground-level interpretations of, and responses to, policy. In this it differs markedly from the concerns of the top-down approach with its focus on the process by which government (or other large organization) executes policy in order to influence delivery locally.

The distinction between the bottom-up and top-down approaches could be seen as merely the adoption of a different level of analysis, the different perspectives offering alternative but not incompatible ways of seeing the same phenomena. Alternatively the different approaches could be viewed as conflicting interpretations of the locale of power and control in the policy-making and implementation processes. Yanow (1987) views the distinction in the former way and comments that analysis can be conducted at the level of the individual implementer, of the dynamics within and between groups, the organizational/structural level, the inter-relationships between organizations or at the policy culture level. In a later paper she develops this idea, suggesting that there are four 'lenses' or perspectives through which the researcher needs to study policy implementation: human relations, political, structural and systems. The human relations lens looks at the behaviour of individual actors within organizations and traits of interpersonal behaviour. The political lens examines dynamics within groups and relations between and among groups. The structural lens focuses on the organization itself as a designed set of behavioural rules while the systems lens targets organizations as they relate to one another in a particular environment. (Yanow, 1990). This seems an appropriate way to view the study of organizational change. The lens selected will bring some parts of the picture into clearer focus but render others indistinct. Some authors, especially Beckhard and Pritchard (1992), lose sight of this fact in their enthusiasm for the heuristic power of their perspective and tend to see other approaches as fundamentally flawed. This leads them, and those who apply their work, to see the implementation of policy in terms of finding the right levers to pull, 'culture' being the most powerful one available (Newman, 1994). The bottom-up approach, though, offers important qualifications to these kinds of assumptions and gives insights into the power of social actors to amend and even create policy. The top-down approach on the other hand alerts us to the constraints within which they operate and the role of the upper levels in setting the agenda and creating the structural context for action.

The explicit articulation of the bottom-up approach came with Barrett and Fudge's (1981) critique of top-down models, particularly Pressman and Wildavsky's (1975) approach to implementation. Barrett and Fudge (1981: 4) note that:

> . . . much of the existing literature tends to take a 'managerial' perspective; the problems of implementation are defined in terms of co-ordination, control or obtaining 'compliance' with policy. Such a policy-centred or 'top-down' view of the process treats implementers as 'agents' for policy makers and tends to play down issues such as power relations, conflicting interests and value systems between individuals and agencies responsible for making policy and those responsible for taking action.

Marsh and Rhodes (1992), drawing on the work of Lipsky (1978, 1980), Barrett and Fudge (1981), Elmore (1982), Hjern and Hull (1982) and Sabatier (1986), summarize the criticisms made from this perspective of the top-down approach. The following is an adaptation of their points:

1. Too much attention is given to the goals of central actors (ignoring the adaptive strategies of those lower down).
2. Conditions necessary for effective implementation are unrealistic.
3. Discretion in order to cope with uncertainty is inevitable in all organizations.
4. The unintended consequences of policies are ignored.
5. Some policies do not have specific objectives; they tend to evolve through the interactions of a multiplicity of actors and outcomes and cannot be evaluated because objectives are not explicit or are multiple. Majone and Wildavsky (1986: 182) write: 'In most policies of interest objectives are characteristically multiple (because there are many things we want, not just one), conflicting (because we want different things), and vague (because that is how we agree to proceed without having to agree on exactly what will be done)'.
6. The distinction between policy formulation and its implementation is artificial; policy is re-made as it is implemented. This rejects simple linear models of the policy-making process like Alexander's (1985) which sees it as moving through four stages: stimulus, policy, programme, implementation, and even Hogwood's (1987) more complex model which identifies the stages of agenda setting, processing of issues, selection of

option, legitimation of option, allocation of resources to policy, implementation, adjudication, impact, evaluation. Instead all stages are seen as being part of the policy-making process. What can be distinguished is official, manifest and specific policy-making from above as against unofficial, latent and implicit policy-making from below.

The first of these points is, perhaps, the most important for the current discussion. Palumbo and Calista (1990: 11) note that: 'Opening the [policy process] black box now reveals that formulation is clearly a small part of policy making . . . Much policy is made during implementation itself. Although this occurs in various ways, the principal way is by street level bureaucrats who create policy through the multitude of decisions they make in interacting with the public'.

The bottom-up model of change, then, sees the process of policy implementation resulting from the multiple interactions of numerous actors, each with their own agenda, definition of the situation, perceived interests and so on. Policy implementation essentially results from a web of political acts as Michael Lipsky's classic text *Street Level Bureaucracy* (1980) shows in some detail.

However, bottom-up approaches to policy implementation have not been without their critics. Sabatier (1986) and Marsh and Rhodes (1992) usefully summarize the critique mounted by proponents of the top-down approach as including the following points:

1. Bottom-up approaches overestimate the discretion of the lower-level actors and fail to recognize sufficiently the constraints on their behaviour.
2. They do not explain the sources of actors' definitions of the situation, perceptions of their own interests etc. In fact these may come, directly or indirectly, from above.
3. The upper levels set the ground rules for negotiation and this is not recognized by these approaches.
4. Bottom-up theorists are not really engaged in 'implementation analysis'. Actually they do not focus on the implementation of policies but on 'understanding actor interaction in a specific policy sector' (Sabatier, 1986: 35–6).
5. The criticisms of the top-down model are overstated. One criticism is that policy-making at the top is characterized by multiple agendas and ambiguities creating room for interpretation and manoeuvre below, for example Majone and Wildavsky, quoted above. However during the Thatcher period, for example, policies tended to have very clear objectives. Also, as suggested in points 1, 2, and 3, the upper levels structure the environment for lower-level actors.

The first point is a criticism which Marxists and others have levelled at interactionist and other phenomenologically-oriented perspectives which adopt a micro rather than macro level of analysis. Clearly there is always a danger of losing sight of structural constraints on behaviour when studying social action at the ground level, but this is not an intrinsic flaw of all studies at that level as, for example, Corrigan's (1981) study amply demonstrates and as Ozga (1990) argues more generally. The second point, though, could be levelled at many of the bottom-up theorists. Lipsky's (1980) study, for example, simply does not offer us enough information to be able to judge how far 'street level bureaucrats'' motivations and interpretations may be conditioned from above. The third point is closely related to the first and second and like those is not necessarily a characteristic of bottom-up approaches, but I will argue in Chapter 5 that some professionals at the ground level (the 'policy reconstructers') take control over the agenda in quite active ways. The fourth criticism essentially attacks a straw person version of bottom-up theory. Understanding actor interaction in a specific policy sector is a necessary but not sufficient component of the study of the implementation in that sector. The final point is important. The coherence of top-level policy-making varies over time, place and issue. In contexts where policy-making is coherent, power is concentrated at the top and there are strong and rigorously controlled implementation procedures, the top-down model may apply relatively well. None of these circumstances apply, in universities, however, though there have been changes in this direction since at least 1985.

Synthesizing the accounts

The division between top-down and bottom-up approaches is, of course, a rather simplistic way of characterizing thinking about policy change and its implementation. The latter can be subdivided into variants, for example: 'bureaucratic process', which focuses on the interaction within organizations between routines and discretion (for example, Lipsky, 1978, 1980); 'organization development', which focuses on the interaction between personal and organizational needs (for example, Argyris, 1962); and 'conflict and bargaining', which focuses on bargaining processes and outcomes between competing interest groups (for example, Bardach, 1977).

Majone and Wildavsky claim to adhere to a third perspective, referred to as 'implementation as evolution'. This attempts to synthesize the top-down and bottom-up approaches and its adherents suggest that:

> At one extreme, we have the ideal type of the perfectly formed policy idea; it only requires execution, and the only problems are ones of control. At the other extreme, the policy idea is only an expression of basic principles and aspirations . . . In between, where we live, is a set of more or less developed potentialities embedded in pieces of legislation, court decisions and bureaucratic plans. This land of potentiality we claim as the territory of implementation analysis.
>
> (Majone and Wildavsky, 1978 quoted in Jordan, 1982: 117)

I would argue, however, that this characterization of the top-down and bottom-up approaches represents, again, the construction of straw targets.

While some studies do have the characteristics Majone and Wildavsky ascribe to them, many are more moderate in their claims, including Lipsky's. The 'implementation as evolution' approach should therefore be seen as a sensible and moderate approach to implementation analysis, one which takes into account the insights from both polar perspectives. Its application can be seen in the work of Elmore (1982), Hjern and Hull (1982), Thain (1987) Palumbo and Calista (1990) and Stringer and Williamson (1987). It is also the approach taken here.

Education policy-making

I now move from the consideration of policy implementation at a general level to consider its application within research in the compulsory education sector where, in marked contrast to most of those concerning higher education, many studies recognize the importance of agency stressed by bottom-up policy theory despite the absence of close linkage between the two areas of literature (Deem, 1996c). Michael Apple (1989), for example, tracks aspects of the proletarianization of schoolteachers in the USA, articulating similar arguments to those UK critics of our own NHE such as Jary and Parker (1994, 1995), Wilson (1991) and Ritzer (1993). Yet Apple (1989: 48) notes that: 'Teachers have not stood by and accepted all this . . . militancy and political commitment are but one set of ways in which control is contested. It is also fought for on the job itself in subtle and even "unconscious" (one might say "cultural") ways . . .'.

Similarly, Michael Fullan's important and well-known work has shown the importance of schoolteachers in the implementation of policy, drawing attention to the importance of the *meaning* of educational change held by those on the ground (Fullan, 1991). He and Pomfret usefully distinguish between adoption and implementation, the latter term taking into account the kinds of points made by Lipsky:

> Implementation refers to the actual use of an innovation or what an innovation consists of in practice. This differs from both intended or planned use and from decision to use, the latter being referred to as adoption. As will become clear, the definition does **not** assume that an innovation is defined in advance by developers and then disseminated to several schools [or other educational institutions]. It merely says that regardless of who develops an innovation, when it is developed or how it is developed, some implementation will have occurred at the point when certain new characteristics are actually in use in the social system.
>
> (Fullan and Pomfret, 1977: 336)

Writing along the same lines in the context of British primary education, Reynolds and Saunders have contributed the useful notion of the 'implementation staircase', arising from their study of the development and implementation of curriculum policy. This gives concrete form in the school context to Giddens' (1984) notion of the 'dialectic of control'. Policy travels up and down the implementation staircase, changing all the time; parts of it are overlooked and drop out of sight, other parts are reinterpreted, still other parts are implemented in ways not foreseen by policy-makers at the top. In all this the interests, values and particular perspectives of actors at various positions on the staircase are important. The finished product (in this case curriculum policy as implemented) turns out to be quite different from its creators' vision. Reynolds and Saunders (1987: 44) explain why this is the case:

> . . . policy is expressed in a number of practices, e.g. the production of texts and rhetoric and the expression of project and national policy management, in school, in classrooms, and in staffrooms. Policy is also expressed by different participants who exist in a matrix of differential, although not simply, hierarchic power. Finally, participants are both receivers and agents of policy and, as such, their 'production' of policy reflect priorities, pressures and interests characterising their location on an implementation staircase.

Andrew Pollard's (1985) work also traces how teachers' actions, conditioned by their particular situations, can have important influences on the whole school experience for children. Based primarily on a symbolic interactionist perspective, Pollard argues that 'Action is viewed as a creative response by each unique individual to their structural and material position in the classroom. Thus action and constraint, biography and role are linked' (p. xiv). Of particular relevance to this study is his notion of 'coping strategies': the patterned and active adaptations to situations which result in the development of acceptable ways of working within situational constraints.

For Pollard, the 'work' done by teachers (and pupils) in given situations is central to the understanding of them: the fine-grained study of this work is important if we are also to understand how and why policy changes in its implementation. Deem and Davies' (1991) case study of the implementation of aspects of the 1988 Education Act carries a similar message, though in their case the emphasis is on the role of governors rather than teachers, on politically and ideologically motivated behaviour rather than personal coping strategies. However, for these authors too, 'educational change does not conform to a purely rational model but . . . is significantly influenced . . . by ideology . . . [and] . . . by human agency and meaning' (p. 153).

Stephen Ball (1994), in discussing the issue of the power of local actors, distinguishes between policy as text and policy as discourse: a useful perspective which attempts not to lose sight of the importance of structures (understood here as properties which lend coherence and relative permanence to social practices in different times and locales), nor the influence of ground-level actors.

Viewing policy as text refers to the contested, changing and negotiated character of policy, which is always the outcome of struggle and compromise.

The contested character of policy is evident at the initial stage of formal policy-making: the point of 'encoding' the representations of the actors involved, as Ball puts it. It is also evident at the point of 'decoding' the text: actors at the ground level interpreting it in relation to their own cultural, ideological, historical and resource context. Just as when an audience watches and 'decodes' a television programme, this process is highly unpredictable and differs according to the characteristics of the audience viewing the programme, or 'text'. To summarize, then:

> [Policies] are the product of compromises at various stages . . . They are typically the cannibalized products of multiple (but circumscribed) influences and agendas. There is ad hocery, negotiation and serendipity within the state, within the policy formulation process . . . [Likewise, once formulated] policies shift and change their meaning in the arenas of politics; representations change, key interpreters (secretaries of state, ministers, chairs of councils) change . . . Policies are represented differently by different actors and interests.
>
> (Ball, 1994: 16–17)

In order to understand the processes by which the local 'secondary adjustments' to education policy take place we need to study, analyse and theorize the cultural 'underlife' (Riseborough, 1993) within the contexts where policy implementation takes place. Examples of this kind of study are relatively sparse in the compulsory phase of education, but this is even more the case in the study of universities. If regarding policy as text stresses the importance of social agency, of struggle and compromise and the importance of understanding how policy is 'read', then this is balanced somewhat by an understanding of policy as discourse (Ball, 1994; Bowe *et al.*, 1994). Here the constraining effect of the discursive context set up by policy-makers comes to the fore. Ball draws on Foucault who argues that discourses are: 'practices that systematically form the objects of which they speak . . . Discourses are not about objects; they do not identify objects, they constitute them and in the practice of doing so conceal their own invention' (Foucault, 1977b: 49).

Adapting discourse analytical and postmodern approaches, with Foucault, Ball is here suggesting that discourse does not just represent reality, but helps to create it and, at the same time, disguise its socially-constructed nature by denying the discursive repertoires necessary to envisage alternatives. Norman Fairclough (1993: 137, 153) makes a similar point in discussing the new discourse found in higher education; the imported commercial and managerial language of 'franchising', 'credits', 'cost-centres', 'management teams' and the rest:

> . . . control over discursive practices can helpfully be seen in terms of hegemonic struggle over orders of discourse, and . . . hegemony and hegemonic struggle in a broader sense may involve discourse to a substantial degree . . . Doing one's job entails 'playing the game' (or various

connected games), and what may feel like a mere rhetoric to get things done quickly and easily becomes a part of one's professional identity.

Ball's discussion of the distinction between policy as text and policy as discourse demonstrates that it is perfectly feasible for ground-level studies to maintain an awareness of both, demonstrating the ways in which actors may, at the same time, reinterpret and change policy while being to a greater or lesser extent 'captured by the discourse' (Bowe *et al.*, 1994).

In compulsory and further education in the UK there has been a systematic attempt to remove the discretion of those at the ground level. The power of the LEAs has been curtailed, a national curriculum imposed, conditional funding has been introduced, centrally-defined competence-based training models developed and so on. Despite all this, street-level implementers, governors and others still develop routines, shortcuts and political strategies for coping with and improving the situation as they perceive it, 'exploiting the gaps and contradictions that any major set of educational reforms is likely to contain' (Deem and Davies, 1991: 154). Their reluctance to simply accept policy as laid down has forced changes further up the implementation staircase, for example to the national curriculum as a result of Ron Dearing's consultations and subsequent recommendations (Dearing, 1994) and to the initially very behaviourist model of competence adopted by the National Council for Vocational Qualifications (NCVQ) (Crawley, 1994; NCVQ, 1994).

Emphasizing the actor in higher education

It is strange, then, that in the field of higher education where such constraints on action have come much later and in diluted form there is much less recognition of agency. Of course, to characterize all studies of policy change in higher education as inappropriately adopting a top-down approach would be incorrect. There are notable exceptions in the literature; authors who recognize that academics have a number of resources at their disposal which makes them important social actors and that the loosely-coupled characteristics of many university contexts give them greater room for manoeuvre than many other workers or even professionals. It is even less true there than elsewhere that Elmore's (1978) four assumptions of the rational model, described in Chapter 2, hold true.

What Bardach (1977) describes as the 'classic symptoms of under-performance, delay and escalating costs' are very familiar in the academic environment. But as Easterby-Smith (1987: 51) notes, attempts to tackle this from the top can have deleterious effects for the higher education sector:

    ... it is the values of staff and students that can be the greatest source of, and barrier to, change and innovation. Senior managers get easily excited at the possibilities of being able to 'manage' the values of their organisations. But this is much more difficult than the popular text books would have us believe, and very dangerous. The danger is that if one simply attacks the existing values of an organisation – say those of scholarship, colleagueship and individual freedom – one runs the risk of destroying individuals' sense of purpose, and thus creating a highly demoralised organisation. If values are to be shifted, say towards a greater commercial orientation – then this must be done in a way which allows for retention of the original values in parallel.

Richard Winter (1995: 130) cautions against a fatalistic approach towards change which may be unwelcome to most academics:

> . . . although we are indeed faced by *attempts* to impose an industrial, profit-oriented logic on to higher education, this situation is not without real educational opportunities, both to shed some of the oppressive practices enshrined in higher education's traditional forms and to begin to realize some innovative and progressive possibilities . . . Contradictions not only generate 'problems' . . . they also generate spaces within which power can be contested and reforms can be won.

Taking up this same theme from a feminist perspective, Celia Davies and Penny Holloway (1995) note that the changes that are happening in British higher education also involve a change in the gender regime (Connell, 1987) in universities. This often involves an improvement for women academics given the fact that previous gender regimes were 'profoundly unwelcoming' to them. The Research Assessment Exercise (RAE) and the careful monitoring of teaching loads, for example, make transparent and create space for opposition to patriarchal practices such as allowing the 'grand old man' of the department to exploit, unacknowledged, the work of (often female) junior staff while simultaneously offloading the bulk of the teaching onto them (Davies and Holloway, 1995: 16).

Similar ideas around the notion of change creating oppositional space, explored at the national and institutional levels, are expressed by Pratt and Silverman (1988) who tracked how further and higher education institutions responded in very different ways to a period of resource constraint during the early to mid-1980s. They found very different outcomes in different institutions to what was meant to be a uniform, centrally administered instrument: the funding and student places policy emanating from the National Advisory Body for Local Authority Higher Education (NAB), set up in 1982. Pratt and Silverman find Popper's (1975: 179) notion of 'situational logic' useful in theorizing about responses to public policy. This involves examining the problem the policy was designed to solve and assessing the situation in which the actors find themselves on the assumption that actors will follow the logic of their situations: '. . . thus "rationality" lies in people's problem-solving rather than in a model of "perfect administration" which assumes that only the rationality of top policy-makers is at issue' (Pratt and Silverman, 1988: 7).

Likewise even those who adopt a view of changes to the academic labour process which stresses its degradation, commodification and at least partial de-skilling and proletarianization, do occasionally nod in the direction of the ability of academics to contest such trends. Both Miller (1995b: 54) and Shumar (1995: 96) do so but they do not attempt to develop theoretically this important insight or explore its ramifications.

Pritchard and Willmott (1996: 1) make the important point that 'contradictions and struggles make this broad shift [towards 'Fordist' mass production arrangements] unstable, partial and by no means inevitable'. Their empirical study of university managers gives a perspective from the 'top' of the difficulties faced in implementing change and demonstrates that these managers themselves are also engaged in the 'struggle' that Pritchard and Willmott describe. Not even they are passive agents of hard managerialism and New Right ideology.

Yet Pritchard and Willmott note that we lack data on the discursive positions taken up by rank and file academics (p. 3). Like so many others (for example, Weil, 1994; Miller, 1995a; Slowey, 1995) their study focuses on senior post holders. The logic of the notion of ground-level struggle implies that we need the kind of data that they call for, as I argued in discussing Lipsky's work. Sheldon Rothblatt, like Trow an American observer of the British scene, also noted in the *Times Higher* that while we are 'inundated with information about nearly every aspect of higher education, we lack sustained discussion of the changing inner culture of universities' (Rothblatt, 1996: 18). Of course there have been such studies both in the UK and abroad (for example, Meek, 1984; Harman, 1988; Becher, 1989; Alvesson, 1993; Ainley, 1994; Selway, 1995), sometimes applying the insights obtained to the understanding of change within the context studied (for example, Aune, 1995). There have also been some useful studies of parts of university cultures (Evans, 1990a, 1990b, 1993; Greed, 1991). These often contain interesting insights meriting further development, such as Evans' brief discussion of the 'adaptive inventions' some language staff develop to strengthen the frame of their discipline (Evans, 1990a, 1990b). As Rothblatt suggests, however, such studies represent only 'good start[s]' (p. 18). There were several in-depth and useful studies of American higher education institutions in the 1960s (for example, Clark, 1960; Clark and Trow, 1966), perhaps stimulated by the rapid changes occurring then. It is time for more sustained research of this type in the UK, as Rothblatt suggests. The following chapter shows how such a project can lead to fundamental realignment of our thinking about the importance of change in higher education.

5

Reconceptualizing Academic
Responses to Change

This chapter explores in detail NewU academics' responses to changes in their working contexts, particularly the introduction of the credit framework of the NHE. A categorization is developed of different types of response to these changes and each is described in detail. More attention is given to the categories of response which are not significantly addressed in the literature on higher education, particularly the creative forms of response which some academics at NewU engaged in to reconstruct policy.

In discussing the role of individual and small groups of academics in reconstructing policy it is not my intention to underplay the importance of organized action through professional associations and trade unions, which is not the focus here. Nor in stressing the strategies adopted by academics in response to changes in higher education do I minimize the deleterious impact of those changes. The data speak loudly and clearly about this from the perspective of academics on the ground and (by implication – I have not focused on this in terms of data collection) from that of students. As I outline in the following sections, several respondents were suffering quite badly in the changed circumstances of higher education. My aim here is to moderate the monochromatic picture painted by both the proselytizers and critics of those aspects of the NHE which are the focus of this study.

Four broad categories of response to the new environment found at NewU can be discerned from the data. For clarity I term these sinking, swimming, coping and reconstructing. Figure 5.1 represents a summary of these different categories of response to changes at the university.

These categories are not mutually exclusive. Academics move from one category to another in their professional lives, reconstructing in some areas and using coping strategies in others, for example. The categories represent types of behavioural response, not types of academic. Nor are the lines between them as clear as Figure 5.1 would indicate. Some academics, however, represent very defined examples of individuals who are firmly in one or other

Figure 5.1   Categories of response to the credit framework in an expanding
institution during a period of resource constraint

	Accept status quo	Work around or change policy
Content	Swimming	Policy reconstruction
Discontent	Sinking	Using coping strategies

of these categories and have little contact with the others. The following
sections illustrate each of these categories with examples from the data.

Sinking

I argued in earlier chapters that the majority of studies of higher education
do not regard the individual academic as an important social actor and that
this was as true of authors critical of the credit framework as of those who
were proselytizers for it. The former group of authors tend to characterize
the academic as 'sinking', essentially as 'mutely accepting' (McMurty, 1991:
216) worsening job conditions, a point of view I was critical of. In this
chapter I present evidence to refute 'sinking' as a generally applicable
description. Nonetheless there was evidence from the data that some academics responded to a greater or lesser extent in this fatalistic and personally damaging way. I briefly describe these here but give more attention
to other categories and to the nature of movement out of this category as
the depiction of academics as 'sinking' is so well covered elsewhere. Using
Merton's (1968) categories of responses to cultural goals and the means to
achieve them, those academics who were 'sinking' engaged in conformity,
ritualism and even retreatism. Intensification in workload, decline of resources, de-skilling in some cases, increase in student numbers and general
degradation of the labour process as well as specific features of the credit
framework have led to weariness, disillusionment and even illness for these
academics.

The most extreme example is respondent 14. I quote from her at length
here to give a flavour of her response:

The comparison [with when I was a student] is so negative, I just think that the quality [of higher education] with increasing student numbers has deteriorated quite frighteningly. I wouldn't want to be a student now . . . we've increased our numbers far in advance of having the facilities to deal with them . . . [The staff in my department] are all absolutely run into the . . . ground. We're all exhausted, we're all demoralized . . . An awful lot of us have lost our enthusiasm and energy . . . The impact that has on the students is that we're not available and when they can find us we're not so nice to the students because we rather dread all the interruptions . . . I feel we are not well enough briefed on the CAT system . . . an awful lot of staff don't know what the regulations are . . . We're all chasing round and nobody's quite sure that we've got the right answer . . . It's all a bit of a nightmare . . .

I haven't had any coping strategies [for my own survival] . . . I'd leave today if I could . . . I've also seriously considered working half time . . . but I'd be doing the same job for half the pay . . . It really has damaged my health; I've been quite ill as a result of having to work far too hard. But that's because I do tend to be a perfectionist . . . I've tried not to let my standards drop so I'm always quite meticulous about things like handouts and references and keeping things up to date . . .

I love my job, I love [my discipline], I love teaching. I get a terrific amount of stimulation and satisfaction out of the job but what I want is the job as we used to know it, not as it is now. That's why I would like to get out. I would come back to it if I could come back to things as they were, not as things are now.

Respondent 14 was, however, almost unique among those I interviewed in the degree of her passivity in the face of unwelcome change. She was in a classic Robbins trap situation: she largely subscribed to a traditionalist ideology, wanting to maintain academic standards and close contact with students, yet she was in favour of broadening access. She was thus caught between a desire for access and expansion in higher education and a traditionalist conception of it. This trap brought her more work than she was able to cope with and she was unwilling to compromise by adopting the coping strategies that she reported (in a critical way) her colleagues to have used. The consequences have been threatened health and a considerable amount of stress.

Faced with a dilemma of another sort is the respondent in journalism described in Chapter 3 (p. 71) who subscribed to a progressivist ideology and hence rejected some of the pedagogical coping strategies available for dealing with increased student numbers, especially those centred around information technology and other techniques which 'dehumanize' the teacher–learner relationship from her point of view. The results for her could be stress, overwork and 'sinking' too, but this was not the case because

she and her colleagues were able to argue for the capping of student numbers and a somewhat privileged treatment in terms of resources because of
the high status of journalism within the institution.

However, many respondents reported having been in the kind of impasse
I showed respondent 14 to be in at one stage in their careers, but then
developing more active forms of response. For some the trigger was a crisis
of some sort, as it was for respondent 32, discussed in Chapter 3 (pp. 82–3).
After a health crisis she came to the realization that she had to change her
attitudes and behaviour towards the job. For others, such as respondent 10,
the switch was a result of quiet reflection on the situation. He felt that:

> My professional role ha[d] been eroded by the system such that I'[d]
> become more and more required to be not only an administrator,
> which we all have, but also required to be in a sense less creative, in
> other words to be much more of a functionary as a teacher. To go in,
> do it, and come out again. That's been brought about by changes to
> the system including the increase in student numbers.

In his account his reflection on these processes, perhaps deepened by his
social science training, continued for some time and he began to formulate
and experiment with a number of active responses, discussed below. A
respondent in accounting reports a similar process, indicating that while
a social science training may be helpful in this it is not essential.

Sometimes the switch from a passive to an active stance is the result of
experiential learning by a group of colleagues, facilitated by the rate of
change at NewU. This was the case for respondent 16:

> [Having successfully ignored CATS 1] we were dragged kicking and
> screaming into CATS 2. The then HoD resisted CATS in any way he
> could. Because he wanted to operate an integrated course, he wanted
> to go much more towards [a project-based course] ... CATS really
> destroyed that in his eyes completely and so he resisted it as far as he
> possibly could and then of course at the end we had to CATify the
> course and what we ended up with was something we didn't really like.
> And so when NEWCATS came about we more or less ignored the
> things we'd done for CATS 2. We went back to the course we had and
> then thought about how we wanted to develop that course and devise
> a NEWCATS course which was really what we wanted.

The resources available to academics, either individually or collectively,
are important in being able to make this transition from passivity to activity
(Middlehurst, 1993, especially: 74–5). Mechanic (1962) suggests that informal
power should not be disregarded in that context and cites the sources of
it as including: expertise; effort and interest; attractiveness; location and
position; coalitions; and knowledge of rules. Some of these personal resources
come with experience of the organization. The comparison between respondent 17 and 23 is instructive here. Respondent 17 discussed the administrative fallout of CATS and the excessive paperwork and bureaucracy which he

regarded as inevitable in any large organization. But he noted that: 'It used to be that you could send people memos and they would act on them. Now they don't . . . [However] I do know the people who can make changes, but often . . . you've got to go straight to them' (17). However, his experience in the institution gave him an understanding of who can get things done for him and he got to know these people personally. For example, he shared an interest in *The X-Files* with one key administrator and this established a bond between them which facilitated things for him:

> That's part of the human interaction . . . and I must admit I quite enjoy that . . . If I do it by memo it just doesn't get done because [she] has just as many problems as me. And in order to do it by memo I've got to submit it through the HoD, and then it's got to go through faculty and then from faculty it's then got to come down to planning and these things never happen. So I say 'Right I'll forget that' and I go and talk to [her] and then we discuss *The X-Files*.

Respondent 24 and others with a long history at NewU told similar stories. Without these resources, however, respondent 23 was in a relatively weaker position and had to adopt a more passive stance: '[Correcting students' profiles] takes an awful lot of time and . . . you are not sure when they should be done and who should do them. And it's even not knowing people's names, who to contact in various departments. People are most helpful when you do, but it has been difficult and it's still quite difficult' (23). As respondent 36 put it: 'Once you understand the rules you can play the game' (36).

Respondent 31 also noted that power came with time spent in the organization and accumulated knowledge about it and security in her own position. She felt weak and disempowered at first and: '. . . it was a long time before I was able to work through the process and tamper with things and say "I'm not going to do this, I want to do that"' (31).

The sources of informal power that Mechanic (1962) identifies are, however, only part of the story. He focuses on the characteristics of the individual, but contextual characteristics are important too. In a large, loosely-coupled organization such as NewU there is considerable 'space' for the social actor to operate if they have the necessary resources and choose to do so. This can, paradoxically, simultaneously create a sense of powerlessness and alienation but also create the conditions for the creation of reality by the social actor. This indicates that the site and level of analysis is important in considering the question of actors' passivity or activity. Although academics can feel powerless at one level they may be active in developing or adapting policy at another. Respondent 6, for example, said that: 'I don't feel in a position to drive those sort of changes [mass access]. At the end of the day what happens to the funding council affects how the institution moves and what I think is neither here nor there so I don't have a strong position on it. We're the pawns in that way, aren't we?' However, she spoke passionately about seeing her work as empowering women and she had begun a number of initiatives with this agenda uppermost. In her work practices, then, it is clear that she neither felt nor acted as if she were a pawn.

A respondent in social science also felt a sense of powerlessness at one level in the organization but was by no means passive as an academic:

[At the last RAE in 1992] I was amazed that they put forward people as [from my discipline but they were actually from another]. We got a [grade] one. I have over 30 refereed publications and I wasn't put forward . . . Then there were some comments made by people up front: 'you are not recognized internationally' . . . [But] here on my desk I have faxes from people inviting me to international conferences . . .

This same respondent was quite explicit about his perception of the different levels of identification in the institution:

I see two tiers of interaction for me here, or perhaps even three. One is with colleagues. And I must confess colleagues who I have contact with, I think they give me the respect I think I deserve . . . Secondly in terms of my immediate line management, my HOD, he has been wonderful with me, he sees me as a major contributor in research and teaching . . . But beyond that I think the institution does not understand, in fact they don't know what to do with [my discipline].

Respondent 7 put it in even stronger terms:

The worst thing about [this] . . . institution . . . is just the feeling that as a management structure, as a culture, [it] is almost counterproductive. You know, the feeling that if you'd wanted to do it badly you couldn't have done a better job . . . I've actually seen it from several points of view because I worked on a project for two years . . . If I'd handed in blank sheets of paper for the whole of the two years it would have made not a bit of difference because nothing ever happened . . . There is a great gulf between management and admin and lecturing . . . There's such antagonism and a lack of communication that it is quite pathological really – everybody blaming everybody else for problems rather than getting a grip on them . . . I just find it totally depressing.

This theme of close identification with local colleagues but alienation from the institution recurred very frequently in the interviews. It was a clear finding, too, of the Ethics and Values Audit (EVA):

There is evidence of mutual respect and trust inherent within an informal community network . . . [But there are] insignificant organisational communication networks . . . poor information flow . . . [and] non-participation in important decision making processes . . . [with] some abuse of both power and role, when management practices and styles are inappropriate, resulting in the individual feeling undervalued.

(Henry *et al.*, 1992: 6)

The 'values identification grid' used by the EVA, an adaptation of Kelly's (1955) repertory grid, demonstrated very starkly this local collegiality and therefore potential for social action, but alienation from levels above the departmental one (Henry *et al.*, 1992: 56–67). Clearly, academics on the ground draw strength from collegiality at NewU which helps them to move out of the 'sinking' category.

Swimming

For some academics the NHE in general and the development of the credit framework in particular create an environment in which they can thrive. They essentially accept the spirit of the NHE and the flexible, credit-based curriculum, and act within that paradigm. The credit proselytizers discussed in Chapter 2 tend to assume that most academic staff belong in this category, though they do subscribe to the 'bad apple' theory often used in cases of civil unrest and police corruption which suggests that a few individuals (resisters in this case) with contrary views and actions can and do wield a disproportionate amount of weight.

The reasons why the environment is so amenable to academics in this category vary. One is the fact that the introduction of the credit framework has allowed some, often women, to create new Subjects within the combined honours scheme, and eventually defined fields, through the gradual development and accretion of modules: 'This is an institution that has given those people who wanted to [take it] the opportunity to develop the kinds of courses which could not exist in the old universities or in many of the new ones and I think that is something I am eternally grateful for' (27).

Many have gained course leaderships, promotion and the prerogative of being able to determine their own fields of teaching and research. Examples here include women's studies, race and ethnic studies and design history. The latter is now a self-standing degree, a defined field, but grew out of servicing art and design courses: 'Design history developed out of art history, which was very well established. [Both] developed in the 1970s to service teach' (design history).

It was CATS which provided the opportunity for this 'promotion' to happen:

> When CATS came in . . . people in the department had to write modules that they knew about and give [the aggregated modules] . . . some kind of title . . . Suddenly you think you can offer a Subject, which is all we did at first, and . . . work away from history of art and design because [my colleague] and I (who developed it) believed that it could be a separate Subject. But I never envisaged the two [would] become so separate. (Design history)

Three defined routes within the design history programme were being planned at the time of the interview: material culture; film and media studies and museum and heritage studies. It seemed clear that these again had the potential for development into self-standing degrees in the future just as design history and the related visual studies are now separate. What has happened, then, is what Clark (1987a) refers to as substantive growth in the discipline. 'Parturition' (dividing off into separate segments), 'dignification' (achieving high enough status to be taught in a higher education context), 'dispersion' (disciplines extending the ground they cover) and 'programme affiliation' (HEIs adding more to the curriculum) are all involved here and the credit framework facilitates them all, often to the advantage of the academics involved.

Other 'swimmers' had found themselves in disciplines in decline in terms of recruitment of students and in resources. They too have used the flexibility of the credit framework and the marketization of higher education to develop new, niche, 'sexy', programmes of study which attract new resources and larger numbers of students. Audio-visual media studies is the best example of this. Two respondents had essentially set up this Subject (and then a degree – BSc media technology) as a result of dissatisfaction with the prospects of the 'mother' discipline, engineering, which had been the background of their own training, research and teaching. The enthusiasm for their new Subject was palpable in both respondents:

> ...I love it. And the students love it too...they're enjoying themselves...I get to play with the toys I could never afford...it's good fun. (Audio-visual media studies, respondent a)

> We've spent seventy-thousand pounds on equipment this year. Nobody else asks! (Audio-visual media studies, respondent b)

Still others, particularly in foreign language departments, relied on the 'elective' element of the combined honours system for their very large overall student numbers: 'We know our department is very heavily dependent on the electives programme. Almost fifty per cent of our FTEs at the moment come from electives... structurally speaking the idea of modules is not a bad thing' (languages).

However, the department was successful in keeping group sizes down because of being able to argue for the special pedagogical requirements of their discipline. They were also in a prime position to take advantage of the push towards income generation.

Others in a less fortunate position with regard to student recruitment were able to take advantage of elements of the credit framework to recruit and to achieve efficiencies and economies in just the ways described in Watson's 1989 text: using generic modules within the department, recruiting new types of student through more flexible delivery patterns and so on. In specific contexts, used in limited ways (particularly limiting the sharing of modules to students in generic disciplines or sub-disciplines), the credit framework can work in the ways described by its supporters and it acts as a buoyancy aid for some 'swimmers' who might otherwise drown. This was the case in one applied science department I observed in detail (field-note 27.4.95.) which reduced the range of modules available but increased the number of students on them by making them generic to a number of courses within the department in order to cope with growing student numbers within a virtually static resource level. The same department also reduced by half the amount of laboratory experience it provided, explicitly redefining its essential goals in teaching so that its academics began to see themselves more as involved in fostering generic graduates with skills of independent study than scientists with particular disciplinary skills. As a result it became possible for students to graduate in that discipline without doing laboratory work: they could complete a research dissertation instead (fieldnote 28.4.95.). The external adviser panel member at a review of that department thought that this development was 'to be deplored', but the departmental staff were more sanguine and frank: 'the dissertation is a mechanism for getting out of the resource issue we're faced with', as one of them said (fieldnote 28.4.95.).

Similar strategies were evident elsewhere in the university, allowing both individuals and departments to 'swim' in what otherwise would be difficult waters. A respondent in legal studies (subscribing to a progressivist ideo-logy) adopted a similar perspective to the teaching of law as that described above in the applied science department: an emphasis on generic skills rather than disciplinary content. This meant that he did not see the increase in student numbers, the introduction of the credit framework and the decline in resources in such hopeless terms as he reported his colleagues doing. The complaint that there is no longer enough time or adequate resources to cover the content properly is nullified if disciplinary content is not considered particularly important. A respondent in another applied science reported that his department had developed a new masters degree and was also increasingly seeing the BSc in the generic terms, changing their practices accordingly.

Respondent 43 is an example of someone who was very clearly in the 'swimming' category, someone who thrives in the NHE and has risen very quickly within it. It is notable that this respondent has a background out-side of higher education and brought to this context a set of values and atti-tudes very different from many academics who had come to it from more traditional routes, demonstrating again the importance of 'presage' as well as disciplinary knowledge structures in conditioning responses to change.

I do find the balance of the work activities very stimulating. I really enjoy what I have to do and I think that an awful lot of my job now really involves spending time with people . . . which involves being avail-able for people, talking to colleagues an awful lot and observing their classes. We've started a scheme of voluntary peer observation this year which is turning out to be quite stimulating. Now that is very time consuming so I wouldn't particularly define my job in terms of teach-ing and then admin., because there's teaching and then there's all the sort of people work and a lot of my admin. or paperwork is connected with . . . trying to communicate effectively within the department . . . Right from the very first year I was aware that I would have to work through the summer to bring in the income. So the whole thing hasn't been much of a shock to me in the sense that I haven't known a previous system, and I've always known, ever since working here, constant change and constantly having to adapt to new ways of thinking in senior management, new political climates . . . and so on. It's obvious that the whole world [of higher education] . . . is in a 'period of change', which is obviously a euphemism. I suppose the people who are going to survive are the people who thrive on change, enjoy it, welcome it and I suppose I see myself as one of those.

Using coping strategies

More negatively, many academics I collected data from had developed 'coping strategies' (Lipsky, 1980; Pollard, 1985) to deal with their new environment, particularly the administrative fallout from the credit framework, increasing student numbers and a declining resource base which together resulted in increased workload. While these helped to release them from the stress and illness suffered by respondent 14 and some of her colleagues, they often had negative consequences for students and others.

Academics reported retreating from innovation in some areas in order to be able to cope with the administrative and other pressing demands they had: '[I use] notes and overheads that were prepared last year and teach from those whereas previously I'd have probably redesigned the lecture each time I gave it' (22).

Some had started unofficially 'working to rule' – for instance, calculating the number of assignments they had to mark, the amount of official work-time they had available for it and then (in the words of one respondent) 'whamming through it' (13). Another said that: 'Some of my colleagues who have small children just say "no we are not doing that, we don't get paid to do that" so they are probably more inventive about the strategies they use during the week' (31). Respondent 48 reported a similar kind of response in himself and his colleagues: 'What has happened over the last few years is I've cut down my working week, from about fifty hours a week I cut it down to the contract and I don't do any more, and I know a number of people who are doing that and of course that's one of the reasons that the system isn't working' (48).

Others had deliberately made themselves unapproachable and their teaching and assessments very difficult in order to reduce the intolerably great demands made upon them by the greatly increased number of students. The note respondent 14 sent me after the interview described this happening, as I described in Chapter 3, and she wondered whether these new young staff are typical examples of Thatcher's children:

. . . indoctrinated with formative years where the doctrine is to look after number one. Their level of un-caringness about student experience I find horrific. However, one of them received PRP [performance related pay] despite constant student complaints about the appalling standard of teaching and feedback on the course for which this member of staff was awarded PRP. Students on this course are considered pathetic whingers! This is why I am so disillusioned!

Many had given up trying to follow the complex and changing rules of the CAT system and signed virtually any CAT-related form students asked them to, regardless of its purpose and whether they were the correct person to do so (fieldnote 3.2.94.). Much the same had recently begun to occur at Oxford Brookes University according to a senior administrator there: 'they designed these rules; they can sort it out' was the attitude of many staff according to him (fieldnote 1.4.95.).

Very many of those I spoke to had, as a matter of course, started to put material which appeared in their pigeon hole into the waste basket with only a cursory glance. A large number of them said words to the effect 'if it is important enough it will come back'. Respondent 36 was explicit about this: 'I cheat the system and I just do what I want, but I think everybody else does. I will throw away some admin., I just can't be bothered with it. Because it is redundant . . . and even if you do do it you end up doing it two or three times. You've just got to close your eyes and get on with it and not worry about the other bits and pieces'.

Many had started to avoid meetings and generally refuse as a matter of course any invitations to become involved in special projects where once they would have accepted: 'I'm getting very good at avoiding meetings. If it clashes with teaching I don't go to the meeting' (29).

Setting up departmental procedures to eliminate the need to deal with the central administration was also a common strategy. Conducting in-class tests rather than formally organized exams helped the department of applied biology and the English staff to avoid the administrative difficulties and timing constraints that using formal examination procedures would have involved (fieldnote 27.4.95. and a respondent in English). Changing assessment strategies too can help alleviate workload. Respondent 31 reported introducing in-class objective tests in many modules: 'That has made a difference to marking: so much quicker'. But she noted that: 'There is resistance [for example from franchised college staff] when you try to be strategic about your teaching and your assessment'.

Some, for example respondents 15 and 39, used 'technical solutions' to the intensification of work. These included resorting to open learning and course books, though this was not always successful, as respondent 15 reported. She wrote two second-year distance learning packs because, as she said: 'I was going to have to prepare it anyway so I thought why not prepare it . . . and get someone else to type it up?' However, the outcome was disappointing from every point of view:

So we wrote it and tested it out on our students who almost universally disliked it . . . Comments that came back were, well from one particular student: 'You're here to teach us. You don't expect us to just go away with this bundle of crap' . . . It didn't work very successfully for them. As many of them passed that year as usually passed . . . but they didn't like it . . . Its sickening [to have done all that work for nothing]. (15)

Eventually, only one franchised college used the packs, and then with only six students. The packs were not used at all on the University's main campus.

As I indicated in Chapter 3, there has been a reduction in the overall amount of class contact with students over the years and this had been another way of dealing with increasing student numbers and relatively declining resources: 'I suppose with one or two other things we've actually reduced the amount of teaching we do and I think that that is common throughout the university' (48).

Some academics had changed their pedagogic techniques in ways which they regretted but which they thought necessary in order to cope. Apparently paradoxically, these included adopting both 'student-centred' independent study techniques (sometimes referred to as 'FOFO' approaches) for some, while for others it involved heavily didactic ones. Respondent 7 was particularly explicit:

I can think of lots of better ways [of delivering the module] but to actually handle that many students any other way than sending them off to do it and only seeing the ones who actually knock on the door, having admittedly told them 'this place is rough you are only going to survive it by knocking on people's doors and asking people' . . . It's the best there's going to be.

Respondent 7 is an example of someone who imports strong cultural currents from beyond the academy walls which affect his work and his attitudes towards and implementation of policy. Quite different from the 'invisible college' which sustains an essentially compatible cultural current to that of the elite academy, respondents like 7 looked at their work in quite a distinctive way. He eschewed research-based organizations and conferences in his discipline but was an active member of non-governmental organizations dedicated to change in his field of study and in the world at large. These organizations sustained his standpoint and the norms and values give him an anti-hegemonic perspective. He was able to innovate and had no problems developing coping strategies as long as these did not compromise his fundamental aims in working in higher education.

All the academics I had contact with regretted having to adopt these kinds of strategies, seeing them as essentially compromising their professionalism. Those who used them, however, did so as a last resort to deal with what they saw as the problems associated with increasing student numbers, declining resources and various aspects of the credit framework, either to preserve their own health and life outside the institution or to allow them to concentrate on those aspects of their work which meant most to them, or both. These strategies had been forced on them and having to adopt them left them with an unpleasant taste in the mouth. Some tacitly used the criteria of impact on students – if coping strategies were deemed deleterious to the student experience then they were not used:

> I try to [take a determined line in regulating workload] because other-
> wise it will take over . . . Providing at the end of the day I can say 'my
> students have been well treated' that's OK. (35)

> Under the circumstances I've taken these decisions to try and protect
> the student experience but they're not the things I would ideally want
> to do. (10)

Others, like respondent 7, were less scrupulous, however, and in such cases there are important implications for the student experience. Students' possession of cultural capital (Bourdieu and Passeron, 1977), particularly confidence and articulacy, becomes paramount in the kind of Hobbesian environment that results from this kind of response. This is ironic as the expansion in higher education and the development of the credit frame-work were at least partly predicated on the notion of reducing the import-ance of characteristics derived from social background in determining access to higher education. Respondent 13 is another example of an individual in this category:

> I'm having to adopt survival strategies that I would be embarrassed to
> admit. The goodwill has gone; there's an assumption that we're in this
> for a vocation as much as anything else, and we'll happily do our mark-
> ing well into the evening and we'll happily do our research as a labour
> of love on top of it . . .

> You have seminar groups of maybe 20 – and that's supposed to be a
> seminar? And if you have over that, they're not going to hire someone
> else to teach it so you're going to have to teach another hour. So your
> teaching hours go up. So the point is that now I'm not as generous
> with my goodwill as I used to be. If they're going to be so damn
> pernickety about . . . claiming days away and a certain amount of re-
> search days and having to log leave and things like that, well fine I'm
> going to work to a thirty-seven hour contract and if that means mark-
> ing twelve five-thousand word essays in an hour, whamming through it,
> reading the first paragraph and the last paragraph and putting a damn
> number against it, well fine . . .

> What they're forcing us to do is to go back to the complete lecture
> system which as far as I can see runs utterly counter to all the educational
> developments that they are trying to promote here . . . It's becoming
> like a correspondence course for some students . . . My difficulty comes

in promising seminars [to students] . . . you're supposed to give them a
number based on listening to them speak for two or three minutes
. . . Bullshit.

A minority of respondents were in disciplinary areas which had had to
struggle for survival rather than being in an expansionist phase. In these
cases they adopted coping strategies which had implications for the implementation of curriculum policy too. For example, decisions about increasing
or decreasing the flexibility of programmes through loose or rigid application of co- and prerequisites for studying modules were conditioned by the
supply and demand context of the discipline: 'Maybe people have been
more inclined not to build in rigid pre- and corequisite structures because
they see that students were being excluded and as it's very much a numbers
game that we're in nowadays, maybe people have been a bit more . . . liberal
with their pre- and corequisites' (37).

The same sort of instrumentalism was also observed coming into play
when considering the issue of accrediting prior learning for admission:
'[Using APL/APEL for] gaining admission I'm quite happy with and it's a
well-established practice . . . perhaps because we are short of applicants. We
tend to take people onto the courses if we think that they can cope with
it. We'll look at what they've done before, sometimes we'll even give them
a test' (34).

Policy reconstruction

This is probably the most interesting category, and potentially the largest,
given that many academic staff engage in some aspect of policy reconstruction as well as developing coping strategies. In Mertonian terms they are
either rebelling or innovating or both. Policy reconstruction is used here,
then, to refer to the processes academics engage in when they reinterpret
and reconstruct policy on the ground, using strategies to effectively change
the policy, sometimes resisting change, sometimes altering its direction. As
respondent 28 put it: '[If you say] "oh no these things have been imposed
on me" and get pissed off about it you end up like the old gits [in discipline
X]' (28).

These academics, then, took a robust approach to their working context, acting as movers and shakers. The 'work' they did in this respect was
much more proactive than the theories of change which incorporate passive
models of the academic would recognize. This 'work' was more creative,
too, than the strategies of resistance in non-academic environments which
are described and discussed in Jermier *et al.* (1994).

The reconstructive strategies uncovered by the fieldwork can be categorized under the following headings: curriculum innovation; syllabus innovation; reinterpretation of policy; policy manipulation; and reprofessionalization.
I will deal with each of these in turn.

Curriculum innovation

There were a number of examples of academics using their latitude for innovation to develop what Robertson (1994a) calls 'regressive' strategies: ones which move away from the claimed flexibility and other advantages of the credit framework 'back' to a more traditional model. Increasingly there was a move towards the validation of defined fields (as the relative decline in the numbers of students in combined honours at NewU shows – see Chapter 1), often involving the two or three stage 'drift' discussed above from the development of individual modules to the creation of a Subject within combined honours to, finally, a defined field. While the first two stages are within the letter and spirit of the credit framework, the last, potentially at least, is not. When academics move into this arena, as was the case, for example, in design history, they are effectively moving from the 'swimming' category to the 'reconstructing' one. As well as a means of gaining promotion, increasing their own status and enabling them to concentrate on areas of their discipline they were most interested in, academics used curriculum manipulation as a means of wresting control (from the centre) of a number of aspects of their work. The move from Subject to defined field, in particular, gave them much more latitude once they were outside the constraints of the combined honours system.

Syllabus innovation

Regressive strategies were also being employed within syllabuses. Reducing the number of optional modules available is one way in which academics can reduce their teaching workload. This is done either by simply deleting options from the programme, or even removing the element of optionality altogether in one or more years. A second strategy is to 'tighten up' the co- and/or prerequisites required to study any particular module, thus constraining choice and effectively structuring students' programmes much more stringently.

Respondent 33, a head of department, noted that increasingly researchers were being appointed, but then: 'We . . . proceed to kill them off by loading them up to the eyeballs with teaching' (33). This respondent clearly felt that the university was trying to do too many things and not doing any of them well: 'I would be grateful if the university would come up with a model for [the balance of work]. Periodically it emphasizes different aspects of the job and it cannot settle in its own mind, it seems, what aspects it regards as having priority'.

This lack of focus, a common complaint among Burton Clark's (1987a) sample of American academics in lower-status institutions, was, however, something that respondent 33 and the department took action to tackle locally: 'Within this department we've taken a machete to the teaching commitment over the last eighteen months and we've reduced it very substantially and we've done that really by cutting down the class contact and by cutting out a very large proliferation of options which should never have been allowed to grow up in my view'.

This kind of strategy is within the letter but outside the spirit of the credit framework scheme as it operates at NewU because of the reduction in choice for students. The same is true of the tightening up of co- and prerequisites for studying particular modules, effectively constraining student choice. This could (and theoretically should) be done only for reasons related to the coherence of study. However, the data indicate that academics constrain choice in this way for other reasons, in particular as a method of reducing the workload in the face of job intensification. There was a clear push in this direction within the department of education studies, with a view forming that this strategy should be used to develop constrained pathways with choice only available in the third year: a very traditional syllabus structure (fieldnote 25.10.95.). Interview data suggested that this was also happening in French: 'It's tightening up, it's becoming more kind of hierarchical in terms of prerequisites' (French).

Other syllabus-related strategies were clearly outside the letter of the university CAT system. One common one was the creation of numerous whole-year modules to avoid the problems presented to academics by the semester system. A respondent in accounting reported this strategy and a less detectable variant of it was used in education studies with a single module nominally split into two half modules. Each ran for one semester, assessment being weighted at the end; in all but name it was a year-long module. Also having a 'regressive' effect, such structures were discouraged by university policy but with little apparent effect, either because the transgression went undetected or unenforced or because good arguments had been developed by the academics to justify 'exceptional' cases.

Academics in general were unhappy with the clear specification of learning outcomes that the credit framework encourages. They felt this restricted their teaching and assessment strategies and also, as I showed in Chapter 2, they were aware of the increased surveillance over them that the publication of this kind of syllabus detail facilitated. Two creative responses to this were common. The first was to keep learning outcomes and other syllabus details as vague as possible and to develop good arguments for this for use at validation events, a strategy I noted being used to good effect at the validation of a BSc degree in a humanities discipline (fieldnote 24.3.94.). This tends to be particularly effective where members of the validation panel share worries, based on accumulated experience, about the deleterious effects of highly pre-structured courses. This appeared to be the case at the validation event in question. The second is to use the traditional freedom of the teacher to control what happens inside the lecture and seminar room, allowing that to change and develop regardless of the outcomes stated: 'We probably don't teach what's on the syllabus anyway . . . you have to [specify learning outcomes] for the sake of the paperwork' (34). Again, educationally sound reasons can easily be marshalled to justify this, particularly the need to be responsive to changes within the discipline and to student need.

Reinterpretation of policy

As with almost all policy areas, most aspects of the credit framework defy policy-makers' attempts to articulate every detail of what is intended in unambiguous terms. Where there is apparent success the specificity itself can become a problem. The attempt to define 'one credit' is a case in point. An early regulatory attempt to define credit value in terms of quantified student work hours over an academic year proved so unworkable that it was abandoned. In many cases, too, policy-makers are unsure or divided about exactly what is intended and their solution is to draft regulations in an ambiguous way. The same 'credit' issue is a case in point: an enthusiast for the credit framework would see the attempt to define it in terms of work-hours unwarranted, given the opposition to 'time-serving' inherent in the philosophy of the credit framework, while those looking at the issue from a managerialist perspective would see doing so as providing a useful quantitative measure of student work-time.

These characteristics of policy give considerable latitude to policy implementers on the ground. Moreover it is extremely difficult to enforce the day-to-day operation of policy across a large university, so even where actors' operations clearly move outside formal policy this goes unnoticed or is ignored in the interests of maintaining good relationships which may be important in other matters.

To explore this aspect of policy implementation I used a case study of two elements of the credit framework: the accreditation of prior learning (APL) and the accreditation of prior experiential learning (APEL), and gave this particular attention in my fieldwork and interviews. My findings are more fully explored in Trowler (1996a) and I will only briefly summarize them here.

I showed in Chapter 2 that there had been a bureaucratization of the APEL process at NewU and central attempts to control a 'system' which had, prior to 1992, been conducted on a very *ad hoc* and localized basis, often with the individual course leader making admissions or exemption decisions on criteria known only to him or herself. This centralization was manifested in the setting up of a university credit exemption and transfer (CXT) committee, the appointment of a CXT officer and secretary, the development of very specific university-wide CXT regulations incorporated into the general regulations, the writing of a handbook for course leaders and others, and the setting up of regular training events. In addition to this effort to impose consistency through bureaucratic means there was also an attempt to promote the use of CXT across the university, as this paragraph from the CXT staff guide indicates:

> The University is committed to the recognition of learning wherever it occurs and to giving credit where such learning can be evidenced in a manner which is academically valid. The principles of credit exemption and transfer are clearly embedded in the philosophy of the Credit

Accumulation and Transfer Scheme (CATS) and are written into the University's Academic Regulations.

(NewU, 1994i: A1)

Despite all this, actors on the ground continued to ignore or selectively interpret the policy. In psychology it was effectively ignored, partly because: '. . . there is a terrific sense of elitism about the subject, a terrific amount of almost snobbery about it' (psychology). It was also ignored in that discipline because there was no perceived need for it: there were many more applicants for the programmes offered than there were places.

Some claimed it was inappropriate for their discipline. One reason was the view that in their discipline experiential learning does not occur: 'People do not get experiential learning in maths basically. It just doesn't happen. People don't wander round the streets picking up maths books' (maths). Though there were other reasons given too: 'It's not really happened that APL has been appropriate . . . mathematical skills get rusty . . . and also there's quite a lot of benefit in going through the educational process again with somebody else giving you a different input and also students might see APL as an easy process and it's not' (electronics).

Where formal learning in other institutions was concerned, some academics suggested that it was too difficult and/or unreliable to check that the content studied matched that on the NewU course. Others used APL/ APEL procedures more for latent functions such as 'cooling the mark out' (Goffman, 1962b) than for their manifest purposes. A number, especially in fashion and art and design areas, said that while they asked candidates to construct a portfolio for admission or exemption, they often based their decisions on an assessment of character at interview. One in another discipline admitted that while he and colleagues sometimes run an aptitude test: 'We will back it up with an interview [and this] can be useful if you've got someone who isn't appropriate and they've scored twenty-two per cent on the aptitude test. You can . . . use that as supporting evidence' (22).

Others applied only the 'credit-exchange' version of APEL, while others again used a very sophisticated 'developmental' model for all their students: 'All our practitioners come in with advanced standing to level two. All of them. Regardless of when they qualified' (nursing studies).

Some (for example in audio-visual media studies) insisted on careful matching of the learning outcomes obtained prior to admission with those on the NewU course, while others (e.g. in education studies) did not. Some insisted on the APL portfolio being written in an academic style with references to the literature made in the same way as one would in an essay (for example, in development studies and nursing studies) while others (for example, in business economics and journalism) did not.

Some of these academics, then, were reinterpreting and reconstructing the APL/APEL policy as formally stated. Despite the fact that the regulations 'strongly encourage' APL/APEL applications (academic regulations note N1.4 to regulation D1.4), many academics discouraged them, would not accept them or used them for purposes other than those intended. Similarly, while regulations state that a 'subject or defined field panel' should consider credit exemption and transfer cases and make decisions (regulation D1.4 6d), course leaders often continued to make decisions (or avoid doing so) on their own account. Finally, although the regulations give some latitude to academics on the assessment of prior experiential learning, the model outlined there is clearly the 'developmental' one (Butterworth, 1992), involving the extraction of learning from experience through reflective writing. As I demonstrated above, however, some academic staff were using a credit exchange model, a simple mechanical matching of knowledge, understanding and abilities to course requirements. A very important factor in conditioning responses was the educational ideology of the particular academic responsible for the implementation of APEL policy. This affected not only their broad attitudes towards the policy but the detail of its implementation. For example traditionalists like respondent 13 tended to require an academic essay in the normal academic style as part of the APEL portfolio whereas progressivists did not. Progressivists like 23 did not require precise matching of previous experience or qualifications against university modules' learning outcomes whereas those subscribing to the enterprise ideology, such as respondent 25, tended to do so.

Policy manipulation

Some of the academics I spoke to were behaving extremely strategically with regard to the regulations. In taxation terms this is the category in which avoidance moves into evasion. This often meant creating local practices and understandings in order to bypass central ones, usually considered to be ineffective or producing undesired effects in some way. Interview and observational data revealed several instances of this sort of strategy.

The university regulations require that 'electives' be incorporated into programmes to broaden students' educational experience. It is also expected that programmes make some of their modules available to 'elective' students: non-specialists who study only that one module in the discipline. Both of these aspects of the principle of electives meet opposition from many academic staff because they are perceived to dilute student quality, make teaching more difficult and to reduce the ability to convey new subject content given that it becomes impossible to assume any prior knowledge. The elective programme, therefore, provides fertile ground for policy manipulation. One particularly inventive way of doing this was reported by one respondent who admitted that: 'We actually cheat a little bit' (35).

Staff made sure that the modules were known to be electives *only* by students in a particular discipline by putting them onto the computer after the course catalogue had been published, then taking them off the computer before the next catalogue was prepared. If this had not been done 'you just couldn't cope with the numbers' (35) and the benefits of having students from this cognate discipline (who were already familiar with the background of the substantive content of the modules) would have been lost, as would potential later recruitment of some of them onto the degree programme of the area of study offering the elective. The effect was to make the programme appear 'legal' in terms of providing elective elements to the university yet to avoid suffering the consequences of just that.

Another, less complex strategy, was simply to inform defined-field students that a particular module was the elective that they must take, thus creating an oxymoron: a compulsory elective. This is what occurred in an applied science department I observed with a module giving what was considered an essential grounding in another scientific discipline and offered by that other department (fieldnote 28.5.95.). Though completely outside the regulations, this strategy prevented what was seen as a watering down of the degree with irrelevant material and an opportunity to pack more subject-specific material into the first year of a content-loaded discipline.

A further example, again to control student numbers, was the setting up of '. . . our own little progression exercise' (22). This was done because: 'If you simply allow the students to pick the modules they want [as the philosophy of CATS suggests] you can't guarantee to be able to staff all the [computer] labs' (22).

A further example in this category is the stretching of the definition of a credit: 'credit inflation'. It was widely acknowledged across the university that a credit in engineering, for example, required far more work from students and input from staff than was the case in many other disciplines. The engineers themselves recognized this and in fact had designed their programme in this way: 'In CATS 2 there were too many subjects [partly because of IMechE requirements and our own desire to cover a lot of material] which were two and three credits. In other areas of the universities they would be five or six credits. And the students were all saying "well why are you doing this?"' (engineering).

A final example relates to 'difficult' elements of core modules in a science discipline that was finding it difficult to recruit 'strong' students. Too many students were failing these modules because of their inability to cope with the difficult elements. This was threatening the viability of the department and would ultimately threaten academics' jobs. The solution was to reduce their presence so that they both appear less significant to prospective students and so that students stand a better chance of getting through: 'Things on core modules that are difficult to pass, we've tended to squash those into modules, which artificially reduces the emphasis . . . [on them] . . . [They are] a smaller element in our course than [they] . . . otherwise would be' (science discipline).

Reprofessionalization

Descriptions of the deprofessionalization, even proletarianization, of the academic profession provided by Jary and Parker and others and described in

Chapter 2 would be very familiar to many of the academics at the research site. Many felt that they were in danger of becoming mere 'deliverers' of modules, interchangeable teachers perceived as having no special skills or qualities and merely there to satisfy the whims of the student 'market'. Some felt that students were seeing them in this way already, treating academics not as professionals and disciplinary specialists but as generally available to help resolve any problem.

However, the causes of these attitudes among academic staff do not simply lie in the particularities of the organizational culture at NewU: the credit framework itself is strongly involved also. For example, many staff felt that modularity meant that students did not identify with any particular discipline and that disciplinary knowledge was becoming increasingly fragmented and 'regionalized' (Bernstein, 1990). As a result students were less likely to see themselves as being socialized into a discipline by specialists, or as following in others' footsteps (a matter of particular regret for those academics subscribing to a traditionalist ideology). Many staff regretted too that there was now limited time for personal relationships to develop with students. In short, many of the traditional attractions and pleasures of the academic life were felt to be waning.

Policy reconstructers tended to be those who reflected on these kinds of issues and took action to reprofessionalize both their work and the perceptions of it held by others. Respondent 10 is a very clear though not unique example and I will use extracts from that interview to demonstrate some of the measures taken. Respondent 10 had consciously moved towards what he calls 'taking control' in the face of deprofessionalization. He wanted students to feel that:

> They weren't just taught by a functionary, they have been taught by people who've got real things to offer, who've written, researched, give papers at conferences, are respected in their own field whatever it is . . . So what I've been trying to do over the last year is to . . . think through what would that mean, for me to take control of my professionalism? What do I have to do in practical terms to do that? And basically it's about putting *me* back in the process. Me as an identifiable person, with a personality and a character and an academic background. I want to put all that back in for the students . . . That's a concrete example of where I'm trying to take control again of the identity of the subject from the student's perspective.

He gave a hypothetical scenario to illustrate the problems he perceived with higher education simply responding to market demands:

> Does that mean then that people are coming along saying 'I don't want to learn about Marxism . . . these ideas are not relevant any more. Communism's on the decline everywhere so I'm not interested in it'? Well my answer to that is: 'Fine, you're not interested in it. But it's my academic judgement that there are important lessons to be learned

here and therefore it's going to be on the course'... We shouldn't allow ... ourselves to be demand-led because ... that works to the disadvantage of some types of knowledge and to the advantage of others, inevitably ... People's views about what they would like to know about ... or skills they would like to acquire isn't neutral. Their decisions about that are influenced by the media, by politics, by ideology and so on.

Respondent 10, like many others, used coping strategies that he was not happy with, but increasingly he is turning to this aspect of policy reconstruction as a key feature of his work. He contributed teaching and research in two domains of study, each of which draws from a number of disciplines. Epistemologically there is considerable attraction in the credit framework for academics working within such domains: one is that with their integrative rather than collection code (see Bernstein, 1971: 53; Becher, 1989: 14) academics can develop modules in areas of interest and potentially encourage curriculum promotion up the modules > subject > defined field ladder, as I noted above.

However, respondent 10 very clearly subscribed to a social reconstructionist ideology. This was evident both from his interview discourse and from observant participation data. From this perspective the undermining of disciplinary knowledge, the decline in the status of academics as experts and in the power of their symbols (Rustin, 1994) serves to neutralize a potential force for opposition to class (or other minority or majority) rule. The credit framework in particular results in an incoherent and inferior degree delivered by proletarianized full-time teachers mostly in under-funded, overcrowded further education (FE) colleges, as Robson (1992) put it. Thus this academic's educational ideology, his personal interests and the epistemological characteristics of his area of specialism contained inherent incompatibilities: exactly the sort of set of ambiguities or dilemmas which Newman recognizes as imposing 'conflicting injunctions on organizational members' (Newman, 1994: 62). He was in a potential trap, in the sense that there are elements of incompatibility in his structural and ideological context, but a very different one from the more famous 'Robbins trap' in which respondent 14 was caught. However, as I have shown here, he was able to use reprofessionalizing strategies to take measures to resolve these dilemmas. He appeared to have succeeded in applying these without compromising his values, harming students or jeopardizing his career (soon after the interview he gained a promoted post in another institution). It is interesting, however, that he did all this alone: no other member of his department, which I observed in detail, appeared to have been aware of his strategies. Such individualistic, adaptive responses are perhaps made more apparent by the nature of my research design which largely adopts the methodological individualism inherent in most of the fine-grained studies of higher education (though observant participation and the analysis of secondary data did allow me to access departmental responses to some extent too).

However, it is clear that this individual and many others I obtained data from illustrate the veracity of Ball's observation that: 'A response [to policy] must . . . be put together, constructed in context, offset against other expectations. All this involves creative social action, not robotic reactivity' (Ball, 1994: 19).

6

New Light on Old Issues

I remarked in the introduction to this book that the empirical and theoretical account of higher education provided by research has so far been rather partial and inappropriately extended to cover a complex, differentiated and changing system. The research project discussed here has provided an ethnographic account of an institution, disciplines and domains of study and of individuals at the lower-status end of the system. It is important that this be done because, as Geertz (1983: 143) reminds us: 'Most people are not settled at or near the top or center but at some region lower down, further out'.

It is important too because of the light such a study sheds on the system as a whole. Just as Delamont recommends a focus on gender as one way to make a familiar setting 'anthropologically strange' (Delamont, 1996: 145), so a focus on another area of cultural difference may render problematic features of everyday life taken for granted by academics. While I do not claim that the conclusions reached are generalizable in detail to other institutions of higher education, even lower-status ones, they can usefully illuminate the way we think about both the system as a whole and its component parts. They may also help shed some critical light on the predominant ways of knowing in higher education and so move the debate forward in that field as it has already been moved in others, particularly in the study of the compulsory education sector. This chapter, then, focuses on areas of thinking about higher education which urgently need reconceptualizing.

Structure and action: structuration, attitudes and behaviour

In Chapter 3 I set out the structures which condition responses to the implementation of the credit framework. In doing so my main purpose was to illustrate the insufficiency of an account predicated on epistemological factors alone. However, the account set out in that chapter itself requires elaboration. As it stands it gives priority to structure and therefore to stability,

Figure 6.1 Structures, structuration and the credit framework at NewU

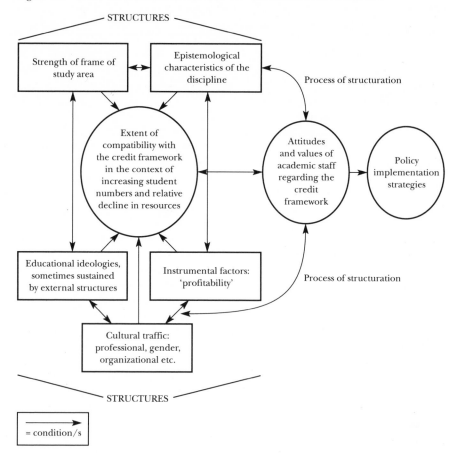

coherence, and forces beyond the control of individual actors, accepting rather than challenging the structuralism inherent in much of the higher education literature. Figure 3.1 needs amending and Figure 6.1 offers a more sophisticated representation of the situation.

In the conception of the processes at work illustrated by Figure 6.1, the influences are iterative: different aspects of structure interact with each other while agency and structure also interact in important ways. This view derives from Giddensian structuration theory, the sophistication of which lies in the insight that structure and action are interdependent and mutually causative so that good social theory must appreciate both. Giddens (1976: 121) writes: '"structuration", as the reproduction of practices, refers abstractly to the dynamic process whereby structures come into being. By the "duality of structures" I mean that social structures are both constituted "by" human agency, and yet at the same time are the very "medium" of this constitution'.

Similarly, Bhaskar (1979: 43), taking a position close to Giddens' but one which gives structure a stronger ontological grounding, writes: 'Society is both the ever-present "condition" (material cause) and the continually reproduced "outcome" of human agency'.

In developing a more powerful theory of the relationship between social structure and social action in higher education the metaphor of the relationship between speech and language is illuminative. Giddens shows that language has the characteristics of social structure: it is an abstract property of a community of speakers and is 'outside of time': it exists only insofar as it is known to its speakers with no specific socio-temporal location. Speech, on the other hand, has the characteristics of social action. It is situated socio-temporally and presupposes a specific subject who produces it. Language (structure) is a prerequisite for the production of speech, but is not speech itself. Neither is it dominant: language in a sense is merely the collective understanding of 'how things are done' and as speech (social action) changes in the routine practices of the speech community, so language (social structure) changes also. Thus language (structure) changes over time as the recurrent practice of speech evolve, as for example has occurred over time in the USA and in the UK, making American English different from British English. Regional and social groups develop their own dialects and even individuals their own idiolects. Conversely, individual speech acts require the shared understandings of language for communication to occur and, in particular socio-temporal locations, may be considered poorly or incorrectly formed as a result of reference to the common understandings of language.

Importantly, however, linguistic (structural) change can also occur as a result of conscious determination of social actors, as occurs in France as a result of the decisions and actions of the Académie Française in its defence of French culture and language, particularly in the face of American culture and American English. This is a useful metaphor for one aspect of the contested nature of cultural production and enactment. Such conscious change in routine behaviour was observed occurring on numerous occasions. Probably more than other social groups academics are likely to reflect on their situation, form a view and then take action to change it if they consider it necessary. Respondents who provide very clear examples of this among my sample are 10, 32 and 31 ('Miss Disempowerment' as she reported her colleagues calling her, for the fact that she regularly discussed academics' position in the university and the possibilities of change). Many other examples can be found in the literature, for example Gayle Letherby's discussion of various aspects of her experience as a woman academic in an unchartered university and the proposals for action she makes (Letherby, 1996: especially 14). The consequences of such actions are not always those which were predicted or intended, but they do have important effects.

Of course, discourse analysts take the language/speech-structure/action discussion one stage further in that they stress the *constitutive* nature of discourse, that is they argue that discourse not only *mirrors* or is analogous to social agency but that it is itself socially constitutive (Potter and Wetherell, 1987: 2; Fairclough, 1993: 134). Adopting such a position means that conscious or unconscious changes in speech acts not only change the language but may also result in (and not just reflect) wider social structural change, just as I have argued may occur with other sorts of acts. The position adopted here, then, takes from Giddens and Bhaskar a perspective which stresses the continuing reproductive and inherently mutually causal relationship between agency and structure, a theoretical position others have also applied in alternative contexts to the one considered here (Smith, 1983; Porter, 1993).

I showed in Chapter 3 that the important structures in the site under examination together condition the likely degree of coherence between the attitudes, values and behaviour of academics in particular locations and the changes in higher education which have been the focus of this study: the implementation of the credit framework in the context of expanding student numbers and declining resources. Where there is a coherent 'fit', academics are likely to find the new policies and environment congenial; where there is incongruity they will find it a less amenable environment. In these circumstances they are likely to find themselves in danger of falling into 'traps' or dilemmas of one sort or another. However an appreciation of the importance of agency means that the story is more complex than that in two senses. First, the structures so described are not autonomous from human agency, and second where there is incongruity in an academic's structural location they are often able to adopt coping and even reconstructing strategies to deal with the situation. I will consider these two points in turn.

In Chapter 3 I developed the argument that the epistemological nature of academic disciplines should not be seen as 'objective' phenomena in the way that essentialist positions tend to do. Rather, I argued (with Evans, 1993) that they are socially constructed and socially understood 'stories' or discursive products which are often the subject of negotiation or contest, as I showed was the case in English and engineering. The essentialist notion of 'linearity' in fact turns out to be a social construction, a story which is itself conditioned to a large extent by educational ideology. These 'stories' are no less 'structural' in nature than 'real' epistemological determinants: they constrain and condition behaviour in the same way and give it regularity and, to some extent, predictability. They are therefore 'real' in their consequences. The point I am making is that they are amenable to change by actors and are themselves influenced by other structures.

The social actor, then, has a degree of 'choice' in thinking about their discipline and, as a corollary, about whether it 'fits' into the credit framework or not in terms of its supposed epistemological properties. This choice itself, of course, may be conditioned by other structural characteristics of the context, for example by academic ideologies, but these too are recursively influenced by agency. The picture is a far more complicated one than that painted by authors writing from an essentialist position who do not problematize to any extent the divisions between academics on epistemological or ideological grounds. Recognizing these kinds of intra-disciplinary differences, which partly result from agency and partly from the interaction of structural characteristics, suggests the need for caution about making generalizations about academic disciplines and in particular the 'academic profession' as a whole, as for example Harrold (1992: 1472) tries to do: 'Research is of prime importance in academics' value systems . . . Academics must teach but they prefer to engage in research'.

The importance of recognizing agency applies as much to the other significant structural characteristics in operation at NewU as to epistemology. I argued in earlier chapters that organizational and other manifestation of culture should be regarded as both enacted (structural) and constructed in nature. Social agency may be manifested in numerous ways: by the more or less conscious decisions to break the cultural mould of recurrent behaviours, for example, or as a result of changing practices which themselves are the product of a changed perception of circumstances, perhaps precipitated by a period of crisis, external events or simply reflection on the sources of current travails, as is instanced in the previous chapter.

In a similar fashion, while educational ideologies impose structure in the sense the word is used here, particularly in terms of their normative elements and codes of signification, the reality is that individuals do not in general blindly subscribe to one or another ideological position but move between them, adopting different discursive repertoires in different situations, as I argued in Chapter 3. The material needs and interests of academics, particularly in this context in terms of the market position of their disciplines, on the other hand, appear to have greater ontological depth and to constrain the individual in quite real ways. Giddens argues these translate into more subjective 'needs dispositions' but this is to under-emphasize the degree of constraint that such structural characteristics impose: a criticism that has been levelled at structuration theory in general (Craib, 1992: 50). The resource aspect of structures is in practice less amenable to the influence of social agency than their rule dimensions, though academics in different social locations may be more, or less, aware of and concerned about them. Much the same applies to the strength of frame issue. With regard to this, academics seem to be most aware of and concerned about the impact of professional bodies in constraining their power to determine the structure and content of academic programmes rather than, for example, the influence of the developing 'quasi-market' in higher education. However only a few (nine) of the interviewees reported significant syllabus control by external bodies (for example IMechE, BPS, ENB, BTEC and the Law Society), three reported some control but qualified this in some way, and twenty-six reported no significant control. However, without detailed examination of exactly what each of these bodies require, and how rigorously they enforce their requirements, it is difficult to establish how far respondents' perceptions of influence accurately reflect the regulations. I have a suspicion, shared by more than one respondent, that the symbolic importance of professional bodies, particularly the weight they lend to an argument for a particular direction of change, is at least as important as the actual effect of their stipulations. Frame strength, too, is partly a constructed 'story' which individuals may or may not subscribe to as well as a 'real' characteristic of disciplines in a given context.

Academics, then, occupy particular locations within the specific cultural configuration of their university. As they address or are faced with new issues, aspects of that configuration and of the structural circumstances more generally recede or advance in terms of their relevance and importance and, especially in the long term, the context itself is changed by the actions of the individuals within it, alone or (more especially) in groups. Both structure and agency are important in that sense.

But agency is important in another sense: the power of the actor to influence policy in its implementation. Much of the literature I reviewed in Chapter 4 portrays academics as passive in the face of change, most of which is unwanted by them. Much of the literature too is predicated on a rationalist top-down model of change based on an implicit railway signal-box metaphor: successful organizational, cultural and curriculum change involves finding the appropriate levers and pulling them at the right time. By contrast the previous chapter has shown that many academics do in fact act in important ways to influence the shape of change and respond to policy in ways that are not predicted by policy-makers. Attitudes, values, how people think and 'the way things are done around here', in a word *culture*, are not changed by fiat from above (as Beckhard and Pritchard would have us believe). People learn new patterns as they interact with others at work and elsewhere, meet new problems, tackle new circumstances and reflect on their practices and ideas. They construct culture as well as play it out, as Giddens shows us. Seeing organizations and the cultural configuration which exists within them in this way has important implications for our understanding of educational change. A full appreciation of the policy process needs to encompass the implementation stage, or rather to see policy implementation as another aspect of policy-making.

The findings about how academics react to curriculum policy in the context discussed here lead me to question the bleak view of the 'decline of donnish dominion' which is so prevalent in the literature. Clearly in recent years a combination of factors at both the national and institutional levels has meant that many aspects of academic work have suffered degradation and deprofessionalization. These factors have included the relative reduction in public funding for higher education, changes in the nature of funding mechanisms which have led to a reduction in university autonomy, the decreased power of professional associations to defend members' pay and conditions, New Right and 'postmodern' undermining of the status of forms of knowledge traditionally offered by universities as well as the effects of changes in the curriculum structure mapped here. Certainly the status and rewards of the profession as a whole have diminished. Certainly, too, more labour is being extracted from academics by 'management' (whether seen as government or within the university), to put it in Braverman's (1974) terms, and the discursive repertoires in use within universities are increasingly managerial ones. It may be that we are merely seeing the first stage of the extension of control over and proletarianization of academics: what Derber (1983) calls 'ideological proletarianisation', to be followed at a later stage by 'technical proletarianisation'. Yet unalloyed images of 'traps' and 'decline' fail to take into account the resources that academics have to respond to curriculum and other forms of change which mitigate their effects or turn them to their own advantage. This side of the equation needs as much theoretical work as the other side, but so far little of this has been done.

Academics' responses themselves have effects on the direction of change just as much as formal policy does. Some of these are intended, as is the case with many of the policy reconstruction strategies discussed, but some are unintended: for example those which may occur as a result of the coping strategies adopted by some academics. Judged from the point of view of the student experience there seems little doubt that many of them have a deleterious effect, as of course do many of the wider higher education policy changes. How far students, too, are able to respond effectively to these changing circumstances has not been the focus of this study, but my suspicion is that the effect of the changes has been to diminish access to good quality higher education for those lacking the cultural capital necessary to develop strategies for success in this new context.

Culture and policy

Craig McInnis notes that given the interest in organizational cultures over the last decade, 'the lack of interest in the role of the collective in discussing the policy implementation process generally, and especially in the worlds of higher education, is rather surprising' (McInnis, 1996: 99). The previous section has demonstrated that the linkages between culture and change are both complex and important. In order to understand the ways in which policy is interpreted and effectively changed at the ground level during the process of 'implementation' it is necessary both to develop a more sophisticated appreciation of cultures in higher education organizations than has been deployed so far and to consider the consequences of this for the policy implementation process.

In the study of culture in higher education there has been a heavy emphasis on the ideational dimension: on symbols, sagas, images and icons. This is seen, for example, in the work of Becher (1989) and Clark (1987a; 1987b) and may derive from the work on culture in other corporate settings in which 'the management of meaning' through manipulation of such symbols is an important strand in the management literature (Alvesson, 1990a). However, such accounts detract attention from the more important aspects of cultures, the values, attitudes and recurrent practices which permeate everyday life. Seeing cultures in this way brings to the foreground their importance in structuring the interpretation of policy change, the attitudes taken towards it and subsequent implementation behaviours. In Chapter 1 I highlighted other deficiencies in the way the concept of culture has been applied to higher education to date. Together these points make clear the importance of viewing cultures in organizations as substantive rather than ideational phenomena, of seeing them as open to influence and change from outside and inside the organization, of recognizing that they are not always consensual or functional in nature but multiple and sometimes conflicting. Most important is the need to recognize their importance in shaping policy outcomes locally, in creating (or minimizing) the 'implementation gap' between policy intentions and policy outcomes.

Gender issues

Becher comments at the end of his 1989 text that if he were to conduct his study again he would 'want to build in some more systematic allowance for gender' (Becher, 1989: 179). Becher is not alone in the omission of gender issues from research design and data analysis. Few studies of professional cultures explicitly take gender issues into account in any detailed way, though a notable exception is Cullen's (1994). Until recently only those studies of higher education specifically addressing gender issues as research questions gave it any detailed attention (Acker and Piper, 1984; Sutherland, 1985; Thomas, 1990; Bannerji *et al.*, 1991; Greed, 1991; Acker, 1994; Davies *et al.*, 1994). Studies of cultures in organizations and organizational analysis generally tended to ignore the gender dimension until the early 1990s (Acker, 1992b; Hearn and Parkin, 1992; Mills, 1992; Itzin and Newman, 1995). However if cultures concern the shared symbols, discourse, practices, beliefs, values and attitudes of social groups, then it is clear that gender, defined as 'patterned, socially produced distinctions between female and male, feminine and masculine' (Acker, 1992b: 250) permeates most aspects of them. Indeed, Delamont (1989: 29) argues that it is precisely these cultural aspects, the 'taste of a group, its characteristic taken-for-granted view of the world' and its 'tacit, indescribable competencies' which are the most important aspects of patriarchy because they prove so elusive to women. Mainstream approaches to the study of higher education, then, have also tended to be 'malestream' ones, and have, as a result, systematically ignored the gendered nature of the issues they explore.

The importance of foregrounding gender issues was illustrated in Chapter 3. I argued there that norms, values and attitudes associated with gender are an extremely important part of the cultural flow into, within and through higher education institutions and have very important consequences for the work of women academics in particular. Because of the patriarchal nature of contemporary British society a cultural perspective on women academics' work tends to highlight the deleterious aspects of their position.

However, the story is not a completely negative one in which women are the victims of the patriarchal context in which they operate. In returning to this issue I wish to stress the 'social action' side of the structuration equation in this regard. The data from this research project lead me to believe that women are benefiting more than men from the introduction of the credit framework, and in large part due to their taking the initiative. In Chapter 5 I showed that for some academics the credit framework environment is a particularly hospitable one. I argued there that one of the reasons for this is the opportunity the credit framework offers to develop modules, often to service other disciplines, and then to slowly accumulate them to create new Subjects within the combined honours scheme and eventually whole degree schemes, defined fields. At a personal level those academics who do this can gain course leaderships, promotion and the prerogative of determining their own areas of teaching and research as they move their field up the module > Subject > defined field ladder. One of the design history respondents said:

> I think to some extent [the credit framework is] . . . quite empowering because it means that individual members of staff can kind of take hold of a whole chunk of the curriculum and . . . redesign it and improve it as they go along on the basis of experience . . . From that point of view it works quite well . . . My subject . . . developed within the context of modularization, and probably wouldn't have been there if we hadn't modularized. So, in effect the introduction of CATS was taken, I think, as an opportunity by a lot of people, including myself, to introduce new courses and new Subjects and so on. (Design history)

In general the women in my sample were more likely than the men to have had personal benefit from this kind of experience: women respondents 5, 25, 27, 38, 39, 42 and (to a lesser extent) 11 and 23 are examples compared to only two men in an analogous situation (28 and 35). The programmes involved are women's studies, journalism, race and ethnic studies, public relations, design history, nursing studies, and (for the men) audiovisual media studies. Another programme area which has undergone this kind of development is physiology/pharmacology, a male-dominated area at NewU, but the individuals concerned did not express the view that they had personally benefited from it.

The reasons for the gender differences in the opportunities presented by the credit framework are, ironically, related to the fact that women have traditionally been concentrated in the lower-status, newer and more 'marginal' disciplines and domains, relegated to 'servicing' other disciplines (the traditional women's role) not considered 'proper' fields of study in their own right. Even within this context women have often been largely confined to the lower-status areas of the discipline, for example applied rather than theoretical work (Deem, 1996a: 7), and to teaching rather than research (p. 10). The introduction of the credit framework simultaneously puts traditional academic hierarchies to some extent in a state of flux and at least temporarily makes the curriculum structure fluid enough for there to be some realignment in epistemological structure and its presentation. Blau notes that a flexible departmental structure in universities is important in that it 'mitigates the dead hand of tradition and the power of vested interests that tend to evolve in institutional structures' (Blau, 1973: 207). The same is true of flexible curriculum structure which, at NewU, presented an opportunity to at least some women academics to work for professional advancement and to redefine the 'border territories' (Deem, 1996a).

It is important to stress, however, that I do not claim that these findings necessarily apply elsewhere. To use the language of Raffe *et al.* (1994), the 'institutional logic' of the context of modularity (and other aspects of the credit framework) at NewU is reasonably compatible with the 'intrinsic logic' of the framework itself and these combined have on balance worked in women academics' favour. One aspect of this is the fact that areas of study which have issues of equality of opportunity as a prime focus, for example women's studies and race and ethnic studies, find fertile ground at NewU where this is, at least front-of-stage, a central concern: it is a key theme in its mission statement, other official documents and in the public discourse of senior managers. Another is the absence there of the more extreme manifestations of 'masculinist managerialism' (Blackmore, 1993; Deem, 1996b; Leonard, 1996) often especially associated with the new managerialism developing in other contexts. This feature of the institution is the result of a long-standing concern with equal opportunities issues at senior levels at NewU (Cockburn, 1988a, 1988b). Even merely rhetorical concern with these issues within an institution (and at NewU it is more than this) can create space for manoeuvre for those at the ground level.

My research at NewU leads me to agree with Davies and Holloway (1995) that curriculum and other forms of change in universities also result in change in their gender regimes (Connell, 1987). Given the patriarchal nature of previous gender regimes in universities such change is likely to have beneficial as well as negative effects for women academics. However, for staff on fixed-term and part-time contracts, disproportionately women, the benefits are likely to be less tangible as the higher education system as a whole becomes increasingly post-Fordist in character (Davies and Holloway, 1995: 15).

Culture and presage

I showed in Chapter 3 that the data from this study firmly align it with that part of the literature which stresses the importance of 'presage': the social background of the academic as an important influence on their attitudes and behaviour within the academy. Social class background, ethnicity, industrial and commercial experience and so on are all important influences which affect in important ways the cultural flow within the academy. Clark (1987a: 107) is wrong, then, when he claims that 'characteristics imported into the academic profession by individual members from their personal

background and prior experiences are relatively unimportant in conditioning their subsequent attitudes and behaviour'.

However, my conclusions lead me to go beyond the claims of, for example, Huber (1990), Joseph (1978, 1980) and Greed (1991) who also disagree with Clark's position but tend to stress only the origins of academics
as influencing early choices of discipline. This limits in an unrealistic way
the influence of background only to recruitment to the academy. The cultural traffic that flows into the academy with the individuals and groups who
come to it is an extremely important but neglected aspect of the cultural
configuration of higher education institutions. Personal experience of access
to higher education as a route to social mobility among academics can shape
educational ideology, providing an enduring commitment to access issues,
to franchising and other aspects of the credit framework as well as an anti-
pathy to elitist traditions in higher education, as was the case for respondent 3, for example. Gender-role socialization can likewise have enduring
effects within the university on female and male academics' attitudes towards
the relative emphasis they place on various dimensions of their job role,
for example the pastoral and teaching side as opposed to the administrative
or research side. Students too come into the context with highly gendered
sets of expectations which affect their behaviour and so the circumstances
encountered by male and female academics respectively.

Professional socialization goes on, of course, from the moment the new
entrant steps foot in the university, but this by no means wipes clean the
norms, attitudes and values acquired in other contexts. With their emphasis
on the 'organizational saga' (Clark, 1972) and the 'invisible college' (Crane,
1972) higher education researchers have stressed the distinctiveness and
separateness of academic culture from the wider community, seeing it as
united by a common culture involving guiding principles, codes and myths
as well as a deeply-rooted occupational ethos which transcends these divisive
elements, the 'small and different worlds', and integrates the profession.

Donald Light (1974), in critically appraising studies of the 'academic
profession' (so-called: for him the plural is obligatory) in particular and
research on higher education in general, makes comments which are relevant and important today, especially in the context of this study. Taking
Parsons and Platt's (1968) work to illustrate some general issues, he points
out that these authors assume that research-based universities and research-
oriented academic staff are the norm and see their 'culture' as the ideal
type (in a non-Weberian sense). Parsons and Platt's depiction of the American academic profession, based on this assumption, therefore applies only
to those staff in a minority, elite, structural location though they wrongly
attempt to generalize from this. For Light 'the academic man [sic] is a
myth' (1974: 14): academic staff in different structural locations (in terms
of the institution they work in, the nature of their employment and their
own characteristics) develop different cultures. Moreover the structures
which support these cultures may be peripheral, or even oppositional, to the
academic enterprise as traditionally conceived, unlike the 'invisible college'

which receives so much attention in the higher education literature. Parkin (1972) alerts us to the role of institutions in sustaining counter-hegemonic or at least alternative versions of reality, and these were found to be important at NewU too. Academic staff in development studies, women's studies, fashion design and accounting each referred to important organizations and activities outside the university which sustained them in terms of their attitudes and values. In some cases these could be usefully thought of in terms of 'invisible activism': for example in the case of staff involved in non-governmental development agencies working in the Third World, in women's movements or in charitable work through their church. In others the link was more commercial and less change-oriented, for example in the continuing links with industry and commerce and the attitudes and values imported into the academy from them (for example in terms of the very nature and purposes of higher education itself). Again, such findings emphasize the importance of the actor and agency in the higher education context as opposed to the enactment of institutional and professional culture. They point up, too, the pluralistic nature of the cultural configuration in any context: even where cultures *are* merely enacted, there is a complex pattern of sometimes contradictory forces bearing on a given issue rather than a unitary, coherent set. Likewise the discursive repertoires available are multiple rather than unitary in nature and this in itself lends power to actors over structures, as postmodernist theory (with all its weaknesses) suggests.

The study of higher education

Graham Allison (1971: 4) notes that what we find as researchers depends upon how deeply we cast our nets, how narrow their mesh is and which ponds we choose to fish in. To date much higher education research has involved casting nets near the surface, exploring the system level and catching the 'public' rather than the 'private' lives of universities (Trow, 1975); the front-of-stage discourse rather than what is happening behind the scenes in the day-to-day lives of those involved. The literature is replete with calls for more efforts to trawl further down with finer nets (Becher, 1989; Walford, 1992; Smyth, 1995; Cuthbert, 1996; Rothblatt, 1996) but so far comparatively little of this has been done and where such research has been conducted it has mainly been based on interview or questionnaire data collection techniques (for example, Becher, 1989; Halsey, 1992). However, the understandings of cultural production and enactment arrived at as a result of this study raise important questions about how far research based on interviews alone can go in accessing the multiple cultural configurations which inevitably exist in higher education institutions and in uncovering the nature and significance of the complexities of the skilled performances, language games, different levels of practical activity and movement between discursive repertoires which constitute social life.

Giddens argues that:

The production of society is a skilled performance, sustained and 'made to happen' by human beings . . . a grasp of the resources used by members of society to generate social interaction is a condition of the social scientist's understanding of their conduct in just the same way as it is for those members themselves . . . To be able to describe a form of life correctly, including its tensions and ambiguities, the social analyst has to learn what it is to 'go on' in the activities which constitute that form of life.

(Giddens, 1976: 15–16, 1983: 75)

His argument is that a full understanding of social life requires a hermeneutically-based description of human conduct, given the power of social actors over time to stamp a unique character on each apparently similar structural context. Access to 'mutual knowledge' is a central feature in this endeavour. This is the taken-for-granted knowledge that social agents assume is possessed by those they are interacting with if they are seen as competent members of society (Giddens, 1976: 107). It is most effectively mobilized to the benefit of the quality of research outcomes in insider, participant, research through the use of what Stenhouse (1979) calls the 'second record' of accumulated knowledge of participants' meaning systems in order to interrogate, understand and interpret data fully (Hull, 1985). This research strategy has the important benefit too of accessing not only discursive consciousness, the form of data collected by studies of higher education based on interview and questionnaire data collection techniques (as the majority are), but practical consciousness: that which actors know but cannot necessarily put into words about how to 'go on' in the many contexts in which they operate. Not to take account of practical consciousness as well as discursive consciousness is, as Giddens (1983: 76) says: '. . . like supposing that what the speakers of a language can articulate about the rules and procedures they use in speaking or writing is all they "know" about language'.

An insider account based on multiple methods of data collection also has the potential of allowing us to move beyond the meanings, understandings and intentions of actors, giving insight into the structural contexts in which they operate and the unintended consequences of their actions. If, as Giddens argues, the reproduction of social practices coordinated in structured social systems should be seen as resulting from a conjunction of deliberate and unreflective behaviour and the intended and unintended outcomes of conduct, then the methods traditionally adopted by social researchers in the higher education field have had serious limitations because they are better suited to accessing some of these than others. There is a clear need for more anthropologically-oriented studies which are able to apply a more subtle understanding of the complexities of discursive production and of social life than has been the case in the study of higher education hitherto.

Of course, the approach recommended by Giddens is not without its critics (for example, Hammersley, 1993), but these criticisms can be effectively countered in many cases, often through instancing studies which have foreseen and avoided the problems supposedly intrinsic to this form of research (see for example, Trowler, 1996e: Chapter 10). This is not to say that such criticisms are without foundation, only that the researcher needs to be aware of and take into account the problems that have been identified with the methodological approach recommended here.

7

Conclusions and Implications

For university managers and others attempting to achieve the successful adaptation of institutions of higher education to changing contexts the key finding of this study revolves around the understanding of cultures within the university. In developing the implications of the concept of the multiple cultural configurations invariably found in higher education contexts and in fleshing it out with empirical detail from one location, I have highlighted the one-dimensional nature of much previous thinking about 'organizational culture' which has in fact often addressed only 'corporate culture'. Here I want to explore the implications for work and change in university contexts.

I showed in Chapter 4 that much of the literature on change in higher education cites Beckhard and Pritchard's managerialist approach to changing the culture as providing a useful practical guide for managers. I argue that their ideas are steeped in the corporate culturism (Willmott, 1993), typical of much of the work of popular management gurus such as Deal and Kennedy (1982). In this account the kinds of cultural traffic I have identified at NewU are a sign of cultural 'weakness' with the consequence that the organization has difficulty defining and achieving its goals. I argue, however, that the understanding of 'culture' underpinning this perspective and the managerialist approach to 'changing the culture', with its assertion of managerial prerogative in the governance of employee values, are both simplistic and flawed. The following sections demonstrate why, and go on to elaborate an alternative approach to change.

Understanding cultures in organizations

The discussion throughout this book has emphasized the need to conceptualize organizations as open systems and cultural configurations within them as multiple, complex and shifting. Differentiation and conflict as well as coherence and consensus is encompassed within their walls. Beckhard and

Pritchard, by contrast, see the organization as a closed system and organizational culture as monolithic. In this regard their perspective lies in the nomothetic and functionalist tradition which underpins an earlier management literature (e.g. Tichy, 1983; Kilmann *et al.*, 1985), though one which is by no means dead (e.g. Hooijberg and Petrock, 1993; Fidler, 1996; Sporn, 1996). The approach they adopt represents a particular strand in thinking about cultures, one which could be described as 'pragmatic' rather than 'pure' (Alvesson, 1990b: 39). Their model of cultural change is also rooted in early, and now superseded, behaviourist and social learning psychological theories which stress the importance of behaviour modelling and imitation, rewards and sanctions (but go beyond such approaches through the aim of attempting to secure 'personal commitment' as well as behavioural change). In the study of the mass media, for example, such perspectives have come to be replaced by audience reception approaches which emphasize the heterogeneous nature of media audiences and the importance of their prior attitudes and values for the differential reception, interpretation and effect of media messages. Commenting on this change of perspective and its implications for our understanding of the power and effects of the mass media in changing attitudes, values and behaviour, Cashmore's (1994: 95) comment that '[w]e are not as empty headed and manipulable as many . . . seem to think' could apply equally well to academics 'receiving' policy developments as to the television audience.

The pre-existing values and attitudes of staff, both academics and others, need to be understood and addressed when considering change. Individuals and groups are far from 'empty-headed', especially those in universities. They have values and attitudes which are often deeply rooted in early and later socialization and reinforced by daily recurrent behaviours and these are used to facilitate critical thinking and deploy arguments in support of their point of view. Organizations beyond the individual can serve to sustain oppositional points of view and structures compatible with pre-existing sets of attitudes and values are often actively sought out by individuals to sustain them in what may be a work environment which is otherwise not conducive to them. Universities provide the context for multiple discourses and attempts to impose a dominant discourse are likely to result in failure.

These points undermine to some extent the relevance in a university context of Stephen Ball's (1994) points about the structural characteristics of policy considered as *discourse*. For Ball, policy in this sense sets the discursive context, conditioning what can be said and thought. The locus of legitimacy is the production of text. In this sense discourse does not just represent reality, it also constitutes it. Discourses are: 'practices that systematically form the objects of which they speak . . . Discourses are not about objects; they do not identify objects, they constitute them and in the practice of doing so conceal their own invention' (Foucault, 1977b: 49).

For Ball, the discursive context is circumscribed by policy and limits the power of actors: 'We read and respond to policies in discursive circumstances that we cannot, or perhaps do not, think about' (Ball, 1994: 23).

The scope for interpretation of the text and the parameters of resistance to and change of it are, therefore, delimited in this account. However, to view discourse in this way is to ignore the multi-dimensional nature of cultures within universities and the processes of discursive resistance, creation, contest and displacement which occur there. Important processes occur backstage and under-the-stage as alternative discursive repertoires are developed and used, a social reality represented and constructed. Examples of institutions and other structures outside the immediate context which have an important bearing on these processes include the church and religious belief (as in the case of respondent 48), non-governmental development agencies (as in the case of the development studies respondent) and the conferences and events organized by and for the early CATS proselytizers in an unsympathetic environment described by Allen and Layer (1995). As Willmott (1993: 535) says: 'employees are exposed to, and constituted by, other relations and discourses, such as feminism and environmentalism. Beyond the immediate control of corporate culture designers, these discourses serve to relativize the authority of corporate culture . . .'.

The lack of serious research and theorizing about the underlife of organizations has led higher education researchers to largely ignore these aspects of culture, ideology and discourse and to ignore the alienation from, opposition to and effective change of curricular and other policies. A developed understanding of the underlife of higher education can highlight more clearly the ways in which action is implicit in structure, how structures are perceived, socially constructed and responded to in variegated ways. The ideologies, beliefs, assumptions, values, principles, tastes and the taken-for-granted recurrent behaviours stemming from them which comprise culture are not easily disposable. In fact they are remarkably durable, and this durability stems from their social rather than individual character. They do change of course, as I have shown in earlier chapters, and I have argued that to represent academic staff, or anyone else, in terms of a socially determined 'homo sociologicus' would be to ignore the importance of agency and cultural construction. But agency is not as easily 'shaped' as Beckhard and Pritchard would have us believe. Moreover, the ethical underpinning of a project to do so is questionable. As Fitzgerald (1988: 13) puts it: 'If I view as essentially insulting an uninvited attempt to make me over into someone else's version of a better human being, should it be any less offensive to the hired hands?'

In addition to these issues there are more practical problems surrounding the advice to 'change the essence', such as the difficulty of shining visionary light from the top in large, complex organizations like universities, the multiple criteria for rewards which university managers must take into account, and indeed the very role and importance of 'top managers' in university contexts even in the unchartered universities. Top-down approaches suffer from the bind that in order to be effective they require the kinds of conditions they are trying to bring about to already be in existence. Instead, actors at the ground level are as likely to adapt policy as adopt it, to shape and reshape it as they 'implement' it, or in some cases attempt to block the implementation process altogether. Even where change can be imposed, under-the-stage aspects of cultural articulation will prevent the type of fundamental acquiescence to change envisaged in the 'cultural manipulation' approach.

Moreover, that approach omits other factors which condition responses to change. Perhaps most important among these is the perceived profitability of an innovation for those charged with implementing it. Where an innovation is potentially profitable it may be adopted relatively unproblematically even where there are incompatibilities with existing cultural characteristics on the ground, but where this is not the case there is likely to be resistance and/or policy reconstruction. In the case of the adoption of the credit framework the level of valence is also affected by disciplinary epistemological characteristics, whether 'real' or socially constructed. Other policy areas will 'activate' their own relevant issues in a similar way.

It is clear, then, that a university-wide innovation such as the decision to adopt some or all of the components of the credit framework will elicit a wide variety of responses among the organization's staff. These will be largely but not wholly conditioned by the configuration of the cultural traffic flowing into and through the organization. The staff's response will be articulated on multiple levels: front-stage; back-stage and under-the-stage. The attempt to implement the policy will meet with compliance (both enthusiastic and reluctant), with resistance, with coping strategies, and with attempts to reconstruct the policy during the implementation phase. Which type of response is adopted by staff, both individually and collectively, will be conditioned by the valence between their current situation and the innovation, and by pre-existent cultural characteristics. The effects of these responses will be difficult to predict and will involve outcomes not intended by any actor. These may have more impact than the intended outcomes in both the short and (particularly) the long term. There are likely, for example, to be important effects on the student experience, on equality of opportunity for both staff and students and, in the longer term, on the success of the institution in terms of attracting students and achieving its goals in terms of teaching, research and other work. The cultural configuration of the institution will undoubtedly change also, but not necessarily in ways that were originally intended or that are desirable.

An alternative approach

So far the general message of this book has been a negative one (seen through a manager's eyes): the story has concentrated on the ability of academic staff to obstruct and change policy during its implementation phase. However, there is another, more positive side to that same coin: precisely that academic staff, and others, are not passive role players who simply enact cultural norms and values. Rather, they can be actively involved in their creation on a day-to-day basis. This is unlikely to happen, however, if staff are simply asked to sign up to a 'vision' imposed from the top. The alternative, as Senge (1990), Fullan (1993) and others point out, is to encourage the development of a shared vision, one that attracts broad commitment because it reflects the personal vision of those involved.

Establishing this kind of ownership of change is difficult. Ownership is mercurial in character and understanding is almost always fuzzy initially. Both are developed and sustained by hands-on experience and by giving room for experimentation and adaptation. Moreover, ownership cannot be achieved *in advance* of learning something new: successful implementation is more likely to be achieved by the sequence 'ready, fire, aim' than 'ready, aim, fire' (Fullan, 1993: 31).

Stressing the importance of establishing a consensual vision for the future does not absolve senior management of the responsibility for goal setting. Over-centralization leads to over-control and resistance but on the other hand solutions which are too decentralized lead to anarchy and chaos. Many authors stress the importance of 'trialability' in introducing policy and of initial small-scale experimentation, one of the strengths of the incrementalist approach. Yet without support from above this risks the danger of 'enclaving' and the project becoming stalled. Senior management needs to provide leadership, but where goals are provided they need to be limited, achievable and provide room for negotiation and accommodation locally. Successful change is more likely to come about when there is consensus above and pressure below, a 'change sandwich', rather than simply flow from above.

The top-down/bottom-up relationship needs to be one of dialogue, negotiation and learning from experience. Dialogue is usually best conducted on the basis of mutual comprehension and for managers it is particularly important to understand the nature of the contemporary cultural configuration of their institution. Indeed, this is the first piece of advice which Fullan gives to headteachers committed to building their school into a learning organization (Fullan and Hargreaves, 1992). Conversely, the attention of those at the ground level may need to be directed outwards, to the environment in which the organization is operating and the constraints and forces which are found there. The development of empathy with the need to operate more economically in a resource-constrained environment and to develop a flexible curriculum in a changing economic, social and higher education environment may facilitate negotiation about the implementation of modularity. As NewU's vice-chancellor said: 'Universities must recognise that preferences of students do change, sometimes quite dramatically, over a short period of time. It is important to ensure and maintain flexibility in the range of courses offered and to face up to the implications of some courses no longer being popular' (NewU, 1997: 8).

However, empathy and understanding does not mean acquiescence and acceptance on anyone's part. Too much of the literature on change seems to accept as axiomatic that change is of itself a Good Thing. Clearly, change that is misconceived, inappropriate, that benefits only a particular group or does not lead to improvement is not desirable and too much change introduced too quickly can lead to innovation fatigue which is invariably detrimental to the change process.

The learning university

Robertson argues that as a result of their research for the HEQC into the credit framework in the UK he and his team had come to the conclusion that strategic change is cultural change and cultural change is linked to the mission set at the top: '. . . institutional leaders are encouraged to "lead by example" in order *to commit others to their vision . . .*' (Robertson, 1994: 314, emphasis mine).

However, the fundamental problem with this kind of corporate culturism is that it attempts to suppress competing standpoints and individuals' reflective practice in assessing alternative positions and options. Essentially it is trying to impose a monoculture for management purposes, but in so doing runs the risk of suppressing the possibility of the university becoming, or remaining, a learning organization. Such a project in a university context is particularly disturbing given that learning is a university's *raison d'être*. The danger in such a project is the creation of instrumentality among staff and of an active back-stage and (particularly) under-the-stage culture of cynicism and resistance rather than encouraging commitment, reflection and involvement among individuals who are active in constructing as well as enacting both culture and policy.

If a learning organization is one which encourages its members to reflect on experience in order to improve performance in the future and to draw in new knowledge to inform that process, then there is evidence that NewU has moved towards this in recent years. NewU's University Plan for 1996–2000, formally adopted in July 1996, identified four main objectives providing direction for the period ahead. These were:

Objective 1 – To develop a distinct identity at University level and to promote and market this identity through partnerships with education, industry, commerce, the public services and the community.

Objective 2 – To ensure that each department and research centre develops a distinctive academic profile based on excellence in teaching and research.

Objective 3 – To establish a clear focus on identifying and meeting the needs of students and others who seek to benefit from the activities of the University and in doing so to remove any unnecessary bureaucracy.

Objective 4 – To develop an environmentally and culturally rich campus for students, staff and community.

(NewU, 1996a: 19–23)

Objectives 2 and 3 are particularly interesting for the purposes of this chapter. Objective 2 signals a change of approach away from the 'big bang' towards a decentralized and incrementalist approach, with each department and research centre responsible for setting its own objectives under broad parameters. To support this a series of meetings were held between members of each faculty and members of the senior management to explain and discuss the objectives and to initiate and facilitate the process of formulating the local interpretation of them. The 'big bang' analogy appears to be an apt one: explosions are by their nature unpredictable, destructive and fling large amounts of debris around a wide area. However, there the analogy breaks down: real explosions can flatten, creating clear space for new building. Policy 'big bangs' do not. Pre-existent values and attitudes, remarkably resistant to change, remain and act upon the new structures being erected. Incrementalist approaches, by contrast, can be used in ways which work with the cultural configuration found in a particular context, adapting policy in a nuanced way according to local cultural and other characteristics and facilitating cultural change at the same time. Done well the implementation process becomes an evolutionary, not a revolutionary, one, and the evolution applies as much to the policy as to the cultural configuration at the site. In moving from the 'big bang' to the decentralized incrementalist approach, NewU appears to have learned that 'change is a journey, not a blueprint' (Fullan, 1993: 21).

Objective 3 demonstrates that lessons have been learned at NewU from the experience of the unintended consequences of policy changes, particularly as these relate to the student experience. I showed in Chapter 2 how at NewU and elsewhere the administrative centralization associated with the credit framework had led to administrative fallout, to a decline in effectiveness in some areas of the administrative structure and to a paper-bound organization. The decision to take action on this and to focus on student need demonstrates the enactment of organizational learning.

Adopting the credit framework

The question still remains, however, as to whether the university was correct to adopt the credit framework in the first place. Clearly there has been considerable dissatisfaction with it among sections of the academic staff and there have been some unintended consequences of its introduction which have been deleterious to the student experience and in other ways. However it is worth reiterating here that it is impossible to untangle the threads of causality when considering the impact of the credit framework. A declining resource base, increasing student numbers, environmental changes and other phenomena are all important, though academic staff themselves tend to pin the blame on the nearest candidate, in this case the credit framework as a whole or one or more of its components.

The framework brings its own imperatives. I have already discussed the pluralistic character of the factors which condition the level of valence between the various components of the highly differentiated academic staff body in a university and the framework. Added to these are the highly diverse needs of disciplines and domains which limit the general applicability of a single credit structure across the university as a whole. In Chapter 2 I showed how academic staff in disciplines and domains such as art and design and nursing studies saw their area of study as having unique constraints and characteristics which made them extremely uncomfortable in the credit framework's Procrustean bed. Both in practical terms and in terms of the principles for successful adoption outlined above, the conclusion must be that an homogeneous university-wide scheme should not be a preferred option; a better one is a framework within which disciplines and domains can adapt to their own needs. Successful, smoothly-operating examples of the credit framework operating in a 'mass' context do exist, both in the UK and elsewhere, and this indicates that the administrative fallout which was so much a feature of it at NewU is not inevitable. NewU signally failed to learn from these models of good practice at that time and as a consequence has learned the hard way, a point recognized by the HEQC: 'The University might find it helpful to identify institutions . . . with which it might compare itself, with a view to assisting it to identify appropriate levels of service, and readily available solutions to common matters of concern. [Doing so would also] contribute to the diminution of the [university's] "closed culture"' (HEQC, 1994: 22).

Besides administrative fallout there have been other important unintended consequences of the introduction of the credit framework which were avoidable. These included a reduction in staff-student contact, both quantitatively and qualitatively as the flexibility provided by modularity was used to cope with pressures on staff time caused by increased student numbers and a declining resource base. This aspect of the framework provided a quick and easy solution, but one which is detrimental to the student experience unless managed in a controlled way, for example by other forms of provision replacing the quantity and quality of contact. The framework also resulted in a complex system which was difficult for the student to 'navigate'. Combined with the simultaneous withdrawal of some academic staff from student contact as increasing pressures were placed on them, this put many students in a bind which only those in possession of cultural capital were able to resolve satisfactorily. This set of issues is not unique to NewU: similar concerns have been expressed in other universities, both chartered and unchartered, for example at East Anglia and Oxford Brookes (Marfleet and Kushner, 1995a; Webster, 1996).

The rapid, uncontrolled escalation of the assessment load both for staff and students has been a further common unintended consequence of the introduction of the credit framework as module developers each pile on the work with little regard to the other demands made on the students or for the implications in terms of marking in a context of larger group sizes

(Hounsell, 1996). Again, careful management and coordination between departments can avoid this relatively easily. Emphasis on improving communication and learning from experience can avoid, too, the replication and redundancy which result in the efficiency gains claimed for modularity not being achieved in practice as departments develop their own modules without regard to what is available elsewhere.

Conclusion

To date, thinking about the management of change in universities has tended to adopt a 'policy science' approach (Grace, 1995), one which takes a 'scientific' standpoint in order to formulate a rational, top-down, prescription for action but which, in the process, loses a grasp on the deeply structured historical, cultural, political, ideological and value issues ingrained in social processes. *Policy scholarship* approaches, by contrast, situate an understanding of education policy in the context of the cultural and ideological struggles in which they are located and demonstrate the constraining or liberating effects of wider socio-economic and political relations. Only by properly contextualized policy scholarship can good understanding and policy resolutions be achieved. Research in and management approaches towards higher education are in danger of stumbling into the very same policy-science traps which many of those involved in the study of compulsory education have already climbed out of. The policy scholarship approach may not appeal to university managers in search of the levers of organizational change – its depiction of social reality is an extremely complex one which denies the possibility of controlled, predictable change. It does, however, hold the promise of an improved understanding of social reality in universities as organizations and hence to organizational development in a difficult environment.

Appendix: Research Issues

The Study

Sources of data

This is a single-site ethnographic case study of an institution of higher education. The sources of data used in the study were fourfold and included both primary and secondary data. These were: interviews; observant participation; documents generated within and without the institution; and other studies of it.

Interviews

A total of 50 interviews were conducted, covering 30 disciplines and domains in all, mainly with two academics from each being interviewed (some individuals were serially or concurrently located in two disciplines or domains and so were able to provide data for both). The interviews took a semi-structured form and generally lasted between an hour and an hour and a half. All but one were tape recorded. The first five and the last 14 were fully transcribed with the others being partially (about 50 per cent) transcribed and annotated.

The selection of interviewees was guided by three main considerations: personal characteristics, their 'location' in terms of the credit framework, and disciplinary characteristics. I interviewed roughly equal numbers of women and men and included the full range of age groups and degrees of experience both in HE in general and at NewU in particular. Some key respondents were selected on the basis of their commitment to the credit framework, sometimes having been involved in setting it up (e.g. respondents 3, 33 and 45). No one above head of department level was selected as this was designed to be a study of ground level actors. Four heads of department were interviewed and one other interviewee was appointed to that post shortly after the interview. I included individuals with a variety of backgrounds: those with PhDs and those without; those with long experience of study in elite higher education contexts and those with other experiences of education and training; those with professional or industrial backgrounds, and those who have largely stayed within the education sector. Only academics from Subjects which contributed to the Combined Honours degree were selected for interview. I did not include staff on short-term, part-time contracts on the grounds that they would have limited contact with the framework, though some of those I interviewed had permanent contracts below 100 per cent or were full-time but on short-term contracts. Areas of study taught 'above' or 'below' degree level were not included in the study. I did not extend the study into the partner colleges, first on the grounds of practicality and secondly, because other studies of this type had recently been or were in the process of being conducted in NewU's partners.

The choice-criteria concerning the disciplinary characteristics of the sample selected were fivefold. First I wanted a range of 'areas of study' and Clark's (1987) categories (based on the Carnegie classification) were used to ensure a good range. I also included disciplines and domains which have a variety of levels of strength in terms of Bernstein's (1971) categories of 'classification' (the degree of 'boundedness' of study areas) and 'frame' (the extent to which there is an explicit and agreed content to be transmitted to students in a particular study area and how far this is under the control of academics). I reasoned that these two characteristics may have important implications for academics' attitudes to the credit framework. Likewise the degree of demand for the discipline or domain by students would seem influential in this respect so I ensured that the disciplinary sample included those able to pick and choose their students, those who could not afford to be so selective and many points between. Finally I included areas of study which had been previously under-represented in higher education research (which had predominantly concentrated on high status disciplines). In particular I wanted to include domains of study, especially the more recent entrants to the higher education system such as women's studies and development studies. This was done in order to 'yield new insights into a relatively neglected but none the less substantial sector of academic activity' as Becher (1989: 179) puts it.

Observant participation

This aspect of the research involved observing and making notes about events and comments people made more or less as they happened. I sought out locations which would give me greater insight into work across the university. During the 'survey stage' of research (Fetterman, 1989) my observation was conducted in a fairly unstructured way. However, after completing the literature review and a depth analysis of the first five interviews, observation became increasingly focused. The clear specification of the research questions plus the progressive development of concepts and theoretical approaches led to a far greater sensitivity to what was more, or less, significant for the research. At the same time, however, I was aware of and allowed for the danger of premature cognitive closure. The practice I developed was to jot down observations in a notebook, including verbatim quotes if possible, at the time of observation or immediately afterwards. In the evening I transferred this into my computer file, adding any other comments or observations as necessary as well as the appropriate HyperResearch code (see below). Eventually I accumulated a very large (over 200kb) file of records of observations, thematically organized.

Documentary evidence

Documents produced internally, official and unofficial, were routinely collected to inform the study. Eventually a very large archive of material was accumulated, including anything that appeared even potentially relevant. These documents ranged from formal statements of academic policy to internal memos, from the unofficial staff newspaper (*The New Guardian*) to the official ones (*New Diary* and *Newlook*), from drafts of reports, subsequently amended, to formal and public reports (for example of validation meetings). The documents were both quantitative (for example, the student profile) and qualitative in nature (for example, the vice-chancellor's review of the year). The observant participation and documentary analysis aspects of the study were intertwined – as one of the respondents noted, the institution is 'paper bound' and inevitably attendance at any formal event involved a number of documents, usually a very large number.

Using both official and unofficial documents made me very aware of the various 'stages' of public performance (Goffman, 1959; Bailey, 1977; Becher, 1988), as did observant participation. Comparing, for example, the public utterances of the vice-chancellor on the sexual harassment policy of the university, comments about it in the editorial and letters columns of *The New Guardian* and the discussion of staff over coffee, highlighted the distinctions between and the importance of front-of-stage, back-stage and under-the-stage discourse and made me think more clearly and critically both about received notions of organizational culture and the interpretation of data in the analytical phase.

Previous studies of the institution

The final element of data collection was the use of other studies of the university. Here I include both 'academic' and non-academic studies. The latter included HEQC and HEFCE reports. With these in particular, however, the analysis was conducted with care because of the issue about the 'stages' of action. For example, in a memo of 15 January 1996 circulating the HEQC Quality Audit Report on Collaborative Provision, the pro-vice-chancellor states that: 'I am very pleased to note that the HEQC have taken into account most of the comments which were made to them regarding the draft report . . .' (NewU pro-vice-chancellor, 1996: 1).

The director of the HEQC's Quality Assurance Group, Peter Williams, in a letter to the vice-chancellor about the report acknowledges the essential negotiability of its contents and its public function:

> I am grateful for your comments on the draft audit report of your University, and have taken them carefully into account in the preparation of the final version . . . In accordance with HEQC policy, we shall be publishing the report four weeks after the date of this letter. The four week 'embargo' period is to allow you time to consider whether you wish to prepare a press release or commentary on the report before it is released for general publication . . .
>
> (P. Williams, 1996: 1)

Where I had access to both draft and final versions, I tended to give analytical priority to the former because of the more 'negotiated' character of the latter, particularly where the HEQC was concerned. This was less of a problem, though by no means absent, in the academic studies of the institution and its work which I used. I cannot cite them here to retain the anonymity of the institution but they included two historical studies of the institution, three commissioned reports on equal opportunities issues, one other study of equal opportunities issues, three studies of collaborative provision, one internal study focusing on issues around values and ethics, and one PhD thesis concerning mature students' experiences.

Even these academic reports needed to be treated with some caution. Of one of the commissioned studies of equal opportunities in the institution, for example, respondent 27 warned me that: 'There was a secret version which [was] . . . produced for [the director's] . . . eyes alone' (27). Neither that respondent nor I ever gained sight of this secret version: ethical considerations prevented me from making an attempt to do so (I eschewed attempting to obtain any confidential documents throughout the research on these grounds). However, I did make some fruitless tentative enquiries among those who might have knowledge of it with the intention of gaining a view about the status of the data and conclusions in the publicly available report. Similarly a careful reading of another (uncommissioned) report suggested that its results also needed to be treated cautiously: comments made within it suggested that the researchers had been 'captured' by senior management's perspective as a result of the researchers' dependence upon them for access. This suspicion was strengthened by the fact that one of my respondents (10) had read the report and been an insider during a particular series of events described in detail in it. His interpretation was that the report both reproduces the management perspective of events and is inaccurate in its account of some of the facts. The final grounds for doubt were that the report's account of the role and reception of the work of an equal opportunities officer within the university is also at odds with the under-the-stage currents on this issue which I accessed.

Rather than not use these studies, however, I decided to extend the application of Stenhouse's (1979) notion of the 'second record' (the use of a detailed understanding of meaning systems to 'read' interview data) to this kind of secondary data about the institution. Thus I not only used the data and results of other studies to check my own understandings and interpretations, but also the reverse.

Methods of data analysis

Analysis of the interview transcripts was done partly using the qualitative data analysis package HyperResearch and partly through more traditional means. A total of 157 codes were developed, around 40 of which related to the characteristics of the respondents (their gender, discipline and age) while the rest were thematic. Passages were coded and the software permitted the retrieval of passages on the same subject and some limited cross tabulation. The computer package proved invaluable as a database for retrieving comments, and reading the reports it produced often led to new analytical ideas. My early fears that the holistic nature of the data would be destroyed, the individual lost, as a result of this kind of vertical slicing proved groundless – I made frequent reference back to the original interview transcript, and sometimes the audio-tape itself.

The analysis of the fieldnotes and secondary data, however, was much less structured. I read through the notes from time to time, reminding myself of what they contained and consulted them during the analysis and write-up phases. Later I checked them again to ensure that nothing of value had been missed and that there was nothing that contradicted my interpretation. This analysis procedure can be summed up as familiarization, selection and later checking for missed or contradictory data.

The sheer amount of data collected presented a considerable problem for the data analysis phase. Although theoretically it was possible to engage in a highly systematic procedure as had been done with the interview data, in reality this presented too many practical problems, particularly in the amount of time involved.

Areas for further research

As even a brief analysis of the Society for Research into Higher Education's (SRHE) *Research into Higher Education Abstracts* will show, research into higher education has tended to follow a rather limited number of well-worn tracks: national systems and comparative studies; institutional management and governance; teaching and learning; finance and resources; curriculum issues and so on. Only recently has there been much concerted research effort around the unexplored undergrowth: professional and other cultures within universities; student cultures and the student experience; ethnographic studies of institutional 'underlife' (Riseborough, 1992) or policy sociology studies like those which are currently so active in the school sector. A considerable amount of work in, and development of, these newer areas still remains to be done – for example there is a great need for the sort of policy trajectory studies (Maguire and Ball, 1994) being conducted in the school sector (for example, Lingard, 1997). The SRHE has also indicated the pressing need for more research in a number of areas to improve our knowledge and understanding of the field (SRHE, 1996: 13). These are largely positivist in character. This research project has highlighted the need too for phenomenologically-oriented research in a number of areas around the fields of study discussed in this book. Here I will outline just five:

1. **The phenomenology of specific aspects of the credit framework from the student's perspective.** There is an abundance of assertions about the value, impact and desirability of each component of the credit framework as far as students are concerned but remarkably little hard evidence to support or refute any of them. Such research would address questions such as: the extent to which students actually desire a flexible curriculum and the student characteristics which condition the level of its attraction to them; the nature and effects of the student experience in navigating large, complex, credit systems; the phenomenology of the experience of accrediting prior experiential learning (see Trowler, 1996a: 24–5 for an intimation of the complexity that such a project would probably reveal); the student experience of modular programme provision, and so on.
2. **The gender issues surrounding the changing nature of the higher education system in the UK.** While this research project has maintained a focus on gender as a factor in addressing the research questions outlined in Chapter 1 it was not underpinned with the resources necessary to fully explore this issue. There is a need for research projects which focus on the differential impact on male and female academics of recent changes in the higher education system and on the ways in which they each respond to them, on the gendered nature of the status and reward structures of higher education, on the gender regimes there, and on the nature and impact of sex-role spillover in higher education.

3. **The collective strategies which academics adopt in resisting, reconstructing or coping with policy change.** Most studies of academic professional life have so far been based on research strategies rooted in methodological individualism, predominantly questionnaires and interviews with individual academics. This approach conditions the nature of the results obtained, which tend to emphasize the individualistic nature of adaptive responses to policy. Adaptive responses are, however, often collective because they are rooted in the cultural context just as cultural change is collective in nature. More imaginative ethnographic approaches to data collection in higher education are needed if this emphasis is to be corrected and, for example, the importance of departmental cultures and responses are to be highlighted.

4. **Work on the significance of cultural milieux for policy 'implementation'.** To date, and with some significant exceptions (for example, McInnis, 1996), there has been a gap between work on and thinking about the cultural contexts of higher education and the significance of these for policy 'implementation' (or, better, policy interpretation, negotiation and policy-making at the ground level). Linked to a greater emphasis on fine-grained studies of higher education institutions called for by Sheldon Rothblatt and many others, this could usefully illuminate our knowledge about and understanding of policy outcomes (as against intentions).

5. **Case studies on the changing shape and nature of 'knowledge' in the NHE.** While Ronald Barnett (1990, 1994) among others has been helping us to conceptualize the important epistemological issues in universities today and has mapped in general terms the trends in the relative status and character of different knowledge forms, this has yet to be explored to any extent through descriptively rich case studies at the ground level. If there is a shift towards 'performativity', as Barnett suggests, then this is not going uncontested. The nature and outcomes of this contest need to be understood. Every day in every university in course development committees, assessment boards and elsewhere there are disputes around the priority given to different knowledge forms: propositional knowledge; competence-based approaches; practical knowledge and so on. This highly-contested terrain needs to be mapped through theorized accounts of these events so that we achieve an insight into this important aspect of the 'private lives' of universities.

Glossary

age participation index (API) the number of home initial entrants to full-time higher education expressed as a proportion of the averaged 18–19-year-old population.

APL/APEL accreditation of prior learning and accreditation of prior experiential learning. The former normally refers to learning acquired in formal educational contexts with a qualification awarded for successful completion. The latter refers to experiential learning in work of other contexts.

AUT Association of University Teachers. Professional association of university academics, mainly in the chartered universities.

chartered/unchartered universities chartered universities is used here to mean those institutions designated as universities prior to the 1992 Further and Higher Education Act. Unchartered universities are the institutions designated polytechnics or colleges prior to that date but which subsequently became universities or, in one case, a polytechnic university. These terms are used to avoid the lack of clarity involved in the use of the term 'new universities' or similar phrases which are also applied to the universities built or so designated in the post-Robbins expansion of the 1960s and 1970s.

Council for National Academic Awards (CNAA) the body overseeing the validation and review of programmes in the former polytechnics. Abolished with the disappearance of the binary divide following the 1992 Further and Higher Education Act.

credit accumulation and transfer scheme (CATS) a curriculum structure based on the assignment of credit to assessed learning which allows the progressive accumulation of academic credit and its transfer between programmes and/or institutions.

credit exchange model of APEL based on the National Council for Vocational Qualifications' (NCVQ) job-role notion of competence, this involves the assessment of personal competencies and their matching with the planned learning outcomes of an accredited programme offered by an educational institution. Competencies which can be shown to be already achieved, either through demonstration or via a portfolio of evidence, are exchanged for course credits and may give exemption from part of the programme. This is the model used in programmes leading to National Vocational Qualifications (NVQs). A pre-requisite of this model is the very careful delineation of the outcomes of the programme (usually mapped onto some specified job role) so that the matching, and hence exchange, process can take place. Because it concentrates on assessing skills and abilities through carefully evidenced accomplishments it is sometimes referred to as accreditation of prior achievements (APA) or prior learning achievements (APLA). The term derives from the work of Christine Butterworth (1992).

CVCP   Committee of Vice-Chancellors and Principals.

defined field   used at NewU to refer to a course of study leading to a degree which limits the student's choices of disciplines or domains of study, as distinct from combined honours in which they select from a large number in a relatively unconstrained way. The terminology changed in 1994 so that defined fields became referred to as 'courses', however I have retained the original use throughout this book because of the ambiguity of the word 'course'.

developmental model of APEL   like the credit exchange model of APEL (see above) this involves a process designed to assess an applicant's claim to have already achieved learning appropriate for access to or advanced standing in a programme of study. However there is a crucial additional element in this kind of APEL procedure: the requirement that the claimant reflects on and evaluates their previous experience, identifying in a codified way the learning that derived from it. According to Christine Butterworth (1992) this additional reflective element has the benefit of actually adding to the learning the individual derives from experience, hence the term 'developmental'.

DfEE   Department for Education and Employment, formerly the DfE and before that the DES.

domains of knowledge   used here to refer to areas of study such as women's studies or education studies which are oriented around a particular subject matter and draw from a number of disciplines in the attempt to better understand it. The term derives from the work of Trist (1972) who used it to mean the study of a problem area, such as drug-taking. However, as Kogan and Henkel (1983) point out, this usually mutates into the study of a domain in the sense I am using it. Hirst (1974) uses the term 'field' in the same sense as my 'domain' and distinguishes this from 'disciplines' which are shaped by the forms of knowledge in Hirst's view. A related term is 'subject' (with a small 's') which is used here in Evans' (1995) sense: the institutional enactment of disciplines in the shape of departments.

ethics and values audit (EVA)   a project internal to NewU conducting an audit of the values and practices related to ethical issues there. Published as Henry *et al.* (1992).

FTE   full-time equivalent (students). This figure agglomerates part-time student numbers according to a formula to give a notional figure of full-time students. This is done to assist in the calculation of, for example, SSRs (see below).

HEFCE   Higher Education Funding Council for England.

HEI   Higher Education Institution.

HEQC   Higher Education Quality Council.

MASN   maximum aggregated student numbers. The HEFCE sets this as a target for part-time and full-time student enrolments to be reached by individual institutions each year. Financial penalties are attached for recruitment which is above or below this figure by more than 1 per cent.

Mathew principle   the policy that more resources should be given to those who are already successful. Used in the higher education context in relation to the funding of research and the policy that centres of excellence should be encouraged through the funding regime.

modularity   involves the division of a syllabus into discrete, separately assessed, segments. The modular curricular format is said to promote choice and flexibility,
allowing students to select their own programmes of study, including times and
places, from the options available.

NCVQ   National Council for Vocational Qualifications. A body set up to coordinate
the introduction and oversight of a system of competence-based vocational and
professional qualifications.

NVQs   national vocational qualifications. A system of vocational qualifications based
on a competence model.

new higher education (NHE)   this is a shorthand term borrowed from Richard
Winter (1991) and others, used here to refer to that part of the higher education system which has the characteristics of a curriculum structure based on the
credit framework, epistemological assumptions which value forms of learning
acquired outside the academy, including non-propositional and even demotic
knowledge, responsiveness to what is viewed as a market-place in the context of
a constrained resource environment and large and recently-expanded student
numbers.

Newmanite   derived from the ideas of John Newman, this is used here as shorthand
for the view that university education should be 'liberal' with knowledge an end
in itself, separated from the needs of industrial society and with a goal of intellectual excellence. In personal terms such an education is thought to lead to
intellectual enlargement, an expansion of the mind (Barnett, 1990: 19–21).

older mature participation index (OMPI)   the proportion of those aged 25 or more
entering higher education for the first time as a percentage of the general
population of that age.

profitability   Levine (1980) suggests that the 'profitability' of an innovation is an
important precondition for its successful implementation. By profitability he
means whether or not it can bring such things as security, prestige, peer approval,
growth, efficiency and improvement in the quality of life.

RAE   research assessment exercise: a four-yearly assessment of the research output
of research-active staff in university departments. The outcome of the exercise
is used by the higher education funding councils to determine the allocation of
research funding to individual universities.

Robbins trap   the dilemma resulting from the contradictory commitment to expansion of access to higher education and a traditional conception of its nature.
The concept derives from Trow (1989).

SSR   student to staff ratio.

Subject (capital 'S')   used at NewU to refer to a discipline or domain of study offered
as part of the combined honours programme. A Subject must always be studied
in combination with one or two others and cannot in itself lead to the award
of a degree. The word 'subject' (with a small 's') is used here in Evans' (1995)
sense: the institutional enactment of disciplines in the shape of departments.

unitized curriculum   is similar to modularity (see above) but the use of this term
implies smaller segments of study than modules normally are, with more choice
and flexibility integrated into the scheme.

younger mature entry index (YMEI)   the proportion of 21–24-year-olds entering
higher education for the first time as a percentage of the general population
of that age.

Bibliography

Abramson, M.G., Bird, J. and Stennett, A. (eds) (1996) *Further and Higher Education Partnerships: The future for collaboration*. Buckingham: Open University Press/SRHE.

Acker, S. (1981) No-woman's-land: the British sociology of education 1960–1979. *Sociological Review*, 29 (1): 77–104.

Acker, S. (1992a) New perspectives on an old problem: the position of women academics in British higher education. *Higher Education*, 24: 57–75.

Acker, S. (1992b) Gendering Organizational Theory, in A.J. Mills and P. Tancred (eds) *Gendering Organizational Analysis*. London: Sage.

Acker, S. (1994) *Gendered Education*. Buckingham: Open University Press.

Acker, S. and Piper, D. (1984) *Is Higher Education Fair to Women?*. London: SRHE/NFER Nelson.

Adler, M.E., Petch, A. and Tweedie, S. (1989) *Parental Choice and Educational Policy*. Edinburgh: University of Edinburgh Press.

Ainley, P. (1994) *Degrees of Difference*. London: Lawrence and Wishart.

Albert and Whetten (1985) Organisational identity. *Research in Organisational Behaviour*, 7: 263–95.

Alcoff, L. (1988) Cultural feminism vs post-structuralism, in E. Minnich, J. O'Barr and R. Rosenfeld (eds) *Reconstructing the Academy*. Chicago: University of Chicago Press.

Alexander, E. (1985) From idea to action: Notes for a Contingency Theory of the Policy Implementation Process. *Administration and Society*, 16 (4): 403–26.

Allen, R. and Layer, G. (1995) *Credit-based Systems as Vehicles for Change in Universities and Colleges*. London: Kogan Page.

Allison, G.T. (1971) *Essence of Decision: Explaining the Cuban Missile Crisis*. Boston: Little, Brown.

Alvesson, M. (1990a) Organization: from substance to image?. *Organization Studies*, 11 (3): 373–94.

Alvesson, M. (1990b) On the popularity of organizational culture. *Acta Sociologica*, 33 (1): 31–49.

Alvesson, M. (1993) *Cultural Perspectives on Organisations*. Cambridge: Cambridge University Press.

Apple, M. (1989) *Teachers and Texts*. London: Routledge.

Apple, M. (1990) *Ideology and Curriculum*. London: Routledge (second edition).

Argyris, C. (1962) *Interpersonal Competence and Organizational Effectiveness*. Homewood, Ill: Irwin.

Argyris, C. and Schön, D.A. (1974) *Theory in Practice: Increasing Professional Effectiveness*. San Francisco: Jossey Bass.

Arnot, M. and Barton, L. (1992) *Voicing Concerns: Sociological Perspectives on Contemporary Education Reforms*. Wallingford, Oxfordshire: Triangle.

Aune, B.P. (1995) The Human Dimension of Organisational Change. *The Review of Higher Education*, 18 (2): 149–73.

Austrin, T. (1994) Positioning Resistance and Resisting Position: human resource management and the politics of appraisal and grievance hearings, in J. Jermier, D. Knight and W.R. Nord (eds) *Resistance and Power in Organizations*. London: Routledge.

Avram, A. (1992) The humanist conception of the university. *European Journal of Education*, 27 (4): 397–415.

Bagilhole, B. (1993) How to keep a good woman down: an investigation of the role of institutional factors in the process of discrimination against women academics. *British Journal of Sociology of Education*, 14 (3): 261–74.

Bagilhole, B. (1994) Being different is a very difficult row to hoe: survival strategies of women academics, in S. Davies, C. Lubelska and J. Quinn *Changing the Subject*. London: Taylor and Francis.

Bailey, F.G. (1977) *Morality and Expediency*. London: Blackwell.

Bain, A. (1993) Private sector funding in higher education. Report to the HCFCE, *SHEFC, FCW, and DENI, HEFCE*, mimeo.

Ball, C. (1990) *More Means Different*. London: Royal Society of Arts.

Ball, C. (1992) Opening address. Presented to conference on the new renaissance partnerships in enterprise education: an international perspective, Sheffield, 13 July.

Ball, S.J. (1990a) *Politics and Policy Making in Education*. London: Routledge.

Ball, S.J. (1990b) *Markets, Morality and Quality in Education*. Brighton: Hillcole Press.

Ball, S.J. (1990c) Management as moral technology: a luddite analysis, in S.J. Ball (ed.) *Foucault and Education: Disciplines and Knowledge*, pp. 153–66. London: Routledge.

Ball, S.J. (1994) *Education Reform: A Critical and Post-structural Approach*. Buckingham: Open University Press.

Bannerji, H., Carty, L., Dehli, K., Heald, S. and McKenna, K. (1991) *Unsettling Relations*. London: Women's Press.

Bantock, G.H. (1968) *Culture, Industrialisation and Education*. London: RKP.

Barber, N. (1984) 'The organisation as curriculum', unpublished PhD thesis. Wright College, Berkeley.

Bardach, E. (1977) *The Implementation Game*. Cambridge, MA: MIT Press.

Barnett, R. (1985) Higher education: legitimation crisis. *Studies in Higher Education*, 10 (3): 241–55.

Barnett, R. (1990) *The Idea of Higher Education*. Buckingham: Open University Press/ SRHE.

Barnett, R. (1994) *The Limits of Competence*. Buckingham: Open University Press/ SRHE.

Barnett, R. (1996) Discourse and the university. Conference paper presented at the 'Dilemmas of Mass Higher Education' conference, Staffordshire University, 10–12 April.

Barrett, M. (1980) *Women's Oppression Today: Problems in Marxist Feminist Analysis*. London: Verso.

Barrett, S. and Fudge, C. (eds) (1981) *Policy and Action*. London: Methuen.

Baudrillard, J. (1985) The ecstasy of communication, in H. Foster (ed.) *Postmodern Culture*. London: Pluto.

Bauman, Z. (1988) Is there a postmodern sociology? *Theory, Culture and Society,* 5: 217–37.

Baxter, A. and Bird, J. (1992) *Franchising and Associate College Arrangements in the PCFC Sector.* Bristol: Bristol Polytechnic (draft).

Becher, T. (1981) Towards a definition of disciplinary culture. *Studies in Higher Education,* 6 (2): 109–22.

Becher, T. (1984) The cultural view, in B. Clark (ed.) *Perspectives on the Higher Education System.* San Francisco: University of California Press.

Becher, T. (1988) Principles and politics: an interpretative framework for university management, in A. Westoby (ed.) *Culture and Power in Educational Organizations,* pp. 317–28. Buckingham: Open University Press/SRHE.

Becher, T. (1989) *Academic Tribes and Territories.* Buckingham: Open University Press/ SRHE.

Becher, T. (1990) The counter-culture of specialisation. *European Journal of Education,* 25 (3): 333–46.

Becher, T. (1994a) The significance of disciplinary differences. *Studies in Higher Education,* 19 (2): 151–61.

Becher, T. (1994b) The state and the university curriculum in Britain. *European Journal of Education,* 29 (3): 231–45.

Becher, T. (1995) The internalities of higher education. *European Journal of Education,* 30 (4): 395–406.

Becher, T. and Kogan, M. (1980) *Process and Structure in Higher Education.* London: Routledge.

Becher, T. and Kogan, M. (1992) *Process and Structure in Higher Education.* London: Routledge (second edition).

Beckhard, R. and Pritchard, W. (1992) *Changing the Essence: The Art of Creating and Leading Fundamental Change in Organisations.* San Francisco: Jossey Bass.

Berger, P. and Luckmann, T. (1967) *The Social Construction of Reality.* Harmondsworth: Penguin (first published 1966).

Bernstein, B. (1971) On the classification and framing of educational knowledge, in M.F.D. Young (ed.) *Knowledge and Control,* pp. 47–69. London: Collier Macmillan.

Bernstein, B. (1990) *The Structuring of Pedagogic Discourse.* London: Routledge.

Berquist, W.H. (1992) *The Four Cultures of the Academy.* San Francisco: Jossey Bass.

Beynon, H. (1973) *Working for Ford.* London: Allen Lane.

Bhaskar, R. (1979) *The Possibility of Naturalism: A Philosophical Critique of the Contemporary Human Sciences.* London: Harvester.

Billing, D. (1996) Review of modular implementation in a university. *Higher Education Quarterly,* 50 (1): 1–21.

Birnbaum, R. (1988) *How Colleges Work: The Cybernetics of Academic Organisation and Leadership.* San Francisco: Jossey Bass.

Blackler, F. (1993) Changing organisations. Inaugural lecture, Lancaster University Inaugural Lectures 1993–4, pp. 21–32.

Blackmore, J. (1993) 'In the shadow of men': the historical construction of administration as a 'masculinist' enterprise, in J. Blackmore and J. Kenway (eds) *Gender Matters in Educational Administration and Policy: A Feminist Introduction,* pp. 27–48. London: Falmer.

Blackstone, T. and Fulton, O. (1975) Sex discrimination among university teachers: a British-American comparison. *British Journal of Sociology,* 26 (30): 261–75.

Blau, P.M. (1973) *The Organization of Academic Work.* New York: John Wiley.

Blauner, R. (1964) *Alienation and Freedom.* Chicago: University of Chicago Press.

Bligh, D. (1990) *Higher Education.* London: Cassell.

Bloor, M. and Butterworth, C. (1990) The accreditation of prior learning on in-service education courses for teachers. *Aspects of Educational Technology*, 22: 77–82.

Bocock, J. and Scott, P. (1995) *Redrawing the Boundaries: Further/Higher Education Partnerships Final Report.* Leeds: Centre for Policy Studies in Education, University of Leeds.

Bocock, J. (1994) Curriculum change and professional identity: the role of the university lecturer, in J. Bocock and D. Watson (eds) *Managing the University Curriculum: Making Common Cause.* Buckingham: Open University Press/SRHE.

Bocock, J. and Watson, D. (1994) *Managing the University Curriculum: Making Common Cause.* Buckingham: Open University Press/SRHE.

Bok, D. (1986) *Higher Learning.* Boston, MA: Harvard University Press.

Boud, D., Cohen, R. and Walker, D. (eds) (1993) *Using Experience for Learning.* Buckingham: Open University Press/SRHE.

Bourdieu, P. (1977) *Outline of a Theory of Practice.* Cambridge: Cambridge University Press.

Bourdieu, P. (1981) Men and machines, in K. Knorr-Cetina and A. Cicourel (eds) *Advances in Social Method and Methodology.* Boston, MA: RKP.

Bourdieu, P. and Passeron, J.C. (1977) *Reproduction in Education, Society and Culture.* London: Sage.

Bowe, R., Gewirtz, S. and Ball, S.J. (1994) Captured by the discourse? Issues and concerns in researching 'parental choice'. *British Journal of Sociology of Education*, 15 (1): 63–78.

Brandes, D. and Ginnis, P. (1986) *A Guide to Student Centred Learning.* Oxford: Blackwell.

Braverman, H. (1974) *Labour and Monopoly Capital.* New York: New York Monthly Review Press.

Brookman, J. (1992) Same song but with a different tune, *Times Higher Educational Supplement*, 2 October.

Brown, P. and Scase, R. (1994) *Higher Education and Corporate Realities: Class, Culture and the Decline of Graduate Careers.* London: UCL Press.

Burgess, T. (1977) *Education After School.* Harmondsworth: Penguin.

Burgess, T. (1995a) *Degrees East: The Making of the University of East London 1892–1992.* London: Athlone Press.

Burgess, T. (1995b) *A critical look at new principles of learning in higher education.* Conference paper, Higher Education Foundation annual conference, Keble College Oxford, 1 April.

Burman, E. and Parker, I. (1993) *Discourse Analytical Research.* London: Routledge.

Butterworth, C. (1992) More than one bite at the APEL. *Journal of Further and Higher Education*, 16 (3): 39–51.

Cameron, K.S. and Ettington, D.R. (1988) The conceptual foundations of organisational culture, in J.C. Smart (ed.) *Higher Education: Handbook of Theory and Research*, Vol. 4, pp. 356–96. New York: Agathon.

Cannon, T. (1995) Weights and measures. *Times Higher Synthesis*, 19 May.

Carnegie Foundation for the Advancement of Teaching (1990) Women excel as campus citizens. *Change*, 2: 39–43.

Carr, W. and Kemmis, S. (1986) *Becoming Critical.* Lewes: Falmer.

Carter, C. (1980) *Higher Education for the Future.* London: Blackwell.

Carvel, J. (1997) Interview with Sir Ron Dearing: the Artful Dodger, *Guardian Higher Education Supplement*, 22 July.

Cashmore, E. (1994) *. . . and There Was Television.* London: Routledge.

Cerych, L. and Sabatier, P. (1986) *Great Expectations and Mixed Performance*. London: Trentham.

Chait, R. (1979) Mission madness strikes our colleges. *The Chronicle of Higher Education*, 18 (36): 89.

Church, C. (1975) Modular courses in British higher education: a critical assessment. *Higher Education Bulletin*, 3 (3): 165–84.

Clark, B. (1960) *The Open Door College: A Case Study*. New York: McGraw Hill.

Clark, B. (1963) Faculty culture, in T.F. Lunsford (ed.) *The Study of Campus Cultures*. Bolder, CO: Western Interstate Commission for Higher Education.

Clark, B. (1972) The organisational saga in higher education. *Administrative Science Quarterly*, 17: 178–83.

Clark, B. (1973) The making of an organisational saga, in H. Leavitt and L. Pondy (eds) *Readings in Managerial Psychology*, pp. 232–62. Chicago: Chicago University Press (second edition).

Clark, B. (1980a) *Academic Culture*. New Haven, CT: Yale University Higher Education Research Group, Working Paper no. 42.

Clark, B. (1980b) The cooling out function revisited. *New Directions for Community Colleges*, 8 (4): 15–32.

Clark, B. (1983a) The contradictions of change in academic systems. *Higher Education*, 12 (1): 101–16.

Clark, B. (1983b) *The Higher Education System*. Berkeley, CA: University of California Press.

Clark, B. (ed.) (1984) *Perspectives in Higher Education: 8 Disciplinary and Comparative Views*. Berkeley, CA: University of California Press.

Clark, B. (1987a) *The Academic Life: Small Worlds Different Words*. Princeton, NJ: Carnegie Foundation for the Advancement of Teaching.

Clark, B. (ed.) (1987b) *The Academic Profession*. Berkeley, CA: University of California Press.

Clark, B. (1993) The problem of complexity in modern higher education, in S. Rothblatt (ed.) *The European and American University Since 1800*. Cambridge: Cambridge University Press.

Clark, B. (1994) The research-teaching-study nexus in modern systems of higher education. *Higher Education Policy*, 7 (1): 11–17.

Clark, B. and Trow, M. (1966) The organizational context, in T.M. Newcomb and E.K. Wilson (eds) *College Peer Groups*. Chicago: Aldine.

Cline, S. and Spender, D. (1987) *Reflecting Men (at Twice their Normal Size)*. London: Deutch.

Cockburn, C. (1988a) *Women's Progress, a Research Report: Positive Action for Sex Equality in New Polytechnic*. Newtown: New Polytechnic.

Cockburn, C. (1988b) *Making Policy for Women: A History of Steps in the Process of Policy Making for Sex Equality in New Polytechnic 1983–87*. Newtown: New Polytechnic.

Cockburn, C. (1991) *In The Way of Women: Men's Resistance to Sex Equality in Organizations*. London: Macmillan.

Coghill, C. (1989) Systems, in D. Watson with J. Brooks, C. Coghill, R. Lindsay and D. Scurry *Managing the Modular Course: Perspectives from Oxford Polytechnic*. Buckingham: Open University Press/SRHE.

Cohen, L. and Manion, L. (1989) *Research Methods in Education*. London: Routledge (third edition: first published 1980).

Cohen, M.D. and March, J.G. (1974) *Leadership and Ambiguity: The American College President*. New York: McGraw Hill.

Collier, K.G. (1982) Ideological influences in higher education. *Studies in Higher Education*, 7 (1): 13–19.

Collins, J. (1993) The Wolverhampton experience of CATS and APL for nurses. *CORE*, 17: 2.

Collins, P. (1994) The White Paper and academic research. *Higher Education Quarterly*, 48 (1): 5–11.

Committee of Vice-Chancellors and Principals (CVCP) (1985) *Report of the Steering Committee on Management and Efficiency in British Universities* (the Jarratt Report). London: CVCP.

Committee of Vice-Chancellors and Principles (CVCP) (1991) *Equal Opportunities in Employment in Universities UK Guidance*. London: CVCP.

Committee of Vice-Chancellors and Principles (CVCP) (1993a) *Key Points From DFE Announcement on Planned Spending for 1994/5*, fax to HEIs 30 November. London: CVCP.

Committee of Vice-Chancellors and Principles (CVCP) (1993b) *Review of the Academic Year: A Report of the Committee of Enquiry into Reorganisation of the Academic Year* (the Flowers Report).

Committee on Higher Education (1963) *Higher Education: Report of the Committee Appointed by the Prime Minister under the Chairmanship of Lord Robbins 1961–63* (the Robbins Report). London: HMSO.

Connell, R.W. (1987) *Gender and Power*. Oxford: Polity Press/Blackwell.

Corrigan, P. (1981) *Schooling the Smash Street Kids*. London: Macmillan.

Coser, L. (1974) *Greedy Institutions: Patterns of Undivided Commitment*. New York: New York Free Press.

Cotterill, P. and Waterhouse, R.L. (1996) I don't know how to tell you this but . . . the invisibility of emotional labour in mass higher education. Conference paper 'Dilemmas of Mass Higher Education' conference, Staffordshire University, 10–12 April.

Council for National Academic Awards (CNAA) (1985) *Summary Report of the Institutional Review to New Polytechnic (November 1984–March 1985)*. London: CNAA.

Council for National Academic Awards (1989) *Going Modular: Information Services Discussion Paper 2*. London: CNAA.

Council for National Academic Awards (CNAA) (1990) *The Modular Option: Information Services Discussion Paper 5*. London: CNAA.

Council for National Academic Awards, (undated) *Franchising*. London: CNAA.

Craib, I. (1992) *Anthony Giddens*. London: Routledge.

Crane, D. (1972) *Invisible Colleges: Diffusion of Knowledge in Scientific Communities*. Chicago: University of Chicago Press.

Crawley, R. (1994) A pragmatic truce between knowledge and competence. *Personnel Management*, August: 31.

Cullen, S. (1994) Culture, gender and organisational change in British welfare benefits services, in S. Wright (ed.) *Anthropology of Organisations*. London: Routledge.

Cuthbert, R. (ed.) (1996) *Working in Higher Education*. Buckingham: Open University Press/SRHE.

Dahrendorf, R. (1968) *Homo Sociologicus*. London: Routledge.

Dahrendorf, R. (1979) *Life Chances*. Chicago: University of Chicago Press.

Dale, R., Esland, G. and MacDonald, M. (1976) *Schooling and Capitalism*. London: RKP.

David, M. (1989) Prima donna inter pares? Women in academic management, in S. Acker (ed.) *Teachers, Gender and Careers*. Lewes: Falmer.

Davidson, G. (1994a) *Credit Accumulation and Transfer in the British Universities 1990–1993.* Canterbury: University of Kent.

Davidson, G. (1994b) Can CATS cope? Current changes in higher education. Conference paper, AUA Conference, 29 March.

Davidson, M.J. and Cooper, L. (1992) *Shattering the Glass Ceiling: The woman manager.* London: Paul Chapman.

Davies, C. and Holloway, P. (1995) Troubling transformations: gender regimes and organizational culture in the academy, in L. Morley and V. Walsh (eds) *Feminist Academics.* London: Taylor and Francis.

Davies, S. (1995) Equal opportunities: language policy. Unpublished memorandum, NewU, 28 February.

Davies, S., Lubelska, C. and Quinn, J. (eds) (1994) *Changing the Subject.* London: Taylor and Francis.

Davis, D. and Astin, H. (1990) Life cycle, career patterns and gender stratification in academe: breaking myths and exposing truths, in S. Stiver Lie and V. O'Leary (eds) *Storming the Tower: Women in the Academic World.* London: Kogan Page.

Deal, T.E. and Kennedy, A.A. (1982) *Corporate Cultures.* Reading, MA: Addison-Wesley.

Dean of Faculty of CLASS (1996) Meetings with the Vice-Chancellor. Unpublished memorandum from dean of CLASS to Class HoD enclosing vice-chancellor's memorandum on 'Special meeting of the University Board', NewU, 5 January.

Dearing, R. (1994) *The National Curriculum and its Assessment: Final Report, December 1993.* London: SCAA.

Dearing, R. (1997) *Higher Education in the Learning Society.* Norwich: HMSO.

Deem, R. (1996a) Border territories: a journey through sociology, education and women's studies. *British Journal of Sociology of Education,* 17 (1): 5–19.

Deem, R. (1996b) Women managing for diversity in a post modern world. Adapted version of paper presented at the American Educational Research Association Annual Meeting, New York, 12 April.

Deem, R. (1996c) The future of educational research in the context of the social sciences: a special case? *British Journal of Educational Studies,* 44 (2): 143–58.

Deem, R. and Davies, M. (1991) Opting out of local authority control – using the Education Reform Act to defend the comprehensive ideal: a case study in educational policy implementation. *International Studies in Sociology of Education,* 1: 153–72.

Delamont, S. (1989) *Knowledgeable Women: Structuralism and the Reproduction of Elites.* London: Routledge.

Delamont, S. (1996) Just like the novels? Researching the occupational culture(s) of higher education, in R. Cuthbert (ed.) *Working in Higher Education.* Buckingham: Open University Press/SRHE.

Denzin, N.K. (1983) Interpretive interactionism, in G. Morgan (ed.) *Beyond Method: Strategies for Social Research.* Beverley Hills, CA: Sage.

Department of Education and Science (DES) (1973) *Adult Education: A Plan for Development* (The Russell report). London: HMSO.

Department of Education and Science (DES) (1985) *The Development of Higher Education into the 1990s,* Cmnd 9524. London: HMSO.

Department of Education and Science (DES) (1987) *Higher Education: Meeting the Challenge,* Cmnd 114. London: HMSO.

Department of Education and Science (DES) (1991a) *Aspects of Work Based Learning in Four London Polytechnics.* London: HMSO.

Department of Education and Science (DES) (1991b) *Higher Education in FE Colleges: A Report by HMI.* London: HMSO.

Department of Education and Science (DES) (1991c) *Higher Education: A New Framework*, Cmnd 1541. London: HMSO.

Department for Education (DfE) (1993a) *Letter from Roger Dawe, Deputy Secretary to Graeme Davies, Chief Executive HEFCE* (12 November). London: DfE.

Department for Education (DfE) (1993b) *Realising Our Potential*, Cmnd 2250. London: HMSO.

Department for Education (DfE) (1994) *Student Numbers in Higher Education – Great Britain 1982/3 to 1992/3*. Statistical bulletin, August, no. 13/94. London: HMSO.

Derber, C. (1983) Managing professionals: ideological proletarianization and post-industrial labor. *Theory and Society*, 12 (3): 309–41.

Derrida, J. (1982) *Margins of Philosophy*. London: Harvester.

Dill, D.D. (1982) The management of academic culture. *Higher Education*, 11 (3): 303–20.

Dingwall, R. (1980) Ethics and ethnography. *Sociological Review*, 28 (4): 157–67.

Dockrell, W.B. (1995) Ethical considerations in research, in M. Bird and M. Hammersley (eds) *E835 Educational Research in Action Offprints Reader*. Buckingham: Open University Press.

Donald, J. (1986) Knowledge and the university curriculum. *Higher Education*, 15: 267–82.

Douglas, J. (1976) *Investigative Social Research*. Beverley Hills, CA: Sage.

Dowdeswell, C. (1974) The inter-university biology teaching project, in K.G. Collier (ed.) *Innovation in Higher Education*. London: NFER.

Dressel, P. and Marcus, D. (1982) *Teaching and Learning in College*. San Francisco: Jossey Bass.

Duke, C. (1992) *The Learning University: Towards a New Paradigm*. Buckingham: Open University Press/SRHE.

Durkheim, E. (1938) *The Rules of Sociological Method*. New York: New York Free Press.

Durkheim, E. and Mauss, M. (1969) *Primitive Classification*. New York: Cohen and West (first published 1903).

Dwyer, P.J. (1995) Foucault, docile bodies and post-compulsory education in Australia. *British Journal of Sociology of Education*, 16 (4): 467–77.

Easterby-Smith, M. (1987) Change and innovation in higher education: a role for corporate strategy? *Higher Education*, 16: 37–52.

Eccles, R. and Noriah, N. (1992) *Beyond the Hype*. Boston: Boston Harvard College.

Egerton, M. and Halsey, A.H. (1993) Trends by social class and gender in access to higher education in Britain. *Oxford Review of Education*, 19 (2): 183–96.

Eisner, E. (1985) *The Art of Educational Evaluation*. Lewes: Falmer.

Eisner, E. (1992) Objectivity in educational research. *Curriculum Inquiry*, 22 (1): 9–15. Reprinted in M. Hammersley (ed.) (1993) *Educational Research: Current Issues*, pp. 49–56. Buckingham: Open University Press.

Elmore, R. (1978) Organisational models of social program implementation. *Public Policy*, 28: 185–228.

Elmore, R.F. (1982) Backward mapping: implementation research and policy, in W. Williams (ed.) *Studying Implementation*. London: Chatham House.

Elzinga, A. (1985) Research, bureaucracy and the drift of epistemic criteria, in B. Wittrock and A. Elzinga (eds) *The University Research System*. London: Almquist and Wiksell.

Employment Department (1992) *Embedding Accreditation of Prior Learning*. Employment Department competence and assessment briefing series no. 7, October. Sheffield: Employment Department.

Employment Department (1994) *Higher Education Projects Digest 1.* Sheffield: Employment Department.

Entwistle, H. (1979) *Antonio Gramsci: Conservative Schooling for Radical Politics.* London: RKP.

Entwistle, N., Hanley, M. and Hounsell, D. (1979) Identifying distinctive approaches to studying. *Higher Education,* 8: 365–80.

Eraut, M. (1985) Knowledge creation and knowledge use in professional contexts. *Studies in Higher Education,* 10: 117–33.

Eraut, M. (1995) Schön shock: a case for reframing reflection-in-action? *Teachers and Teaching: Theory and Practice,* 1 (1): 9–23.

Eriksen, S. (1995) TQM and the transformation from an elite to mass system of higher education in the UK. *Quality Assurance in Education,* 3 (1): 14–29.

Evans, C. (1990a) A cultural view of the discipline of modern languages. *European Journal of Education,* 25 (3): 273–82.

Evans, C. (1990b) *Language People.* Buckingham: Open University Press.

Evans, C. (1993) *English People.* Buckingham: Open University Press.

Evans, C. (1995) Choosing people: recruitment and selection as leverage on subjects and disciplines. *Studies in Higher Education,* 20 (3): 253–65.

Evans, G., Leather, S., Smith, R. *et al.* (1991) *Franchising in post 16 education.* Coombe Lodge Report, 22 (9): 743–819.

Evans, N. and Turner, A. (1993) *The Potential of the Assessment of Experiential Learning in Universities.* London: Learning from Experience Trust.

Evetts, J. (1986) Teachers' careers: the objective dimension. *Educational Studies,* 12: 225–44.

Fairclough, N. (1989) *Language and Power.* London: Longman.

Fairclough, N. (1992) *Discourse and Social Change.* Cambridge: Polity Press.

Fairclough, N. (1993) Critical discourse analysis and the marketization of public discourse: the universities. *Discourse and Society,* 4 (2): 133–68.

Fairley, J. and Patterson, L. (1995) *Scottish Education and the New Managerialism. Scottish Educational Review,* 27 (1): 13–36.

Farish, M., McPake, J., Powney, J. and Weiner, G. (1995) *Equal Opportunities in Colleges and Universities: Towards Better Practices.* Buckingham: Open University Press/ SRHE.

Fay, B. (1987) *Critical Social Science: Liberation and its Limits.* Los Angeles: Cornell University Press.

Fennema, E. (1983) Success in mathematics, in M. Marland (ed.) *Sex Differentiation and Schooling.* London: Heinemann.

Fetterman, D.M. (1989) *Ethnography Step by Step.* Beverley Hills, CA: Sage.

Fetterman, D.M. and Pitman, M.A. (1986) *Educational Evaluation: Ethnography in Theory, Practice and Politics.* Beverley Hills, CA: Sage.

Fidler, B. (1996) *Strategic Planning for School Improvement.* London: Pitman/BEMAS.

Finch, J. (1984) It's great to have someone to talk to: the ethics and politics of interviewing women, in C. Bell and H. Roberts (eds) *Social Researching: Politics, Problems and Practice.* London: Routledge.

Finch, J. (1986) *Research and Policy: The Uses of Qualitative Methods in Social and Educational Research.* Lewes: Falmer.

Finch, J. (1988) Ethnography and public policy, in A. Pollard, J. Purvis and G. Walford (eds) *Education, Training and the New Vocationalism,* pp. 185–200. Oxford: Oxford University Press.

Finkelstein, M. (1984) *The American Academic Profession: A Synthesis of Scientific Enquiry Since World War II.* Columbus, OH: Ohio State University Press.

Fitz, J., Halpin, D. and Power, S. (1994) Implementation research and education policy: practice and prospects. *British Journal of Education Studies*, 42 (1): 53–69.

Fitzgerald, T.H. (1988) Can change in organizational culture really be managed? *Organizational Dynamics*, 17 (1): 5–15.

Foster, C. (1994) The brain drain. *Living Marxism*, October: 24–8.

Foucault, M. (1977a) *Discipline and Punish*. Harmondsworth: Penguin.

Foucault, M. (1977b) *The Archeology of Knowledge*. London: Tavistock.

Foucault, M. (1980) *Power/Knowledge*. New York: Pantheon.

Foucault, M. (1982) The subject and power, in H. Dreyfus and P. Rabinow (eds) *Michel Foucault: Beyond Structuralism and Hermeneutics*. London: Harvester.

Fox, C.J. (1990) Implementation research: why and how to transcend positivist methodologies, in D.J. Palumbo and D.J. Calista (eds) *Implementation and Public Policy: Opening Up the Black Box*. CT: Greenwood Press.

Frain, J. (1993) *The Changing Culture of a College*. London: Falmer.

Freire, P. (1972) *Pedagogy of the Oppressed*. Harmondsworth: Penguin.

Fullan, M. (1986) Improving the implementation of educational change. *School Organisation*, 6 (3): 321–6.

Fullan, M. (1991) *The New Meaning of Educational Change*. London: Cassell.

Fullan, M. (1993) *Change Forces*. London: Falmer.

Fullan, M. and Hargreaves, A. (1992) *What's Worth Fighting for in Your School*. Buckingham: Open University Press.

Fullan, M. and Pomfret, A. (1977) Research in curriculum and instruction implementation. *Review of Education Research*, 47 (1): 335–97.

Fulton, O. (1981) Strategies for revival: increasing demand and improving access. *Education Policy Bulletin*, 9 (1): 39–49.

Fulton, O. (1991a) Modular systems in Britain, in R.O. Berdahl, G. Moodie and I. Spitzberg *Quality and Access in HE: Comparing Britain and the US*. Buckingham: Open University Press/SRHE.

Fulton, O. (1991b) Slouching towards a mass system: society, government and institutions in the United Kingdom. *Higher Education*, 21: 589–605.

Fulton, O. and Elwood, S. (1989) *Admissions to Higher Education: Policy and Practice*. Sheffield: Training Agency.

Gaff, J. and Wilson, R.C. (1972) Faculty cultures and interdisciplinary studies. *Journal of Higher Education*, 42 (3): 186–201.

Gardner, G. (1976) *Social Surveys for Social Planners*. Buckingham: Open University Press.

Gaskell, J. (1992) *Gender Matters from School to Work*. Buckingham: Open University Press.

Geertz, C. (1983) *Local Knowledge*. New York: Basic Books.

Geertz, C. (1993) *The Interpretation of Cultures*. London: Fontana (first published 1973).

Gibbs, G. (1994) *Improving Student Learning*. Oxford: Oxford Centre for Staff Development.

Giddens, A. (1976) *New Rules of Sociological Method*. London: Hutchinson.

Giddens, A. (1983) Comments on the theory of structuration. *Journal for the Theory of Social Behaviour*, 13: 75–80.

Giddens, A. (1984) *The Constitution of Society*. Cambridge: Polity Press.

Gilbert, N.G. and Mulkay, M. (1984) *Opening Pandora's Box: A Sociological Analysis of Scientists' Discourse*. Cambridge: Cambridge University Press.

Gillespie, M. (1995) *Television, Ethnicity and Cultural Change*. London: Routledge.

Glaser, B. and Strauss, A. (1967) *The Discovery of Grounded Theory*. Chicago: Aldine.

Glassman, R.B. (1973) Persistence and loose coupling in living systems. *Behavioral Science*, 18: 83–98.

Goffman, E. (1959) *The Presentation of Self in Everyday Life*. New York: Doubleday.

Goffman, E. (1962a) *Asylums: Essays on the Social Situation of Mental Patients and Other Inmates*. Chicago: Aldine.

Goffman, E. (1962b) On cooling the mark out: some aspects of adaptation to failure, in A.M. Rose (ed.) *Human Behaviour and Social Processes: An International Approach*. London: RKP.

Goodson, I. (1990) 'Nations at Risk' and 'National Curriculum': ideology and identity. *Politics of Education Association Yearbook*: 219–32.

Gordon, C. (ed.) (1980) *Foucault: Power/knowledge: Selected Interviews and Other Writings 1972–77*. London: Harvester.

Gouldner, A.W. (1957) Cosmopolitans or locals? *Administrative Science Quarterly*, 2: 281–69.

Grace, G. (1978) *Teachers, Ideology and Control*. London: RKP.

Grace, G. (1995) *School Leadership – Beyond Education Management: An Essay in Policy Scholarship*. London: Falmer.

Gramsci, A. (1971) *Selections from the Prison Notebooks*. London: Lawrence & Wishart.

Grant, R. (1987) A career in teaching: a survey of middle school teachers' perceptions with particular reference to the careers of women teachers. *British Educational Research Journal*, 13: 227–39.

Gray, A. (1992) *Video Playtime*. London: Routledge.

Greed, C. (1991) *Surveying Sisters*. London: Routledge.

Gregg, P. (1996) Modularisation: what academics think, in Higher Education Quality Council, *In Focus: Modular Higher Education in the UK*. London: HEQC.

Grieco, M.S. (1988) Birth marked? A critical view on analysing organisational culture. *Human Organisation*, 47: 84–7.

Griffin, C. (1987) *Assessing Prior Learning: Progress and Practices*. London: Learning from Experience Trust.

Gutek, B.A. and Cohen, A.G. (1992) Sex ratios, sex role spillover, and sex at work: a comparison of men's and women's experiences, in A.J. Mills and P. Tancred (eds) *Gendering Organizational Analysis*. London: Sage.

Hall, S. (1990) Cultural identity and diaspora, in J. Rutherford (ed.) *Community, Culture, Difference*. London: Lawrence & Wishart.

Hall, S. (1993) Thatcherism today. *New Statesman*, 20 December.

Halsey, A.H. (1992) *Decline of Donnish Dominion*. Oxford: Oxford University Press.

Halsey, A.H. and Trow, M. (1971) *The British Academics*. London: Faber.

Ham, C. and Hill, M. (1984) *The Policy Process in the Modern Capitalist State*. London: Wheatsheaf.

Hammersley, M. (1992a) Reflections on the liberal university: truth, citizenship and the role of the academic. *International Studies in the Sociology of Education*, 2 (2): 165–83.

Hammersley, M. (1992b) *What's Wrong With Ethnography?* London: Routledge.

Hammersley, M. (1993) On the teacher as researcher, in M. Hammersley (ed.) *Educational Research: Current Issues*. Buckingham: Open University Press.

Hammersley, M., Bird, M., Carty, J. *et al.* (1995) *E835 Educational Research in Action Study Text*. Milton Keynes: Open University.

Hammersley, M., Scarth, J. and Webb, S. (1985) Developing and testing theory: the case of research on student learning and examinations, in R. Burgess (ed.) *Issues in Educational Research: Qualitative Methods*. Lewes: Falmer.

Handy, C. (1976) *Understanding Organisations*. Harmondsworth: Penguin.

Hansard Society (1990) *The Report of the Hansard Society Commission on Women at the Top*. London: Hansard Society.

Hanson, A.P. (1989) 'Expectations and realisations: experiences of mature students returning to study in an institution of public sector higher education', unpublished PhD thesis. Newtown, New Polytechnic.

Harman, K.M. (1988) 'The symbolic dimension of university organisation', unpublished PhD thesis. LaTrobe University.

Harman, K.M. (1989) Professional versus academic values: cultural ambivalence in university professional school in Australia. *Higher Education*, 18: 491–509.

Harrison, R. (1972) Understanding your organisation character. *Harvard Business Review*, May–June: 119–28.

Harrold, R. (1992) Resource allocation, in B. Clark and G. Neave (eds) *The Encyclopaedia of Higher Education*, Vol. 2, pp. 1353–8. Oxford: Pergamon Press.

Hartley, J. (1983) Ideology and organisational behaviour. *International Studies of Management and Organisation*, 13 (3): 24–36.

Haslum, M. (1994) A course leader's perspective, in J. Bocock and D. Watson (eds) *Managing the University Curriculum: Making Common Cause*. Buckingham: Open University Press/SRHE.

Heafford, M. (1967) *Pestalozzi: His Thought and its Relevance Today*. London: Methuen.

Hearn, J. and Parkin, P.W. (1992) Gender and organizations: a selective review and a critique of a neglected area, in A.J. Mills and P. Tancred (eds) *Gendering Organizational Analysis*. London: Sage.

Henkel, M. (1988) Responsiveness of the subjects in our study, in C. Boys, J. Brennan, M. Henkel, J. Kirkland and M. Kogan *Higher Education and the Preparation for Work*. London: Jessica Kingsley.

Henry, C., Drew, J., Anwar, N., Benoit-Asselman, D. and Campbell, G. (1992) *EVA Project: Report of the Ethics and Values Audit*. Newtown: NewU.

Her Majesty's Inspectorate (HMI) (1991) *New Polytechnic: Building and Surveying Provision in the Department of the Built Environment*. London: DfE.

Hermes, J. (1995) *Reading Women's Magazines*. London: Routledge.

Heron, E. (1991) Credit where it's due, *Times Educational Supplement*, 25 October.

Hewton, E. (1987) Inside knowledge, in O. Boyd Barrett, T. Bush, J. Goodey, I. McNay and M. Preedy (eds) *Approaches to Post-School Management*. Buckingham: Open University Press.

Higher Education Funding Council for England (HEFCE) (1993) *The Review of the Academic Year: A Report of the Committee of Enquiry into the Organisation of the Academic Year* (the Flowers Report), November. London: HEFCE.

Higher Education Funding Council for England (HEFCE) (1994) *Profiles of Higher Education Institutions*. London: HEFCE.

Higher Education Quality Council (HEQC) (1994) *NewU: Quality Audit Report*. London: Quality Assurance Group, HEQC.

Higher Education Quality Council (HEQC) (1995) *Learning from Collaborative Audit: An Interim Report*. London: HEQC.

Higher Education Quality Council (HEQC) (1996a) *Quality Audit Report, NewU: Collaborative Provision*, (draft) January. London: HEQC.

Higher Education Quality Council (HEQC) (1996b) *NewU Quality Audit Report: Collaborative Provision*, January. London: HEQC.

Higher Education Statistics Agency (HESA) (1995) *HESA Data Report: Students in Higher Education Institutions*. London: HESA.

Higher Education Statistics Agency (HESA) (1997) *Students in Higher Education Institutions*. London: HESA.

Hill, D. (1992) What the radical right is doing to teacher education: a radical left response. *Multicultural Teaching*, 10 (3): 31–3.

Hirst, P. (1974) *Knowledge and the Curriculum*. London: RKP.

Hitchcock, G. and Hughes, D. (1989) *Research and the Teacher*. London: Routledge.

Hjern, B. and Hull, C. (1982) Implementation research as empirical constitutionalism. *European Journal of Political Research*, 10 (2): 105–15.

Hockey, J. (1986) *Squaddies: Portrait of a Subculture*. Exeter: University of Exeter Press.

Hogwood, B. (1987) *From Crisis to Complacency*. Oxford: Oxford University Press.

Homan, R. (1991) *The Ethics of Social Research*. London: Longman.

Hood, C.C. (1976) *The Limits of Administration*. London: Wiley.

Hooijberg, R. and Petrock, F. (1993) On cultural change: using competing values framework to help leaders execute and transformational strategy. *Human Resource Management*, 32 (1): 29–40.

Horton, T. and Raggatt, P. (eds) (1982) *Challenge and Change in the Curriculum*. London: Hodder and Stoughton/Open University.

Hounsell, D. (1996) Coursework assignments: redrawing the map. Conference paper delivered to the SRHE annual conference, Cardiff, December.

Huber, L. (1990) Disciplinary cultures and social reproduction. *European Journal of Education*, 25 (3): 241–61.

Huberman, M. and Miles, M. (1984) *Innovation Close Up*. New York: Plenum.

Hull, C. (1985) Between the lines: the analysis of interview data as an exact art. *British Education Research Journal*, 11 (1): 27–32.

Humphreys, L. (1975) *Tearoom Trade: Impersonal Sex in Public Places*. Chicago: Aldine.

Itzin, C. (1995) The gender culture in organisations, in C. Itzin and J. Newman (eds) *Gender, Culture and Organizational Change*. London: Routledge.

Itzin, C. and Newman, J. (eds) (1995) *Gender, Culture and Organizational Change*. London: Routledge.

Jackson, N. (1996) *Modular Higher Education in the UK in Focus*. London: HEQC.

Jary, D. and Parker, M. (1994) The neo fordist university: academic work and mass higher education. Conference paper, BSA Conference, Newtown, NewU, March.

Jary, D. and Parker, M. (1995) The McUniversity: organization, management and academic subjectivity. *Organization*, 2 (2): 319–38.

Jermier, J.M., Knights, D. and Nord, W.R. (eds) (1994) *Resistance and Power in Organizations*. London: Routledge.

Jones, A. (1993) Becoming a 'girl': post-structuralist suggestions for educational research. *Gender and Education*, 5 (2): 157–66.

Jones, I. (ed.) (1995) *Accreditation of Prior Learning: From the Margin to the Mainstream*. Salford: Salford University.

Jones, K. (1989) *Right Turn*. London: Hutchinson Radius.

Jordan, G. (1982) The Moray Firth working party: 'Performance' without 'Conformance'. *European Journal of Political Research*, 10 (2): 117.

Joseph, M. (1978) Professional values, a case study of professional students in a polytechnic. *Research in Education*, 19: 49–65.

Joseph, M. (1980) 'Professional socialisation: a case study of estate management students', unpublished DPhil thesis, Oxford University.

Kanter, R.M. (1977) *Men and Women of the Corporation*. New York: Basic Books.

Kaufman, D.R. (1978) Associational ties in academe: some male and female differences. *Sex Roles*, 4: 9–21.

Keat, R. and Abercrombie, N. (1991) *Enterprise Culture*. London: Routledge.

Kelly, G.A. (1955) *The Psychology of Personal Constructs*. New York: Norton.

Kemmis, S. (1988) Action research, in J.P. Keeves (ed.) *Educational Research Methodology and Measurement: An International Handbook*, pp. 42–9. Oxford: Pergamon.

Kempner, K. (1991) Understanding cultural conflict, in W.G. Tierney (ed.) *Culture and Ideology in Higher Education*. New York: Praeger.

Kenway, J. and Willis, S. (1990) *Hearts and minds: Self-esteem and the Schooling of Girls*. Lewes: Falmer.

Kerr, C. (1972) *The Uses of the University*. Boston, MA: Harvard University Press.

Kerr, C., Dunlop, J., Harbison, F. and Myers, C. (1962) *Industrialism and Industrial Man*. Harmondsworth: Penguin.

Kickert, W. (1991) Steering at a distance: a new paradigm in public governance in Dutch higher education. Paper for the European consortium for Political Research, University of Essex, March.

Kilmann, R., Saxton, M. and Serpa, R. (eds) (1985) *Gaining Control of the Corporate Culture*. San Francisco: Jossey Bass.

King, C. (1994) Opinion. *University Life*, 1 (7): 3.

King, R. (1994) The institutional compact, in J. Bocock and D. Watson (eds) *Managing the University Curriculum: Making Common Cause*. Buckingham: Open University Press/SRHE.

Kirby, A. (1980) An approach to ideology. *Journal of Geography in Higher Education*, 4 (2): 16–25.

Kirk, J. and Miller, M. (1987) *Reliability and Validity in Qualitative Research*. Beverley Hills, CA: Sage.

Knights, D. and Vurdubakis, T. (1994) Foucault, power, resistance and all that, in J.M. Jermier, D. Knights and W.R. Nord (eds) *Resistance and Power in Organizations*. London: Routledge.

Knorr-Cetina, K. (1988) The micro-social order: towards a reconception, in N. Fielding (ed.) *Actions and Structure*. London: Sage.

Kogan, M. and Henkel, M. (1983) *Government and Research: The Rothschild Experiment in a Government Department*. London: Heinemann.

Kogan, M. and Kogan, D. (1983) *The Attack on Higher Education*. London: Kogan Page.

Kolb, D. (1984) *Experiential Learning: Experience at the Source of Learning*. New York: Prentice Hall.

Kuh, G.D. and Whitt, E.J. (1988) Using the cultural lens to understand faculty behaviour. Paper presented to the Annual Meeting of the American Educational Research Association, 5–9 April.

Labov, W. (1969) *The Logic of Non-Standard English*. Georgetown: Georgetown Monographs on Language and Linguistics.

Lash, S. (1990) *Sociology of Postmodernism*. London: Routledge.

Lattuca, L. and Stark, J. (1994) Will disciplinary perspectives impede curricular reform? *Journal of Higher Education*, 65 (4): 401–26.

Lawton, D. (1975) *Class, Culture and the Curriculum*. London: RKP.

Leach, E. (1982) *Social Anthropology*. London: Fontana.

Leavis, F.R. and Thompson, D. (1933) *Culture and Environment: The Training of Critical Awareness*. London: Chatto.

LeCompte, M. (1979) Less than meets the eye, in M. Wax (ed.) *Desegregated Schools: An Intimate Portrait Based on Five Ethnographic Studies.* Washington DC: National Institute of Education.

Leonard, P. (1996) Gendering change? masculinity and the dynamics of incorporation. Paper presented at 'Symposium in markets in education: policies, process and practice', University of Southampton, 4–5 July.

Lessem, R. (1990) *Managing Corporate Culture.* Brooklyn, VT: Gower.

Letherby, G. (1996) Roles and relationships: issues of self and identity at home and at work. Conference paper, 'Dilemmas of Mass Higher Education' conference, Staffordshire University, 10–12 April.

Levine, A. (1980) *Why Innovation Fails.* New York: State University of New York Press.

Levinson, R.M. (1989) The faculty and institutional isomorphism. *Academe,* January–February: 23–7.

Licht, B.G. and Dweck, C.S. (1983) Sex differences in achievement orientations, in M. Marland (ed.) *Sex Differentiation and Schooling.* London: Heinemann.

Light, D. (1974) Introduction: the structure of the academic professions. *Sociology of Education, 47 (Winter):* 2–28.

Lincoln, Y.S. (1991) Advancing a critical agenda, in W.G. Tierney (ed.) *Culture and Ideology in Higher Education.* New York: Praeger.

Linder, B. and Peters, A. Design perspective on policy implementation: the fallacies of misplaced prescription. *Policy Studies Review,* 6 (3): 459–75.

Lingard, B. (1997) Producing and practising social justice policy in education: a policy trajectory study from Queensland, Australia. Conference paper, International Sociology of Education Conference, Sheffield, UK, 3–5 January.

Lipsky, M. (1978) The assault on human services: street level bureaucrats, accountability and the fiscal crisis, in S. Greer, R.E. Hedlund and J.L. Gibson (eds) *Accountability in Urban Society.* Beverley Hills, CA: Sage.

Lipsky, M. (1980) *Street Level Bureaucracy: Dilemmas of the Individual in Public Services.* Beverley Hills, CA: Sage.

Littler, C. (1991) *Technology and the Organisation of Work.* Victoria: Deakin University.

Lodahl, J.B. and Gordon, G. (1972) The structure of scientific fields and the functioning of university graduate departments. *American Sociological Review,* 37: 57–72.

Lyotard, J.F. (1984) *The Postmodern Condition.* Manchester: Manchester University Press (first edition 1979).

McCracken, G. (1988) *The Long Interview.* Beverley Hills: Sage.

McInnis, C. (1992) *Academic cultures and the policy implementation process.* Conference paper, Adelaide, 4 September.

McInnis, C. (1996) Academic cultures and their role in the implementation of government policy, in J. Brennan, M. Kogan and U. Teichler (eds) *Higher Education and Work.* London: Jessica Kingsley.

McLuhan, M. (1964) *Understanding Media.* New York: McGraw-Hill.

Maclure, S. (1988) *Education Reformed.* Buckingham: Open University Press.

McMurty, J. (1991) Education and the market model. *Journal of Philosophy of Education,* 25 (2): 209–18.

McNay, I. (1995) From collegial academy to corporate enterprise: the changing cultures of universities, in T. Schuller (ed.) *The Changing University?* Buckingham: Open University Press/SRHE.

McNeill, P. (1985) *Research Methods.* London: Tavistock.

McPherson, A. and Raab, C. (1988) *Governing Education: A Sociology of Policy since 1945.* Edinburgh: Edinburgh University Press.

McRobbie, A. (1994) *Postmodernism and Popular Culture.* London: Routledge.

Maguire, M. and Ball, S. (1994) Researching politics and the politics of research: recent qualitative studies in the UK. *International Journal of Qualitative Studies in Education,* 7 (3): 269–85.

Majone, G. and Wildavsky, A. (1984) Implementation as evolution, in J. Pressman and A. Wildavsky (eds) *Implementation.* Berkeley: University of California Press.

Malinowski, B. (1948) *A Scientific Theory of Culture.* Oxford: Oxford University Press.

Mansell, T., Becher, T., Parlett, M., Simons, H. and Squires, G. (1976) *The Container Revolution.* London: Nuffield Foundation.

March, J.G. and Olsen, J.P. (1975) *Choice Situations in Loosely Coupled Worlds.* Unpublished manuscript, Stanford University.

Marfleet, A. and Kushner, S. (1995a) *The Common Course Structure at UEA – The Educational Evaluation: An Interim Report Raising Some Issues for Discussion.* Norwich: University of East Anglia.

Marfleet, A. and Kushner, S. (1995b) *The Common Course Structure at UEA – The Space Between the Schools: A Discussion Document.* Norwich: University of East Anglia.

Marland, M. (ed.) (1983) *Sex Differentiation and Schooling.* London: Heinemann.

Marsh, D. and Rhodes, R.A.W. (1992) *Implementing Thatcherite Policies.* Buckingham: Open University Press/SRHE.

Marshall, C. and Rossman, D. (1989) *Designing Qualitative Research.* Beverley Hills, CA: Sage.

Martin, J., Sitkin, S. and Boehm, M. (1985) Founders and the elusiveness of a cultural legacy, in P.J. Frost (ed.) *Organizational Culture.* Beverley Hills, CA: Sage.

Marton, F., Hounsell, D.J. and Entwistle, N.J. (eds) (1984) *The Experience of Learning.* Edinburgh: Scottish Academic Press.

Marx, K. (1970) *Capital.* Penguin (first published 1867).

Masland, A.T. (1985) Organizational culture in the study of higher education. *Review of Higher Education,* 8 (2): 157–68.

Maynard, M. (1993) Feminism and the possibilities of a post-modern research practice. *British Journal of Sociology of Education,* 14 (3): 327–31.

Mazmanian, D. and Sabatier, P. (1981) *Implementation and Public Policy.* Chicago: University Press of America.

Mead, G.H. (1934) *Mind, Self and Society.* Chicago: University of Chicago Press.

Measor, L. (1983) Gender and the sciences: pupils' gender-based conceptions of school subjects, in M. Hammersley and A. Hargreaves (eds) *Curriculum Practice: Some Sociological Case Studies.* London: Taylor and Francis.

Measor, L. and Sikes, P. (1992) *Gender and Schools.* London: Cassell.

Mechanic, D. (1962) Sources of power of lower participants in complex organizations. Paper presented at the Ford Foundation Seminar in the Social Science of Organizations, University of Pittsburgh, 10–22 June.

Meek, V. Lynn (1984) *Brown Coal or Plato?* Victoria: The Australian Council for Educational Research Ltd.

Meikle, J. and Major, J.E. (1997) Dearing's new deal, *Guardian Higher Education Supplement,* 22 July.

Melton, R.F. (1994) Competences in perspective. *Educational Research,* 36 (3): 285–94.

Menter, I., Muschamp, Y., Nicholls, P., Ozga, J. and Pollard, A. (1997) *Work and Identity in the Primary School: A Post-Fordist Analysis.* Buckingham: Open University Press.

Merton, R. (1968) Social structure and anomie, in R. Merton (ed.) *Social Theory and Social Structure.* New York: New York Free Press.

Middlehurst, R. (1993) *Leading Academics.* Buckingham: Open University Press/SRHE.

Miles, M.B. and Huberman, M.A. (1984) *Qualitative Data Analysis.* Beverley Hills, CA: Sage.

Miller, H. (1995a) *The Management of Change in Universities.* Buckingham: Open University Press/SRHE.

Miller, H. (1995b) States, economies and the changing labour process of academics: Australia, Canada and the United Kingdom, in J. Smyth (ed.) *Academic Work.* Buckingham: Open University Press/SRHE.

Mills, A.J. (1992) Organization, gender and culture, in A.J. Mills and P. Tancred (eds) *Gendering Organizational Analysis.* London: Sage.

Mills, A.J. and Tancred, P. (eds) (1992) *Gendering Organizational Analysis.* London: Sage.

Mills, C.W. (1970) *The Sociological Imagination.* Harmondsworth: Penguin (first edition 1959).

Minogue, K. (1973) *The Concept of a University.* London: Weidenfield and Nicolson.

Modood, T. (1993) Subtle shades of student distinction, *Times Higher Synthesis,* 16 July.

Modular Information Network (1995) *Bulletin 15,* January. Guildford: University of Surrey.

Morgan, G. (ed.) (1983) *Beyond Method: Strategies for Social Research.* Beverley Hills, CA: Sage.

Morley, D. and Silverstone, R. (1991) Communication and context, in K. Jensen and N. Jankowski (eds) *A Handbook of Qualitative Methodologies for Mass Communication Research.* London: Routledge.

Morley, L. (1994) *Glass ceiling or iron cage: women in UK academia. Gender, Work and Organization,* 1 (4): 194–204.

Morley, L. and Walsh, V. (1995) *Feminist Academics.* London: Taylor and Francis.

Morris, P. (1992) Modular or integrated? A choice for courses in art and design. *Journal of Art and Design Education,* 11 (3): 327–34.

National Council for Vocational Qualifications (NCVQ) (1994) *A Statement by the National Council for Vocational Qualifications on All Our Futures, a Channel 4 Dispatches Programme on 15 December 1993 and Associated Report.* London: NCVQ.

National Council for Vocational Qualifications (NCVQ) (1995) *GNVQs at Higher Levels: A consultation paper,* May. London: NCVQ.

Neave, G. (1985) Elite and mass higher education in Britain: a regressive model? *Comparative Education Review,* 29: 347–61.

New Chronicle (1994) University to cut pay, *New Chronicle,* 16, Spring.

New Chronicle (1995) A Surprise reform? *New Chronicle,* 21, Summer.

New Polytechnic (1987) *Equal Opportunities Committee Forms of Address Code of Practice* (EOC 87/2), ratified March 1987. Newtown: New Polytechnic.

New Polytechnic (1989) *CATS Summary Documentation,* May. Newtown: New Polytechnic.

New Polytechnic (1991a) *Credit Accumulation and Transfer: A Brief Overview,* March. Newtown: New Polytechnic.

New Polytechnic (1991b) *New Polytechnic Staff Profile.* Newtown: New Polytechnic (first edition 1988).

Newman, J. (1994) Beyond the vision: cultural change in the public sector. *Public Money and Management,* April–June: 59–64.

Newman, J. (1995) Gender and cultural change, in C. Itzin and J. Newman (eds) *Gender, Culture and Organizational Change.* London: Routledge.

Newton, R.J. (1994) Accreditation of prior learning in business schools. *Management Development Review,* 7 (3): 9–16.

NewU (1993a) *Annual Report 1991–2.* Newtown: NewU.

NewU (1993b) Language and equal opportunities policy, in *Equal Opportunities*, January. Newtown: NewU.

NewU (1993c) *Rector's Address to Staff*, 24 September. Newtown: NewU.

NewU (1993d) *Student Profile 1991–2*. Newtown: NewU.

NewU (1993e) *Credit Accumulation and Transfer Scheme: NEWCATS*. Newtown: NewU.

NewU (1994a) *Department of Applied Biology Quinquennial Review Report 1989–1994*. Newtown: NewU.

NewU (1994b) *Academic Policy Statement of NewU*. Newtown: NewU.

NewU (1994c) *Annual Report 1992–3*. Newtown: NewU.

NewU (1994d) *Briefing Document for HEQC June 1994 Audit*. Newtown: NewU.

NewU (1994e) *Flexibility of Course Delivery Policy*. Newtown: NewU.

NewU (1994f) *HEQC Audit June 1994 Briefing Document*. Newtown: NewU.

NewU (1994g) *Strategic Training and Development Plan: Report to Management Team from Staff Development Officer*. Newtown: NewU.

NewU (1994h) *Full-Time Prospectus: 1994 Entry*. Newtown: NewU.

NewU (1994i) *Credit Exemption and Transfer: Staff Guide (NEWCATS Regulations)*. Newtown: NewU.

NewU (1995a) *Annual Report 1993–4 NewU*. Newtown: NewU.

NewU (1995b) *Equal Opportunities*. Newtown: NewU.

NewU (1995c) *Internal Telephone Directory*. Newtown: NewU.

NewU (1995d) *Student Profile 1993–4*. Newtown: NewU.

NewU (1995e) *Part-Time Prospectus*. Newtown: NewU.

NewU (1995f) *Academic Policy and Planning Committee: Responsibility for the Maintenance of Student Records*. Newtown: NewU.

NewU (1995g) *Keeping the Record Straight: A Guide for Students*. Newtown: NewU.

NewU (1996a) *Draft University Plan 1996–2000 28.2.96.* (considered by academic board 7 March). Newtown: NewU.

NewU (1996b) *The Mission Statement*. Newtown: NewU.

NewU (1996c) *Annual Report 1994–5*. Newtown: NewU.

NewU (1996d) *A Guide to the Equal Opportunities Policy Statements and Committee Structures*. Newtown: NewU.

NewU (1997) *Vice-Chancellor's Review of the Year 1995–6*. Newtown: NewU.

NewU academic registrar (1995a) Avoiding the chaos of CATS: keeping the record straight. AUA occasional paper no. 11, from a paper delivered by NewU's academic registrar at the AUA national conference, May.

NewU academic registrar (1995b) *Responsibility for the Maintenance of Student Records*. Newtown: NewU.

NewU academic registrar (1995c) *Academic Year 96/97*. Memorandum, 19 December. Newtown: NewU.

NewU assistant vice-chancellor (1996) *Research at NewU 1996–2000*. Newtown: NewU.

NewU CXT (1994) *Credit Exemption and Transfer Panel document, CXT 94.04 for Meeting on 9.2.94*. Newtown: NewU.

NewU CXT (1995) *Report of the Credit Exemption and Transfer Officer for Meeting 22.11.95*. Newtown: NewU.

NewU Planning Office (1996) *Commentary on the Times League Table 1996*. Newtown: NewU.

NewU pro-vice-chancellor (1996) *HEQC Quality Audit Report: Collaborative Provision*. Memorandum to management team, 15 January. Newtown: NewU.

NewU vice-chancellor (1992) More power to the ex-poly's elbows. *Times Higher Educational Supplement*, 2 October.

NewU vice-chancellor (1995a) *Towards the 21st Century.* Newtown: NewU.

NewU vice-chancellor (1995b) *Towards the 21st Century – Responses.* Newtown: NewU.

NewU vice-chancellor (1995c) *Structure and Responsibilities of Senior Staff.* Newtown: NewU.

Nieva, V.F and Gutek, B.A. (1981) *Women and Work: A Psychological Perspective.* New York: Praeger.

Noblit, G.W. and Hare, R.D. (1988) *Meta-Ethnography: Synthesising Qualitative Studies.* Newbury Park, CA: Sage.

Office for Population Census and Statistics (OPCS) (1995) *Social Trends,* 25. London: HMSO.

O'Leary, V.E. and Mitchell, J.M. (1990) Women connecting with women, in S.S. Lie and V.E. O'Leary (eds) *Storming the Tower: Women in the Academic World.* London: Kogan Page.

Opacic, S. (1994) Franchising: the students' perspective. Conference paper, SRHE Annual Conference, University of York.

Organization for Economic Cooperation and Development (OECD) (1987) *Universities Under Scrutiny.* Paris: OECD.

Ozga, J. (1990) Policy research and policy theory: a comment on Halpin and Fitz. *Journal of Education Policy,* 5: 359–62.

Palumbo, D.J. and Calista, D.J. (eds) (1990) *Implementation and Public Policy: Opening Up the Black Box.* Westport, CT: Greenwood Press.

Parkin, F. (1972) *Class Inequality and Political Order.* St. Albans: Paladin.

Parsons, T. (1960) *Structure and Process in Modern Societies.* Chicago: Chicago Free Press.

Parsons, T. and Platt, G. (1968) *The American Academic Profession: A Pilot Study.* Los Angeles: National Science Foundation, mimeographed.

Pascale, P. (1990) *Managing on the Edge.* New York: Touchstone.

Peters, T. (1988) *Thriving on Chaos: Handbook for a Management Revolution.* London: Routledge.

Peters, T. and Waterman, R.H. (1982) *In Search of Excellence: Lessons from America's Best Run Companies.* New York: Harper and Row.

Phillips, D.C. (1989) Subjectivity and objectivity: an objective inquiry, in E.W. Eisner and A. Peshkin (eds) *Qualitative Inquiry in Education: The Continuing Debate.* New York: Teachers College Press, reprinted in M. Hammersley (ed.) (1993) *Educational Research: Current Issues.* Buckingham: Open University Press.

Plato (1955) *The Republic.* Harmondsworth: Penguin.

Platt, J. (1981) On interviewing one's peers. *British Journal of Sociology,* 32 (1): 75–91.

Plummer, K. (1983) *Documents of Life.* London: Allen and Unwin.

Pollard, A. (1985) *The Social World of the Primary School.* London: Holt.

Pollitt, C. (1990) *Managerialism and the Public Services.* Oxford: Blackwell.

Pope, R. and Phillips, K. (1995) *NewU: A History of the Development of the Institution since 1828.* Newtown: NewU.

Popper, K. (1975) *Objective Knowledge.* Oxford: Oxford University Press.

Porter, S. (1993) Critical realist ethnography: the case of racism and professionalism in a medical setting. *Sociology,* 7 (4): 591–609.

Porteus, J.D. (1990) *Landscapes of the Mind: Worlds of Sense and Metaphor.* Toronto: University of Toronto Press.

Potter, J. and Wetherell, M. (1987) *Discourse and Social Psychology.* London: Sage.

Pratt, J. and Burgess, T. (1974) *Polytechnics: A Report.* London: Pitman.

Pratt, J. and Silverman, S. (1988) *Responding to Constraint: Policy and Management in Higher Education.* Buckingham: Open University Press/SRHE.

Pressman, J. and Wildavsky, A. (1984) *Implementation: How Great Expectations in Washington are Dashed in Oakland.* Berkeley, CA: University of California Press (second edition; first published 1975).

Pring, R. (1984) Confidentiality and the right to know, in C. Adelman (ed.) *The Politics and Ethics of Evaluation.* London: Croom Helm.

Pritchard, C. and Willmott, H. (1996) Just how managed is the McUniversity? Conference paper, 'Dilemmas of Mass Higher Education' conference, Staffordshire University, 10–12 April.

Puxty, A., Sikka, P. and Willmott, H. (1994) Systems of surveillance and the silencing of UK academic accounting. *Labour British Accounting Review,* 26: 137–71.

Raban, C. (1990) CATS and quality. *Social Work Education,* 9 (2): 25–41.

Raffe, D., Croxford, L. and Howieson, C. (1994) The third face of modules: gendered patterns of participation and progression in Scottish vocational education. *British Journal of Education and Work,* 7 (3): 87–104.

Reynolds, J. and Saunders, M. (1987) Teacher responses to curriculum policy: beyond the 'delivery' metaphor, in J. Calderhead (ed.) *Exploring Teachers' Thinking.* London: Cassell.

Richards, H. (1993) State tightens control, *Times Higher Educational Supplement,* 3 December.

Richardson, J.T.E. (1994) Using questionnaires to evaluate student learning: some health warnings, in G. Gibbs (ed.) *Improving Student Learning: Theory and Practice.* Oxford: Oxford Centre for Staff Development.

Riseborough, G. (1993) Primary headship, state policy and the challenge of the 1990s. *Journal of Education Policy,* 8 (2): 155–73.

Rist, R. (1981) On the utility of ethnographic research for the policy process. *Urban Education,* 15 (4): 485–94.

Ritzer, G. (1993) *The McDonaldization of Society.* Newbury Park, CA: Pine Forge.

Robertson, D. (1994a) *Choosing to Change.* London: HEQC.

Robertson, D. (1994b) *Choosing To Change: Executive Statement and Summary.* London: HEQC.

Robertson, D. (1996) An open letter to Sir Ron Dearing. Conference paper, Dilemmas of Mass Higher Education Conference, Staffordshire University, 10–12 April.

Robinson, E. (1969) *The New Polytechnics.* Harmondsworth: Penguin (first published 1968).

Robson, P. (1992) Access to what? *Living Marxism,* 18–20 October.

Rogers, C. (1983) *Freedom to Learn for the 1980s.* New York: Merrill.

Rogers, E.M. and Shoemaker, F.F. (1971) *Communication of Innovation: A Cross Cultural Approach.* New York: New York Free Press.

Rothblatt, S. (1991) The American modular system, in R.O. Berdahl, G. Moodie and I. Spitzberg (eds) *Quality and Access in HE: Comparing Britain and the US.* Buckingham: Open University Press/SRHE.

Rothblatt, S. (ed.) (1993) *The European and American University Since 1800: Historical and Sociological Essays.* Cambridge: Cambridge University Press.

Rothblatt, S. (1996) Inner life of don-dom, *Times Higher Educational Supplement,* 22 March.

Rowbotham, S. (1973) *Woman's Consciousness, Man's World.* Harmondsworth: Penguin.

Ruscio, K.P. (1987) Many sectors, many professions, in B. Clark (ed.) *The Academic Profession.* Berkeley, CA: University of California Press.

Rustin, M. (1994) Flexibility in higher education, in R. Burrows and B. Loader (eds) *Towards a Post-Fordist Welfare State.* London: Routledge.

Sabatier, P. (1986) Top-down and bottom-up approaches to policy implementation research. *Journal of Public Policy*, 6: 21–48.

Sackmann, S. (ed.) (1997) *Cultural Complexity in Organizations*. London: Sage.

Schein, E. (1985) *Organisational Culture and Leadership: A Dynamic View*. San Francisco: Jossey Bass.

Schofield, J.W. (1993) Increasing the generalisability of social research, in M. Hammersley (ed.) *Social Research*. Beverley Hills, CA: Sage.

Schön, D. (1971) *Beyond the Stable State*. New York: Temple Smith.

Schön, D.A. (1987) *Educating the reflective practitioner*. San Francisco: Jossey Bass.

Schuller, T. (1990) The exploding community: the university idea and the smashing of the academic atom. *Oxford Review of Education*, 16 (1): 3–14.

Schultz, T.W. (1961) Investment in human capital. *American Economic Review*, 51 (March): 1–17.

Scott, P. (1995) *The Meanings of Mass Higher Education*. Buckingham: Open University Press/SRHE.

Scrimshaw, P. (1983) *Educational Ideologies*. E204, Unit 2, Block 1. Milton Keynes: Open University.

Selway, I. (1995) Stories from the tower: changes in the academic role in a restructured higher education institution. Conference paper, SRHE conference, December, 13–16.

Senge, P. (1990) *The Fifth Discipline*. New York: Doubleday.

Sharp, R. and Green, A. (1975) *Education and Social Control*. London: Routledge.

Shils, E.A. and Finch, H.A. (1949) *Max Weber and The Methodology of the Social Sciences*. New York: Glencoe Free Press.

Shinn, T. (1982) Scientific disciplines and organisational specificity, in N. Elias (ed.) Scientific establishments and hierarchies. *Sociology of the Sciences*, iv: 239–64.

Shore, C. and Roberts, S. (1993) Higher education and the panopticon paradigm. Conference paper, the annual conference of the SRHE, University of Sussex, 14–16 December.

Shore, C. and Roberts, S. (1995) Higher education and the panopticon paradigm: quality assurance as 'disciplinary technology'. *Higher Education Review*, 27 (3): 8–17.

Shumar, W. (1995) *Higher education and the state: the irony of Fordism in American universities*, in J. Smyth (ed.) *Academic Work*. Buckingham: Open University Press/SRHE.

Simons, H. (1984) Guidelines for the conduct of an independent evaluation, in C. Adelman (ed.) *The Politics and Ethics of Evaluation*. London: Croom Helm.

Simosko, S. (1991) *Accreditation of Prior Learning: A Practical Guide For Professionals*. London: Kogan Page.

Skeggs, B. (1994) Situating the production of feminist ethnography, in M. Maynard and J. Purvis (eds) *Researching Women's Lives*. London: Taylor and Francis.

Skilbeck, M. (1976) (ed.) *Culture, Ideology and Knowledge*. E203, Units 3 and 4. Milton Keynes: Open University.

Skilbeck, M. and Harris, A. (1976) Ideology, educational values and indoctrination, in M. Skilbeck (ed.) *Culture, Ideology and Knowledge*. E203, Units 3 and 4. Milton Keynes: Open University.

Skirrow, G. (1986) Hellivision: an analysis of video games, in C. McCabe (ed.) *High Theory/Low Culture*. Manchester: Manchester University Press.

Slaughter, S. (1985) From serving students to serving the economy. *Higher Education*, 14: 41–56.

Slowey, M. (1995) *Implementing Change from Within Universities and Colleges.* London: Kogan Page.

Smart, J.C. and Hamm, R.E. (1993) Organisational culture and effectiveness in two-year colleges. *Research in Higher Education,* 34 (1): 95–106.

Smith, C.W. (1983) A case of structuration: the pure-bred beef business. *Journal for the Theory of Social Behaviour,* 13: 3–18.

Smith, D., Scott, P. and Mackay, L. (1993) Mission impossible? Access and the dash for growth in British higher education. *Higher Education Quarterly,* 47 (4): 316–33.

Smyth, J. (ed.) (1995) *Academic Work.* Buckingham: Open University Press/SRHE.

Snow, C.P. (1959) *The Two Cultures and the Scientific Revolution.* New York: Cambridge University Press.

Society for Research into Higher Education (SRHE) (1983) *Excellence in Diversity: Towards a New Structure for Higher Education* (the Leverhulme Report). London: SRHE.

Society for Research into Higher Education (SRHE) (1996) *Evidence for the National Committee of Inquiry into Higher Education.* London: SRHE.

Spender, D. (1983) *Invisible Women: The Schooling Scandal.* London: Women's Press.

Spicer, E. (1976) Beyond analysis and explanation. *Human Organization,* 35 (4): 335–43.

Spindler, G. and Spindler, L. (1987) *Interpretive Ethnography of Education at Home and Abroad.* New York: Lawrence Erlbaum.

Sporn, B. (1996) Managing university culture: an analysis of the relationship between institutional culture and management approaches. *Higher Education,* 32: 41–61.

Squires, G. (1979) Innovations in British higher education and their implications for adult education, in OECD *Learning Opportunities for Adults,* Vol. 3: *New Structures, Programmes and Methods.* Paris: OECD.

Squires, G. (1986) *Modularisation.* Manchester: The Consortium for Advanced Continuing Education and Training.

Squires, G. (1987) *The Curriculum Beyond School.* London: Hodder and Stoughton.

Squires, G. (1990) *First Degree: The Undergraduate Curriculum.* Buckingham: Open University Press/SRHE.

Squires, G. (1992) Interdisciplinarity in higher education in the United Kingdom. *European Journal of Education,* 27 (3): 201–10.

Stenhouse, L. (1975) *An Introduction to Curriculum Research and Development.* London: Heinemann.

Stenhouse, L. (1979) The problem of standards in illuminative research. Lecture given at the Annual General Meeting of the Scottish Educational Research Association, University of Glasgow, mimeo cited in C. Hull (1985) Between the lines: the analysis of interview data as an exact art. *British Education Research Journal,* 11 (1): 27–32.

Stringer, J.K. and Williamson, P. (1987) Policy Implementation, Policy Development and Policy Change: The Youth Training Scheme. *Public Policy and Administration,* Winter, 2: 3.

Super, R.H. (ed.) (1964) *Mathew Arnold: Schools and Universities on the Continent.* Dearborn, MA: Michigan University Press.

Sutherland, M. (1985) *Women Who Teach in Universities.* London: Trentham Books.

Tall, G., Smith, C. and Upton, G. (1994) Changes in professional development programmes: moderating a new modular structure. *British Journal of In-Service Education,* 20 (1): 81–93.

Tapper, E. and Salter, B. (1978) *Education and the Political Order: Changing Patterns of Class Control.* London: Macmillan.

Tapper, T. and Salter, B. (1992) *Oxford, Cambridge and the Changing Idea of the University.* Buckingham: Open University Press/SRHE.

Tarsh, J. (1992) Education and the labour market: a view from the economics department, DfE. Talk given at Lancaster University, 29 October.

Teichler, U. (1988) *Changing Patterns in the HE system.* London: Jessica Kingsley.

Tesch, R. (1990) *Qualitative Research.* Lewes: Falmer.

Thain, C. (1987) Implementing public policy: an analytical framework. *Policy and Politics,* 15 (2): 67–75.

Theodossin, E. (1986) *The Modular Market.* London: FESC.

Thomas, K. (1990) *Gender and Subject in Higher Education.* Buckingham: Open University Press/SRHE.

Tichy, N.M. (1983) *Managing Strategic Change.* New York: Wiley.

Tierney, W.G. (1987) Facts and constructs: defining reality in higher education organisations. *Review of Higher Education,* 11 (1): 61–73.

Tierney, W.G. (1988) Organisational culture and higher education. *Journal of Higher Education,* 59 (1): 2–21.

Tierney, W.G. (1989) *Curricular Landscapes, Democratic Vistas: Transformative Leadership in Higher Education.* New York: Praeger.

Tierney, W.G. (ed.) (1990) *Assessing Academic Climates and Cultures: New Directions for Institutional Research.* San Francisco: Jossey Bass.

Tierney, W.G. (ed.) (1991) *Culture and Ideology in HE.* New York: Praeger.

Times Higher Educational Supplement (1992) Research rankings, 18 December.

Times Higher Educational Supplement (1996) University league tables 1996, 17 May.

Timmins, G., Foster, D. and Law, H. (1979) *Newtown Polytechnic: The Emergence of an Institution 1828–1978.* Newtown: Newtown Polytechnic.

Toulmin, S. (1972) *Human Understanding,* Vol. 1. Oxford: Clarendon Press.

Toyne, P. (1979) *Educational Credit Transfer: Feasibility Study.* London: DES.

Toyne, P. (1991) Appropriate Structures for Higher Education Institutions. Paper presented to International Seminar on Management in Universities, British Council, Brighton, 17–19 July.

Trist, E. (1972) Types of output mix in research organisations and their complementarity, in A.B. Chern, R. Sinclair and W.I. Jenkins (eds) *Social Science and Government: Politics and Problems.* London: Tavistock.

Trow, M. (1988) Comparative perspectives on higher education policy in UK and US. *Oxford Review of Education,* 14 (1): 81–96.

Trow, M. (1970) Reflections on the transition from mass to universal higher education. *Daedalus,* 90: 1–42.

Trow, M. (1972) *The Expansion and Transformation of Higher Education.* Berkeley: General Learning Corporation.

Trow, M. (1974) Problems in the transition from elite to mass higher education, in OECD, *Policies for Higher Education.* Paris: OECD.

Trow, M. (1975) The public and private lives of higher education. *Daedalus,* 104: 113–27.

Trow, M. (1979) *Elite and Mass Higher Education: American Models and European Realities in Research into Higher Education, Processes and Structure,* report from June 1978 conference. Stockholm: National Board of Universities and Colleges.

Trow, M. (1987) Academic standards and mass higher education. *Higher Education Quarterly,* 41 (3): 268–92.

Trow, M. (1989) The Robbins Trap: British attitudes and the limits of expansion. *Higher Education Quarterly,* 43 (1): 55–75.

Trow, M. (1992) Thoughts on the White Paper of 1991. *Higher Education Quarterly*, 46 (3): 213–26.

Trow, M. (1994) *Managerialism and the Academic Profession: Quality and Control*. London: QSC.

Trow, M.A. (1991) The exceptionalism of American higher education, in M.A. Trow and T. Nybom (eds) *University and Society: Essays on the Social Role of Research and Higher Education*, pp. 156–72. New York: Jessica Kingsley.

Trowler, P. (1994) Credit exemption and transfer and CATS: operational experience of credit exemption and transfer in undergraduate degree programmes. Conference paper, Association of University Administrators' Annual Conference, Sheffield, UK, 28–30 March.

Trowler, P. (1995) Beyond the Robbins Trap. Paper presented to research seminar, University of Central Lancashire, 7 November.

Trowler, P. (1996a) Angels in marble? Accrediting prior experiential learning in higher education. *Studies in Higher Education*, 21 (1): 17–30.

Trowler, P. (1996b) Presentation to Lancaster University's doctoral programme, 10 January.

Trowler, P. (1996c) Beyond the Robbins Trap: reconceptualising academic responses to change in higher education (or . . . quiet flows the don?). Conference paper, 'Dilemmas of Mass Higher Education' conference, Staffordshire University, 10–12 April.

Trowler, P. (1996d) Beyond the Robbins Trap: reconceptualising academic responses to change in higher education (or . . . quiet flows the don?). Amended version of P. Trowler (1996c), sent to interview respondents, 22.5.96.

Trowler, P. (1996e) 'Academic responses to policy change in a single institution: a case study of attitudes and behaviour related to the implementation of curriculum policy in an expanded higher education context during a period of resource constraint', unpublished PhD thesis. Lancaster University.

Trowler, P. (1997) Beyond the Robbins trap: reconceptualising academic responses to change in higher education (or . . . quiet flows the don). *Studies in Higher Education*, 22 (3): 301–18.

Trowler, P. and Hinett, K. (1994) Implementing the recording of achievement in higher education. *Capability*, 1 (1): 53–61.

Tyler, G. (1972) The faculty joins the proletariat. *Change*, 3 (8): 40–5.

Tysome, T. (1996) Modules stir mixed reception, *Times Higher Education Supplement*, 25 October.

University of Nottingham Union (1993) *Report by the University of Nottingham Union on the Initial Impact of Modularisation and Semesterisation at the University of Nottingham*. Nottingham: University of Nottingham NUS.

Usher, R. (1989) Qualification, paradigm and experiential learning in higher education, in O. Fulton (ed.) *Access and Institutional Change*. Buckingham: Open University Press/SRHE.

Usher, R. and Edwards, R. (1994) *Postmodernism and Education*. London: Routledge.

Utley, A. (1995) Wagner's wish for 'inner life', *Times Higher Educational Supplement*, 13 January.

Wagner, L. (1992) *Wagner on franchising. Access News*, 14. London: University of London.

Walford, G. (1992) The reform of higher education, in M. Arnot and L. Barton (eds) *Voicing Concerns: Sociological Perspectives on Contemporary Education Reforms*. Wallingford: Triangle.

Warner, D. (1996) Coherence or chaos? *Managing Higher Education*, 4, Autumn, 30–1.

Waterman, R.H. (1988) *The Renewal Factor*. New York: Bantam Books.

Watkins, P. (1994) The Fordist/Post-Fordist debate: the educational implications, in J. Kenway (ed.) *Economising Education: the post-Fordist Directions*. Victoria: Deakin University.

Watson, D. (1994) Living with ambiguity, in J. Bocock and D. Watson (eds) *Managing the University Curriculum: Making Common Cause*. Buckingham: Open University Press/SRHE.

Watson, D. (1995) Staff development and the academic professions. Keynote speech for the UCoSDA Annual Conference, University of Southampton, 1 November (printed summary).

Watson, D. (1996) *Unit Public Funding*. Conference paper, 'Dilemmas of Mass Higher Education' conference, Staffordshire University, 10–12 April.

Watson, D., with Brooks, J., Coghill, C., Lindsay, R. and Scurry, D. (1989) *Managing the Modular Course: Perspectives from Oxford Polytechnic*. Buckingham: Open University Press/SRHE.

Weber, M. (1958) *The Protestant Ethic and the Spirit of Capitalism*. New York: Charles Scribner's Sons.

Weber, M. (1979) *Economy and Society*. Berkeley, CA: University of California Press.

Webster, F. (1996) Can academic standards be maintained with a declining unit of resource? Evidence from the field. Conference paper, 'Dilemmas of Mass Higher Education' conference, Staffordshire University, 10–12 April.

Weedon, C. (1987) *Feminist Practice and Poststructuralist Theory*. Oxford: Blackwell.

Weil, S. (1994) *Introducing Change From the Top: 10 Personal Accounts*. London: Kogan Page.

Weiner, G. (1989) Professional self knowledge versus social justice: a critical analysis of the teacher-researcher movement. *British Educational Research Journal*, 15 (1): 41–51.

Wester, F. (1987) *Strategieen voor kwalitatief onderzoek* [*Strategies for qualitative research*]. Muiden: Coutinho.

Whitcomb, D.B. and Deshler, D. (1983) *The Values Inventory: A Process for Clarifying Institutional Culture*. EDRS document, no. ED 254, 113.

Williams, G. (1992) *Changing Patterns of Finance in Higher Education*. Buckingham: Open University Press/SRHE.

Williams, G. (1996) *Paying for Education Beyond Eighteen: An Examination of Issues and Options*. London: The Council for Industry and Higher Education.

Williams, P. (1996) *Letter to NewU Vice Chancellor regarding Quality Audit Report: Collaborative Provision*, 11 January. London: HEQC.

Williams, R. (1962) *The Long Revolution*. Harmondsworth: Penguin.

Williams, R. (1980) *Problems in Materialism and Culture: Selected Essays*. London: Verso.

Willmott, H. (1993) Strength is ignorance: slavery is freedom: managing culture in modern organizations. *Journal of Management Studies*, 30 (4): 515–52.

Wilson, T. (1991) The proletarianisation of academic labour. *Industrial Relations Journal*, 22: 250–62.

Winter, R. (1991) Looking out on a bolder landscape. *Times Higher Educational Supplement*, 18 October.

Winter, R. (1995) The university of life plc: the 'industrialisation' of higher education? in J. Smyth (ed.) *Academic Work*. Buckingham: Open University Press/SRHE.

Woodrow, M. (1993) Franchising: the quiet revolution. *Higher Education Quarterly*, 47 (3): 207–20.

Woods, P. (1984) Ethnography and theory construction in educational research, in R.G. Burgess (ed.) *Field Methods in Educational Research*. Lewes: Falmer.

Wormald, E. (1985) Teacher training and gender blindness. *British Journal of Sociology of Education*, 6 (1): 112–16.

Wrong, D. (1966) The oversocialized conception of man in modern sociology, in L. Coser and B. Rosenberg *Sociological Theory*. London: Macmillan. First published in *American Sociological Review*, XXVI: 184–93.

Yanow, D.J. (1987) Toward a policy culture approach to implementation. *Policy Studies Review*, 7 (1): 103–15.

Yanow, D.J. (1990) Tackling the implementation problem: epistemological issues in implementation research, in D.J. Palumbo and D.J. Calista (eds) *Implementation and Public Policy: Opening Up the Black Box*. Westport, CT: Greenwood Press.

Index

The Society for Research into Higher Education

The Society for Research into Higher Education exists to stimulate and coordinate research into all aspects of higher education. It aims to improve the quality of higher education through the encouragement of debate and publication on issues of policy, on the organization and management of higher education institutions, and on the curriculum and teaching methods.

The Society's income is derived from subscriptions, sales of its books and journals, conference fees and grants. It receives no subsidies, and is wholly independent. Its individual members include teachers, researchers, managers and students. Its corporate members are institutions of higher education, research institutes, professional, industrial and governmental bodies. Members are not only from the UK, but from elsewhere in Europe, from America, Canada and Australasia, and it regards its international work as among its most important activities.

Under the imprint *SRHE & Open University Press*, the Society is a specialist publisher of research, having over 70 titles in print. The Editorial Board of the Society's Imprint seeks authoritative research or study in the above fields. It offers competitive royalties, a highly recognizable format in both hardback and paperback and the worldwide reputation of the Open University Press.

The Society also publishes *Studies in Higher Education* (three times a year), which is mainly concerned with academic issues, *Higher Education Quarterly* (formerly *Universities Quarterly*), mainly concerned with policy issues, *Research into Higher Education Abstracts* (three times a year), and *SRHE News* (four times a year).

The Society holds a major annual conference in December, jointly with an institution of higher education. In 1995 the topic was 'The Changing University' at Heriot-Watt University in Edinburgh. In 1996 it was 'Working in Higher Education' at University of Wales, Cardiff and in 1997, 'Beyond the First Degree' at the University of Warwick. The 1998 conference will be on the topic of globalization at the University of Lancaster.

The Society's committees, study groups and networks are run by the members. The networks at present include:

Access	Mentoring
Curriculum Development	Vocational Qualifications
Disability	Postgraduate Issues
Eastern European	Quality
Funding	Quantitative Studies
Legal Education	Student Development

Benefits to members

Individual

Individual members receive

- *SRHE News*, the Society's publications list, conference details and other material included in mailings.
- Greatly reduced rates for *Studies in Higher Education* and *Higher Education Quarterly*.
- A 35 per cent discount on all SRHE & Open University Press publications.
- Free copies of the Precedings – commissioned papers on the theme of the Annual Conference.
- Free copies of *Research into Higher Education Abstracts*.
- Reduced rates for the annual conference.
- Extensive contacts and scope for facilitating initiatives.
- Free copies of the *Register of Members' Research Interests*.
- Membership of the Society's networks.

Corporate

Corporate members receive:

- Benefits of individual members, plus.
- Free copies of *Studies in Higher Education*.
- Unlimited copies of the Society's publications at reduced rates.
- Reduced rates for the annual conference.
- The right to submit applications for the Society's research grants.
- The right to use the Society's facility for supplying statistical HESA data for purposes of research.

Membership details: SRHE, 3 Devonshire Street, London W1N 2BA, UK. Tel: 0171 637 2766. Fax: 0171 637 2781. email:srhe@mailbox.ulcc.ac.uk
World Wide Web:http://www.srhe.ac.uk./srhe/
Catalogue: SRHE & Open University Press, Celtic Court, 22 Ballmoor, Buckingham MK18 1XW. Tel: 01280 823388. Fax: 01280 823233. email:enquiries@openup.co.uk